MW01625645

“Education is not the learning of facts, it’s rather the training of the mind to think.”

--- Albert Einstein

ENDORSEMENTS

Through my studies, there are many individual statements that seem to always resurface. They just seem to always be relevant or meaningful like your favorite part of your favorite song. One of those statements as it relates to rehab and training is "The target organ of everything we do is the Brain." Certainly this can mean many things to many different people, but the truth of the statement is always quite paramount. All systems of the body will always track back to a level of control or advancement by functions of the brain. This truth may be taken for granted as the brain's role in adaptation may be several layers away from what is normally studied or accepted. The excitement for Adam's book here is highlighting the links of key topics that leave the rank and file explanations or physics and biology and focus on the unique neurology that drives the human machine. Perhaps these highlights will become similar to that favorite part of your favorite song too!!!

Dr. Charlie Weingroff, Physical Therapist
Physical Performance Lead, Head Strength & Conditioning Coach, Canadian Men's National Basketball Team

"So often, we try and simplify a truth to increase comprehension, however, in understanding higher level integration of systems during the human life cycle, there is no simple explanation. This book provides a foundation for critical assessment through the lens of a neurological approach and how to begin investigating system interplay. Adam shares eloquently through his own personal journey, the power of understanding over living reactively. Your current reality does not permanently set your path."

Dr. Megan Young PhDc, MS, MSed, RSCC, SCCC
High Performance Director, Chicago Red Stars
15 Years College and Professional Coach

He is able to quickly integrate the tenants of many human movement sub-disciplines to truly treat the whole person. This latest book honors the complexity of being a moving human beautifully by offering readers an in-depth understanding of inter-relationships among the neurological, physiological, and psychological components of human movement. A tremendous read for those eager to keep growing as a professional and a person.

Dr. Karrie L. Hamstra-Wright, PhD, ATC, University of Illinois at Chicago, Clinical Associate Professor and Director of Undergraduate Studies in Kinesiology

Adam Wolf has seamlessly integrated a variety of complex topics including neurology, motor control, biomechanics, and pain science. Where others in the industry have tried to create divisiveness by only referencing journal research that supports their biases, this book is a true representation of Dr. David Sackett's original definition of evidence-based medicine: the integration of an individual's clinical expertise, the best external evidence (research), married with the client's expectations. Whether you're a movement therapist, clinician, and/or fitness professional and looking to expand your education - and have a willingness to keep an open-mind - this book is going to change how you think and work with your clients.

Dr. Evan Osar, DC, Developer of the Integrative Movement System™ and author of Corrective Exercise Solutions.

We are moving into a remarkably exciting time for rehabilitation and movement professionals as research and clinical experience converge to offer new approaches to working with patients and athletes. In his latest book, Adam has done a remarkable job of merging concepts from multiple disciplines and clearly demonstrates how they can be integrated to create drastically improved outcomes. The blending of functional biomechanics with movement neurology is the next step for modern practitioners and this book offers tremendous insights to follow in this process. Highly recommended!

Dr. Eric Cobb
Founder of Z-Health Performance Solutions

What makes this book exceptional is that Adam ties together critical concepts from many disciplines. Whether he's talking about manual therapies to enhance proprioception and reduce inflammation or the use of isometric contractions to stimulate the cortical reorganization of movement patterns, Adam takes his vast clinical experience to show how proper rehab can actually change the way we move. In the not-too-distant future, these treatment protocols will be mainstream as contrary to what we are taught in school, stretching and strengthening tight and weak muscles is a relatively ineffective way to treat musculoskeletal injuries. To rehab an injured person properly, Adam teaches you that you have to rewire the central nervous system essentially erase all faulty motor engrams. I personally find this process the most challenging component of practice, yet also the most enjoyable. This book shows you that in order to effectively treat musculoskeletal injuries, you have to understand the central nervous system.

Dr. Tom Michaud, Chiropractor,
Author, Human Locomotion

Adam Wolf has proven himself to be a world authority on movement and biomechanics. By restoring proper movement at both a local and global level, Adam has helped people from all over the world with a wide range of problems. I often refer many of my patients to Adam because he understands human movement at both a musculoskeletal level as well as a neuromuscular level. This book will help any manual therapist improve their technique by better understanding the relationship between brain function and movement patterns.

Dr David Traster DC, MS, DACNB, FABBIR, FABVR, CCSP, PAK
Chiropractor, Co-Owner, The Neurological Wellness Institute
Assistant Professor, Carrick Institute

In this book, Adam Wolf walks us through a systematic logic of how to think about, structure and organize interventions which improve our ability to ADAPT optimally. This results in enhanced function, and better results. By prioritizing treatment of PAIN, then HIGHER LEVEL INTEGRATION, then MOBILITY/STABILITY, MOTOR FUNCTION and finally MOVEMENT INTEGRATION, Adam provide us a road map to increase capabilities, which help to improve our outcomes. Congratulations Adam on putting together this important narrative, which will help so many of us.

Michol Dalcourt
Founder, Institute of Motion & VIPR/VIPR Pro

FOUNDATIONS OF MOVEMENT

A BRAIN-BASED MUSCULOSKELETAL APPROACH

AUTHOR: ADAM WOLF

NEURO EDITOR: MICHAEL DRZEWIECKI

FOUNDATIONS OF MOVEMENT
A BRAIN-BASED MUSCULOSKELETAL APPROACH

Author: Adam Wolf
Neuro Editor: Michael Drzewiecki
Cover Picture: Jill Wolf

ISBN Number: 978-1-735437-0-5

First Edition – Printed in the United States

PUBLISHED BY:

TMG PUBLISHING
1659 West Hubbard, Chicago IL 60622
312-489-8579
www.themovementguildchicago.com
info@themovementguildchicago.com

ACKNOWLEDGEMENTS & DEDICATIONS

There have been many who have served as my teachers, influencing the person and clinician I am today. Many are themselves clinicians while others aren't, yet all have taught me valuable lessons. I feel fortunate to know how much I don't know, and also that I have a desire to continue learning. Some of that gratefulness also comes from realizing what I don't want, which has potentially proven more useful than knowing exactly what I want. The body provides an endless source of study, and I feel fortunate to have a desire to continue to improve my skill set.

Over the years, learning has become increasingly important to me. I think, very likely, because it's something I can specifically control in a world where I often feel that I don't control much. It plays out for me socially, as anyone who knows me will testify I prefer quieter, more intimate environments that don't include group dynamics. When I am in group settings, I tend to be very quiet and stand in the corner. Interestingly enough, I wasn't always this way, which will be discussed in depth in Part 6 of this book, which is my personal narrative about my central integration dysfunction. That chapter is different than the other chapters in that Part 6 was co-written about my experience with subclinical integration issues by Dr. Mike Drzewiecki. Mike's influence is found throughout this book via his 'applied neuro' insight, specifically, his thoughts can be found in "gray highlights" in every chapter.

Regardless, there are certain people who specifically deserve my acknowledgement because they've played an influential role in the development of this project. First, thank you to Dr. Mike Drzewiecki, who added both his knowledge and insight into creating this book. I'm honored to call him both a colleague and a friend. Dr. Tom Michaud also deserves special thanks and mention. Tom has been a teacher and guide for me clinically, and also in the development of this book. Early on, he read a few chapters and provided insight and direction while also giving me permission to reference his work and use some pictures from his book *Human Locomotion*, which is referenced throughout this text and specifically in the chapter on treating capacities. Thank you to Carl Ankrum, who took the pictures for the text and also Martin Foner, who formatted and edited for grammar and English. Also, to my sister Jill Wolf, who drew the cover picture. Other special mentions include Dr. Nick Studholme and Dr. David Traster, both of whom I'm lucky to consider friends and mentors, and both of whom have provided me endless hours of 'brain based' conversations. Last, I'd like to thank Physical Therapists Dr. Stuart Fife & Dr. Gary Gray, who have both been influential in my thought process as a movement practitioner.

Lastly, I'd like to thank my family, specifically my wonderful children Elijah, Alexia, and Aiden. I love you.

Very last and most importantly, I couldn't have done this without the love and support of my wife and partner, Jessica Carlin. My consigliere. I'm really not sure how she puts up with me, and I feel very grateful for her in my life.

TABLE OF CONTENTS

WHAT'S IN THIS BOOK, WHO CAN BENEFIT FROM IT, AND WHY

Parts 1-4 introduce, review, and discuss what biomechanics are and why they matter, even when not biomechanically driven. The idea of real vs. relative motion is reviewed including how it can be simply applied. These chapters discuss how my thought process has evolved since the first book, specifically surrounding Transformational Zones as defined by the Gray Institute, compared to treating capacities. We will discuss gait cycle capacities, as well as capacities of various parts of the nervous system and musculoskeletal system. We will also discuss basic strategies to improve these capacities.

Part 5 discusses basic concepts about pain, with emphasis placed on it being an output. There are numerous texts that discuss pain more in depth, and a list of suggested readings are provided at the end of that chapter. Part 5 represents a current understanding of relevant pain science information proven useful in practice. It is a chapter deliberately left out of my first book, *REAL Movement,* and upon reflection, I wish it had been included. It discusses some current research along with relevant clinical applications. In addition, why I believe it is important to understand and incorporate pain science into treatment programs.

Part 6 builds upon the idea of higher level sensory integration, and the importance of the vestibulo-ocular and cerebellar systems in governing movement. With sensory integration dysfunction in these regions, there will inevitably be movement compensation and deficiencies in the musculoskeletal system. Checking higher level sensory integration is something I did not pay much attention to until relatively recently. Since I've begun learning more and integrating, I'm amazed at the difference it has made in my practice, and how many demonstrate subclinical integration disorders. This chapter is co-written with the clinical editor of this book, Dr. Mike Drzewiecki, including a personal narrative of my experience working with him on my 'dysfunction'.

Part 7 discusses topics around mobility and provides a working definition and strategies for the improvement of mobility. Generally speaking, the idea of mobility prior to stability is consistent with my thought process, except for when it isn't, which will be discussed further.

Part 8 discusses motor control theories, put into the context of assessing motor output in various ways including through muscle testing. It's a broad topic and specific thought processes will be discussed that will be helpful in treatment including when and why to stretch vs. strengthen.

Part 9 describes in relative detail the integration through isolation spectrum developed to ensure the individual is working at his/her threshold. It is arranged by body part, starting at the foot and moving up to the brain, including regions I like to work together to ensure capacities are being met.

The final Parts of the book include two case studies from actual patients/clients I've had the opportunity to treat, as well as Dr. Drzewiecki's thought process with those demonstrating clinical (rather than subclinical) dysfunction, including clinical integration case studies. Each section will also include an 'additional readings list' comprised of articles, websites, and recommended material that will go more in depth about each subject discussed.

A brief introduction of each fundamental is discussed below, followed by in-depth discussion of each in preceding chapters. My fundamentals of intervention in order are: treat pain, higher level sensory integration, improving mobility, stabilizing, followed by functional integration.

- Pain
    - deal with it quickly
    - It's an output

- Higher Level Integration. Sensorial experience
    - vestibular/cerebellar/basal ganglia/integrative sensory systems

- Mobility
    - Superficial tissue>>joint/capsule>>soft tissue (muscle/tendon/fascia)>>neural mobilization
        - Has joint passed functional capacities to mobilize?
            - What happens when we provide stability input first?
            - Does mobility improve?
        - Did stability input change mobility deficit?
- Motor Function
    - facilitated<>inhibited relationships. MSK driven?
    - Isolated <> Integrated Relationship
        - Isolated isolation. Stabilizers
        - Isolated integration. Synergies
        - Integrated isolation. Higher level synergies
        - Integrated integration. Active Stabilization

- Movement Integration
    - Load capabilities
    - See Integrated<>Isolated Spectrum
    - Brain Based
    - Endurance
    - Thoughts Feelings

The Integrated <> Isolated spectrum is divided into four parts.

As a young clinician, I felt a consistent disconnect regarding the perception of how muscles work and the exercises often prescribed to 'strengthen' a 'weak' region. Simply put, it didn't add up, and so, over time, I created an outline that has helped me to organize and have better objectivity to regressive and progressive movements.

This has turned into what I call an Integrated<>Isolated spectrum, designed to have strategies and movements that work at the individual threshold, which is described below. It was designed recognizing that pure isolation and pure integration aren't always enough to make desired changes and progressive<>regressive strategies were important to keep it novel, intense, and at a threshold appropriate to change the brain. The integration to isolation spectrum includes two middle steps that provide regressive and progressive strategies. These middle steps ensure it is possible to traverse from one end of the spectrum to the other in measurable, thoughtful, and obtainable ways. Isolation and integration thought processes are fairly obvious; however, the steps in between that best allow working at the individual threshold. All the steps can utilize an isometric hold in some form, which has proven to be a useful strategy in the influencing of the nervous system and creating input change. Isometric engagement is non inflammatory and can be an effective strategy to increase somatosensory representation.
They are:

1. Isolated isolation
2. Isolated integration
3. Integrated isolation
4. Integrated integration

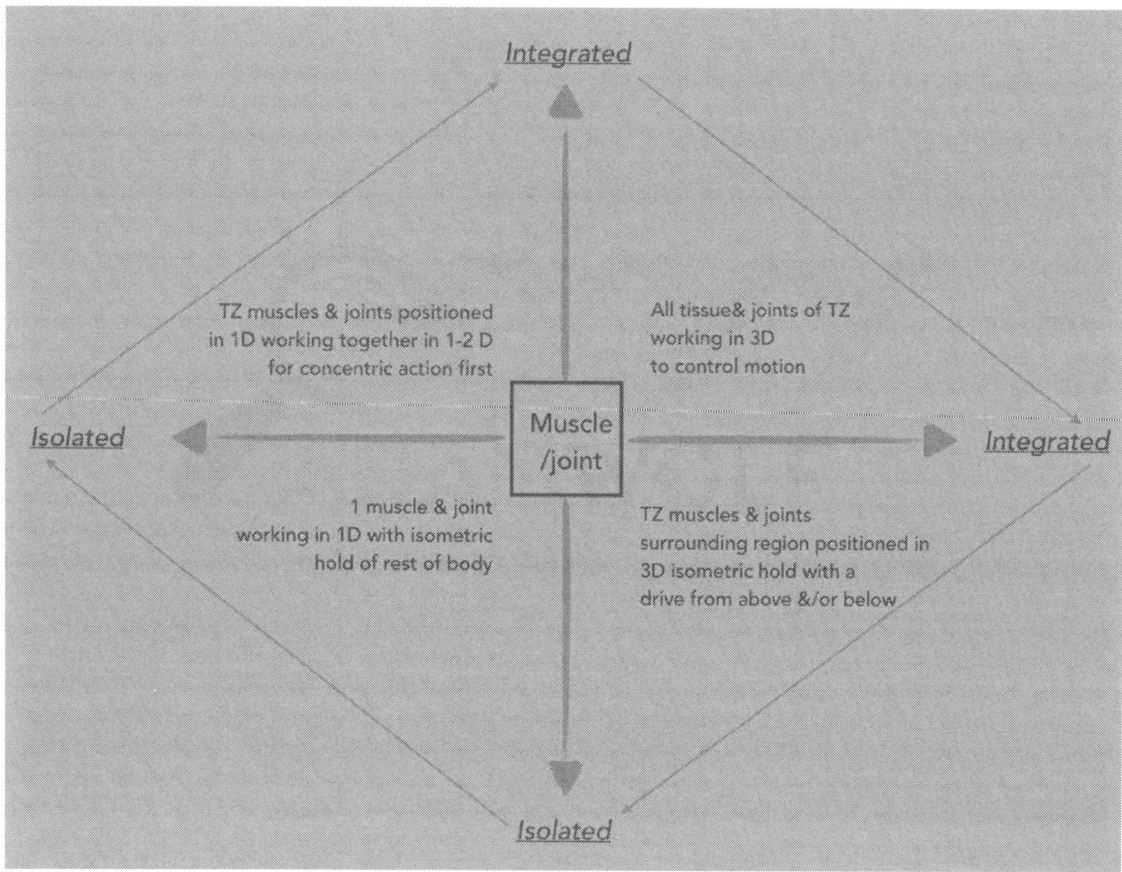

All the stops along the integrated<>isolated spectrum will be discussed in detail in Part 9. They are simply starting points about where to start with someone including progression/regression suggestions in order to work at the threshold of the individual.

Who Can Use This Manual

This manual is designed for movement practitioners who desire a better ability to integrate various thought processes into a workable format. It began as a guide for those working in my clinical practice in Chicago. I realized I am good at synthesizing and conveying information in a workable format, and this manual represents my latest attempt to do both. In clinical, there are some less experienced clinicians I work with and hope to provide them with a thought process empowering them to continue learning on their own, in addition to more experienced clinicians who help me to learn.

It is written with an emphasis on the process, recognizing there is always new information to learn and incorporate. Currently, my education has been focused on a better understanding of the vestibulo-ocular and cerebellar systems and how to apply it in practice. Since I've been looking for it, I have been amazed at the amount of subclinical integration disorders people demonstrate in one or more of these systems. It is also fascinating how they influence each other and can be tested against each other to direct treatment, which will also be discussed.

I feel fortunate to love my profession and that I get to help people every day. My hope is this text serves as an introduction for movement professionals desiring to further their practice. It by no means represents the entirety of any of the subjects discussed, and instead is meant as a jumping off point to learn more in-depth about specifics. To that end, at the conclusion of each chapter is an additional readings list that includes books, articles, blogs, and videos.

This text is more clinical and in-depth than my first book *REAL Movement: Perspective on Integrated Motion & Motor Control*, although it does take some of those concepts and expands on them in order to provide a more comprehensive thought process. It represents my simplified thought processes about how to work with an individual, along with why it's important to do so.

Why Use This Manual?

Having taught numerous courses, I've observed many clinicians having difficulty working within the context of a hierarchical thought process. In addition, many are stuck in a structural, mechanical approach rather than a neurological approach to working with the body. This text is designed to provide the movement practitioner with the tools necessary to hierarchically analyze where and why to start. While we are all unique, there are neurological, physiological, and psychological commonalities in everyone that can be assessed and worked successfully. I am often asked by other clinicians where they can learn more, and this book was written with them in mind. It is written in the order I assess and treat, to improve movement and hopefully decrease pain.

How to Use This Manual

This text is laid out in an order based on my thought process of what to do and when, during rehab, understanding it obviously depends on what is presented. The Parts are divided into information on each specific subject, as well as some current research and synthesis of why it's important. Each Part is designed to stand alone to be referred to when needed. In addition, the back Parts lay out my thought process from isolation through integration, and how and when to progress a patient.

INTRODUCTION – TO THE THOUGHT PROCESS

I have learned from many amazing movement professionals and have arrived at a mindset and knowledge base different from many of my contemporaries. I am lucky to possess a deep desire to continue learning and integrating information to plug the proverbial holes in my understanding of the body. This text is an effort to put down on paper what makes me the clinician I am today, because I don't believe everyone 'needs' Adam, or any specific clinician, as long as they follow a logical thought process that recognizes the governing principles of the body. Represented here is my effort to put into a hierarchy what those principles are, along with a little what, and a lot of why, based on my knowledge and experience up to this point, recognizing I continue to learn and integrate. Right around the time this text was begun, I was encouraged to develop my "fundamentals of intervention" in order to better organize my thought process (thank you Lenny Parracino). With each patient, my fundamentals of intervention are not only a reliable starting point, but also the means by which I determine where to begin and how to proceed, regardless of who is in front of me. This text attempts to explain those fundamentals — along with why I adhere to them — as comprehensively as possible.

Many spectrums exist in the movement profession, static to dynamic, superficial to deep, and isolated to integrated, just to name a few. This is in addition to the countless varieties of movement professionals, including certified professionals such as personal trainers, yoga and Pilates instructors, strength and conditioning coaches, and also licensed professionals such as chiropractors, physical therapists, massage therapists, athletic trainers, doctors, and more. As someone who has spent the past decade in the clinical trenches of the movement profession, I believe it is far more effective to be a part of a loose and coordinated team of professionals than an island unto myself. At some point, everyone reaches their limits to be able to help. Being humble enough to refer out, when appropriate, is critical. It is also a primary driver for me to keep learning.

Currently, my fundamentals of intervention have evolved to include the concepts of treating capacities rather than anatomy, which is a concept I first learned about taking FNOR (Functional Neuro-Ortho Rehab), founded by Dr. David George and Dr. Stuart Fife. Treating capacities allows for a broader, more holistic approach than the more myopic practice of focusing on anatomy, because it is probably not the painful body part's fault. While it is important to free a given body part from pain, it is often even more critical to recognize the site of the injury is not necessarily the cause of pain. Treating capacities, or established movements that have been validated by empirical evidence, provides a consistent thought process anyone across disciplines can come to anchor. Within the paradigm of treating capacities, it doesn't matter what body part is painful, rather it allows one to assess the ability to control certain movements, recognizing that often the breakdown at the painful region is due to too much shearing force and movement of the head of the bones at the joint level. Treating capacities is the paradigm in which fundamentals of intervention should be viewed and will be discussed at length in later parts.

There are many movement certifications to choose; the most popular seems to be the FMS (Functional Movement Screen) and its more clinically oriented version, the SFMA (Selective Functional Movement Assessment), both of which were popularized by Gray Cook and discussed in his book *Movement* (3). Others include Dr. Shirley Sharmahn's *Movement Impairment Syndromes* (4) and the McKenzie method, known as the Mechanical Diagnosis and Therapy (MDT) Method. While there are many effective systems to look at movement, thoroughly understanding a specific system before expanding to other thought process increases the best chance for success. My system is anchored in and started with Applied Functional Science (AFS), which I intensely studied from before PT school and for a good ten years after, taking all their workshops/material offered. This became layered with various other modalities/thought processes, including Functional Range Conditioning (FRC), various soft tissue modalities and increasingly, a brain-based approach learned initially through Functional Neuro-Ortho Rehab (FNOR). It has been expounded upon in the subsequent years and layered with numerous performance and rehab strategies. This has led me more into understanding neuro-anatomy and how to apply it, specifically in a sub-clinical population (i.e. no BPPV or dizziness) that primarily demonstrate musculoskeletal dysfunction. In that spirit, at the time of this publication, I am completing a certificate of competency in vestibular rehabilitation in order to better integrate a brain based approach.

Author's Note:

Anchoring to one system before branching out into other thought processes ensures a greater chance of a thorough understanding. All too often I see people not versed in any one discipline jump between certifications and therefore aren't anchored into one. Get good at one before branching out. I started with AFS and continue to learn it today.

I believe it is our responsibility as "Movement Practitioners" to grasp the intricacies of three-dimensional human motion in order to best serve those wanting to move and feel better. The simple fact of understanding movement almost always combines integrated and isolated, as well as static and dynamic, and helps to create an authentic and individualized movement program. Early in my career I poo-poohed isolation, believing the body only knows motion and how to control forces it is presented with, a topic I discussed in my first book, *REAL Movement: Perspective on Integrated Motion & Motor Control,* which will be reviewed and expanded on in later chapters. However, I've come to realize how important isolation can be, particularly for plasticizing specific parts of the brain to better represent specific body parts. For those in pain, recognizing the pain process results in chemical changes in the brain and less representation to the painful body part. This, combined with the reality that isometrics are non-inflammatory, becomes a powerful way to create increased representation, which is reason enough to utilize isolation.

The reasons medical professionals often give to describe why someone has an issue make me think of the line "I do not think that word means what you think it means" from my favorite movie, "The Princess Bride". In it, the character Vizzini repeatedly misuses the word "inconceivable," until his employee, Inigo Montoya, finally says that famous line. Similar to Vizzini, medical professionals often tell patients/clients about potential mechanisms and what any modality (such as manual therapy or exercise) may or may not do, most times with no benefit for what needs to be accomplished. It often doesn't matter. The quote also makes me think of the stories behind why or why not something is or isn't occurring.

Patients often come with stories about what others have told them about their pain or 'issue'. Much like Inigo Montoya, I often think to myself the same thing, "Your thinking may be incorrect", or maybe not and does it even matter in order to achieve an outcome? Examples include everything from stories about manual therapy interventions (specifically in terms of what may or may not be happening) to the reasons behind why people feel pain in the first place. Increasingly, in my practice, when someone asks about their issue, my response is "I have no idea, but I can make up a story if you'd like, and it will sound really convincing." This typically gets them giggling, upon which point I try to illustrate it really doesn't matter why or how, as long as there is a strategy to move forward. The reality is, often it doesn't matter, and it's the proverbial chicken or the egg.

Clinically, focusing on an individual's pain experience, including treating individual capacities rather than simply looking at anatomy, with an understanding movement is governed by the nervous system, are good starting points. Explaining how pain is an output from a threatened nervous system is also helpful for repatterning, which will be necessary at some level with someone in pain. Therefore, solutions to improving movement should incorporate driving input to the brain. Principles of motor control and muscle testing will be discussed in later sections of this book, without any of the three or four letter acronymed certifications that often are dogmatic in spirit. While there are many ways to 'tie together' information, from a brain-based perspective, motor control principles and applications provide insights into the nervous system and often offer a direction of treatment.

In itself, motor control is a broad topic and can include quantitative and qualitative aspects. Some believe only quantitative should be considered, which can sometimes be limiting. My thought process has evolved to allow the qualitative to guide me when appropriate, as long as I'm anchoring to objectivity and tests that can be reproduced and will be discussed in later parts.

When difficult to objectify, the questions should be:

1. Does everything need to be validated by empirical evidence?
2. How does one know where to start, relative to treatment?

In some cases, producing empirical evidence is challenging simply because some variables can't be isolated. While anchoring to evidence provides a foundation to treatment, not everything needs to be validated through studies and trials, and in fact, can be quite limiting. In short, incorporating objective information consistent across disciplines should always be utilized, and recognizing not everything can be studied allows for individualization and informed improvisation.

One such consistency is pain that produces inhibitions, or latencies, in the response time of the nervous system. The New Oxford Dictionary defines a latency as "a delay before a transfer of data begins following an instruction for its transfer". When pain occurs, the chemistry in the brain immediately changes, and over time these changes result in less brain representation to the painful region. This means the brain's perception of where a painful body part is, in space, becomes skewed and in some cases, can create pain inhibition of movement, further spreading of pain, and abnormal motor patterns of muscles associated with the painful areas.

Pain also creates emotional responses to the movement of a painful body part as a protective mechanism and specific parts of the brain responsible for emotion may need more or less stimulation. These points are vital to remember when working with those in pain. Proper input (treatment) neurologically to an area that has experienced, or is experiencing, improper feedback due to the aforementioned inhibition patterns can help to change output and help the recovery process. In other words, input changes output, and therefore the proper input will help create a desired output, with the trick being to provide the proper input based on observation and understanding. This means brain-based solutions to rehab, performance, and recovery must include driving safe input to the brain in as many ways as possible in order to change the brain's output, many of which are expounded upon in later parts of this text. Simply put, I attempt to assess what region may be less represented in the nervous system in order to drive input to that specific region in as many ways as tolerated. This includes sensory and motor assessments in order to get as much information as possible.

Chiropractor and educator, Dr. David Traster, points out there are many ways to inhibit or facilitate a muscle for a test. It's easy to test a test, and also easy to draw conclusions that may or may not be relevant to the issue. Put another way, motor control theories, including muscle testing, can create a large rabbit hole in which to get lost while also providing a potentially very useful indicator for direction of treatment. Therefore, choosing wisely requires a consistent thought process based on motor control principles, and will be discussed in depth in later parts.

Thresholds

Thresholds, and the ability to find and work at one, is a key to creating lasting changes. The best definition I've found of a threshold comes from The Carnegie Mellon Robotics Academy, which defines a threshold as "values that set a cutoff in a range of values, so that even if there are many possibilities, the value eventually falls above the threshold, or below the threshold. Using thresholds allows you to perform certain behaviors depending on where a certain value falls in relation to the thresholds".

Relative to human movement, there are many kinds of thresholds including muscle recruitment thresholds, oxygenation, lactate, pain, and sensory thresholds, just to name a few. There are also different categories of sensory thresholds including absolute, recognition, differential, and terminal thresholds. Thresholds can sometimes be difficult to quantify, particularly given the time constraints of a clinical situation, the inherent subjectivity of analysis, and no one way to measure movement. Yet, assessing movement is one part of a foundation to obtaining objective information used to direct treatment. Specific thresholds will be discussed in later parts, along with the keys to understanding when an individual has reached her/his threshold capacity. The ability to recognize a threshold allows a more accurate assessment and ability to direct the specific inputs that will most effectively influence the nervous system.

Working at an individual threshold is important in order to create lasting neuroplastic changes. If interventions are too easy, creating desired neuroplastic changes becomes more difficult, conversely, if over the threshold, plasticity can easily be driven in a non-desirable way that perpetuates a negative feedback loop. This is a reason to conceptualize and understand where to start a program and how to progress, with the integrated<>isolated spectrum described in later parts as a good starting point.

The picture above illustrates the concept of staying at or below a tissue tolerance, or threshold, without overstepping the threshold, as described in the book, Explain Pain, by Lorimer Moseley and David Butler. This concept can be expanded to include any threshold because overstepping it often has a non-desirable outcome.

Often, strategies to get someone out of pain as quickly as possible might be counter to the long-term strategies necessary to stay out of pain. Yet, the longer one is in pain, the longer they're going to be in pain, because of the processes of reduced representation to the somatosensory cortex to the painful regions. Superficial nerves get irritated for many reasons, including as a result of the byproducts of the ATP production cycle (energy production), resulting in a lack of oxygen in the tissue, which lowers tissue pH. Lowered tissue pH can easily irritate peripheral nerves and create a pain response.

"Understanding that there are various pain generators is important, including superficial nerve pain, muscular pain, joint pain, referred pain, and psychogenic/emotional pain. Many times, people don't want to talk about pain that might be centrally generated because there is a stigma around psychogenic pain. The reality is, many people have chronic pain that is emotional in nature, either from an injury to an area, or pain that is exacerbated due to unrelated emotional instability causing a plastic nature of pain or lack of inhibition of pain."

Pain is an output and having ways to relax the body via input changes is beneficial, as is the recognition that biology is interrelated to psychology and sociology. In other words, it's impossible to separate the mind, body, and spirit, (or Biology from Psychology from Sociology) which are interrelated, interdependent, and can influence any experience.

This text will go into more depth about each of the topics introduced in this introduction, including pain, defining and outlining motor control concepts, and how to implement these thought processes into a workable format. In addition, we will discuss how to move someone along an integrated movement spectrum, based on objective information.

INTRODUCTION – BY DR. MIKE DRZEWIECKI

"Writing the rest of this book was easy. The Introduction was hardest, and paradoxically, written last. Adam asked me to explain, in his words, "Your history and how you are so good at what you do." Coming from someone like Adam who has proven himself in the physical therapy world both in skill and experience, this is an honor, and also uncomfortable because I generally do not like doing this. I attribute continued accelerated advancement to the environment where I spend most of my waking hours, fortunate to work with some of the most brilliant minds in our field. At any given moment I can have a conversation with ten extremely skilled and unbelievably smart colleagues in our office. The ability to ask questions, bounce ideas around, and have intellectual conversations about patient care, cannot be understated. I'm convinced that it advances everyone's skills exponentially, which is vital in our practice where the cases are more and more complicated with each day.

After graduating from The University of Michigan-Flint, I got married to my beautiful wife, Christie, and moved to Atlanta, Georgia, to start chiropractic school. I started school with the idea of being a sports chiropractor and helping athletes injured through similar ways Chiropractic helped me. It was my all-time dream to someday work with just one professional athlete, especially a pro hockey player. In my novice mind, I thought this would never happen until I was a seasoned chiropractor with many years of experience; that would be the pinnacle of being a sports chiropractor. Incidentally, a bonus at Life University, where I attended chiropractic school, was that they had a Master's Program in Sports Health Science. I enrolled in the Master's Program simultaneously with my Doctorate Program.

About halfway through school I received a phone call from one of my friends who had been very interested and involved in the Functional Neurology Club on campus and told me Dr. Ted Carrick was going to be coming to the school to treat some "high profile people''. He also suggested getting into the neuro world more, as he thought there would be more opportunities in the future to see Dr. Carrick work. I thought it was a cool topic, but I was very busy with my current load and couldn't take on anything more. A couple days later I was standing at a salad bar in a grocery store near campus and looked across and directly into the eyes of Sidney Crosby, arguably one of the best hockey players to ever play. I couldn't figure out why Sidney Crosby was at a salad bar in Marietta, Georgia, and didn't make the connection that this was the "high profile" person my friend referred to until later that when it came out that Dr. Carrick was treating him on campus.

A few days later Dr. Carrick was sitting on stage next to Crosby talking about his concussion and that Crosby was now cleared to return from his near career ending injury. Being an avid hockey fan, I had followed Crosby's injury and knew that this was a monumental time in hockey history. It turned out to be a monumental time in Functional Neurology history as well.

A couple months later it was the week of Thanksgiving and that same friend called me again and asked if I wanted to come help Dr. Carrick for the week. Due to the holiday they were short on help and Dr. Carrick was going to be treating more people on campus. I jumped at the opportunity and spent my first week observing Dr. Carrick in awe. I remember ending the week, exhausted but energized. I had no idea what I had watched for the week but knew I needed to learn all of it. That next week I signed up for my first course with The Carrick Institute and knew that my path had drastically changed.

As a student, I was given the opportunity to observe and treat (under direct supervision), some of the most complicated neuro cases in the world. One of my first direct cases was a fourteen year old patient from France who had come over just to see Dr. Carrick. She was diagnosed with POTS (Postural Orthostatic Tachycardia Syndrome), a condition that left her unable to move from a supine position upwards more than five degrees without having a full tonic-clonic (Grand-mal) seizure that would last from ten seconds to several minutes. The seizure was a result of severe tachycardia and decreased cerebral perfusion due to a dysfunctioning autonomic nervous system. She was having about 60 seizures per day. We treated this patient three times per day for one to two hours per treatment for two weeks. The treatments consisted primarily of tilt table orthostatic tolerance training and various neuro-vestibular rehab techniques. Oftentimes the treatment would set off multiple seizures within each visit. As time progressed, she was able to tolerate more and more elevation without seizing. By the end of two weeks she was able to go from lying to standing position and walk four steps, turn, and sit in her wheelchair without experiencing an episode. Seeing the life come back to a young girl whose parents had been told it was likely that at some point she would sustain severe brain damage or worse from one of her seizures, cemented my drive and passion for what I do now. This young girl is now grown up and living a normal life back in France. It brings tears to my eyes writing this.

Over the next three years I finished chiropractic school, finished the Master's Program, and took 400+ hours of neurology courses on the weekends, including the base neurology courses as well as a specialty course series in traumatic brain injury rehabilitation, taught by Dr. Carrick himself. In addition, I was fortunate enough to attend, participate in, and have a floor management role on all of Dr. Carrick's grand rounds he performed in Atlanta, twelve in total. I learned, in a trial by fire atmosphere, how to manage patients, students, and other doctors who had travelled from around the world to see The Professor's work. These two years were grueling but pivotal in my education. I learned more in this time frame than all of my life prior.

After my first couple years of clinical practice managing a neuro facility, I received a call from my now partner, Dr. George Michalopoulos, asking my wife (also a DC) and me to join his practice in Chicago. We moved and the last few years have practiced in Chicago at The Neurologic Wellness Institute.

Due to the unique nature of our practice, I think an intro to the practice is necessary. Our group, The Neurologic Wellness Institute, is a chiropractic neurology practice with many physicians who treat complicated neurological deficit cases. The vast majority of cases are concussion and post-concussion syndrome cases that are unresolved with traditional management. Other cases include but are not limited to dysautonomia, postural orthostatic tachycardia syndrome (POTS), post stroke, vestibular/balance disorders, Parkinson's disease, autism spectrum disorder, multiple sclerosis, anxiety, depression, peripheral nerve disease, and other rare neurological disorders. The process includes a very detailed history, examination, and diagnostic testing that takes about three hours in total. This lengthy process allows for the patient to fully share all of the details of his/her situation, the doctor to fully assess the function of each patient's nervous system, and the development of an individualized treatment program specific to each patient. There are no protocols depending on the disease process, rather, each of the doctors on staff has a depth of knowledge of the nervous system which allows them to take each of the abnormal objective findings and develop a plan that will, as efficiently as possible, reduce the functional errors through therapeutic activities, without the use of pharmaceuticals or surgery.

Although it is a chiropractic practice, the treatments are much different than what is typically seen in other chiropractic offices. Manual manipulation as seen in traditional chiropractic practices can be very useful and is used in our practice when warranted, but the majority of our therapies consist of physical, vestibular, ocular, and sensory rehab strategies. Patients are typically seen on an intensive basis at first which allows the greatest neuroplastic effect as well as creating a strong doctor-patient relationship. Due to the in-depth knowledge of the complicated inner workings of the nervous system, doctor understands there is a strong psychological connection to being sick, especially when what is injured or not functioning properly is the brain. Like Adam, we stand behind a thought process that our therapies will work quickly, or they will not work at all. Meaning, we would expect there are significant changes during the initial intensive treatment period. If there are no changes seen, then the patient is released, and it is then our job to find a referral that would better fit the patient's needs. We make this promise to every patient, and patients appreciate the honest approach from the beginning.

I met Adam through his referring a patient to our office, a professional ballet dancer with persistent dizziness symptoms. I got to meet him briefly through this as well as another connection through Dr. Nick Studholme who has been friends with Adam for some time. Over time, a relationship was built between

Adam and myself that was friendly and built on a mutual desire to learn more about each other's techniques and clinical gems that could be beneficial in each other's practices.

At some point Adam was dealing with issues he thought were functional in nature and decided that he wanted me to 'take a look at him' clinically to see if there was anything I could find that would help him. He goes into greater detail later in the book and I have the opportunity to break down my thought process with how I examined and treated him. Not only was I happy to help him improve his well-being, I also knew if Adam was functioning more optimally, he would better serve his own patients.

In time this friendship continued to grow, and Adam asked me to help edit and write this book with him, specifically to co-write the chapter that described his personal experience and be a "neuro-editor", providing a more in depth neuroscience perspective. Adam wrote the majority of the book; then I went through and provided my thought process on his standards, which have a tremendous amount in common to mine. The yellow highlights in the book are my voice, and the knowledge is based on years of combined learning in the classroom and in grand rounds from the pioneer in Chiropractic Neurology, also termed Functional Neurology, Dr. Ted Carrick, and The Carrick Institute. I have also learned from mentors and colleagues, Dr. Nathan Keiser, Dr. Jim Duffy, Dr. David Traster, Dr. George Michalopoulos, Dr. Christa Hubbard, Dr. Marc Ellis, Dr. Fili Talamantez and many more. These people have been instrumental in sharing their knowledge of the nervous system, diagnostic evaluation, treatment strategies, and motivation to care for patients not only as cases but as humans in need. Other information that is presented throughout the book is from various articles, texts, and acquired knowledge from treating patients who are not always 'textbook' cases.
My motivation and excitement about being a part of this book was to be able to get the wheels turning in practitioners who are looking to take that next step in providing quality treatment to their patients and who, as one of my mentors would always say, want to "just be better."

PART 1: TO HAVE OR NOT TO HAVE A BIOMECHANICAL ISSUE…

"I am quite correctly described as 'more of a sponge than an inventor….'"

— Thomas Edison

Pain is not always biomechanically driven, however, people often move around, instead of through pain, resulting in biomechanical limitations. Addressing biomechanics creates input change which, even if temporary, can be used to change output. Biomechanical issues can develop when combinations of tissue, both long and short, don't fully lengthen in all three planes of motion. Put differently, tissue that doesn't go through its full range of motion won't experience the pressure change or oxygen saturation levels of tissue that is able to achieve a full range of motion. Lack of pressure difference results in less blood and oxygen reaching the tissue, creating a chemical reaction binding and cross linking tissue layers together. It also means even if not biomechanically driven, it can easily become a biomechanical issue due to asymmetry in tissue/joints/fascial layers and lines that, over time, become densified and matted together.

"However, people move around, instead of through, pain and that can result in biomechanical limitations." But why is this? Pain is a red flag. Pain is perceived only in the brain and is a warning system, a protection system, and a limitation system. Pain is inherently psychological, as it has to be. Pain says, 'Be careful, there is tissue damage happening,' or 'Be careful, the last time we did this there was tissue damage.' The former is what is most widely recognized by the general public and clinicians the same, whereas the latter is less often taken into account.

It is important to remember that the athlete or patient in front of you may be experiencing pain, not because there is actual damage taking place, rather because there is a subconscious perception that tissue damage may occur. This changes activity levels, changes motivation, changes biomechanics, and changes stress, all at a detriment to the patient even when tissue damage is not occurring. Essentially, the protection mechanism, pain, can at times be so protective that it ends up causing exactly what it is trying to avoid.

This is readily seen in athletes who have nagging pain long after healing from an injury, or in patients who say, "Every time I try to get back into working out, I always get hurt." There are subconscious, fear based, pain patterns that often present as musculoskeletal pain, when they are actually an over excitation of the Papez Circuit, which governs memory specific to emotions. Further explanation of the Papez

Circuit will follow, but for now, know that fear of repeated pain, a limbic (aka emotional) response, can change the way someone thinks and can change the way they move."

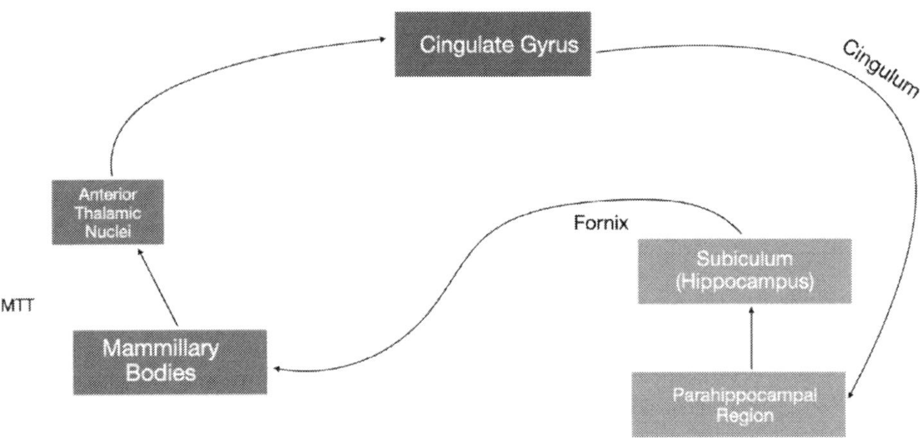

The Papez Circuit governs memory specific to emotions, and often is over excited secondary to subconscious fear based, pain patterns that can present as musculoskeletal pain.

There are numerous consistencies in the body to anchor to; some will be discussed more in depth in later parts. However, generally speaking, longer tissue tends to be less connected to the nervous system as compared to shorter tissue. In other words, longer tissue tends to demonstrate a latency, or delay, in the timing to the muscle relative to shorter tissue. Pain can also produce inhibitions, or latencies, in tissue surrounding the pain, and oftentimes these latencies are found in extensor muscles, which are often positioned longer. When viewed through this lens, restoring length tension relationships and improving tissue layer glide can be helpful for a number of reasons.

Biomechanics can temporarily change input that can help change output. At the very least, biomechanics is an inroad to create immediate afferent changes, which, even if temporary, help to change output. A neurological opportunity is created through manipulation of tissue in various ways, including when improving biomechanics, even if temporary. Creating easier motion leads to greater ease and willingness to continue to move, or as David Tiberio of the Gray Institute says, "motion begets motion". Therefore, it makes sense to change input in multiple ways including through movement. Movement includes a series of alternating compressions and tensions that can be applied in a thoughtful and systematic way. Other inputs include heat/ice, vibration, pressure, tension, muscle contraction thoughts and emotions, all of which can be used as input to try and change the output.

People experience pain differently, yet there are many consistencies. Therefore, early interventions should focus on managing pain and also building trust and confidence, because they go together. In addition, dealing concurrently with both the physical and cognitive aspects of pain allow for an interconnected approach that creates an environment of safe feeling, helping to stimulate parasympathetic responses necessary for learning confidence in activity. It has been beneficial to focus on sensation and the sensorial experience, rather than pain, and I'm cognizant of trying not to use the term pain with those in it.

In the movement profession, most entry points are from an isolated spectrum where a muscle moves a joint through a ROM as the muscle shortens via a concentric contraction. The opposite of isolation is integration, where combinations of tissue work together to control forces associated with eccentric loading best described through the teachings of Gary Gray and Applied Functional Science. While a muscle can move a joint in one direction, typically, combinations of joints/tissue work together to control forces presented before transferring those forces to other tissue and regions via eccentric lengthening and isometric stabilization, before concentric shortening. If one region doesn't move enough, another has to move too much, which can be thought of through a 'victims and criminals' analogy.

From this lens, a majority of injuries occur when forces are presented to the body the body can't effectively handle. Motions (not muscles) should be trained so when forces are presented, combinations of muscles and joints will be able to effectively control the motion rather than causing injury. An understanding of different types of sensations for joint versus muscle versus superficial nerve irritation should also direct treatment.

Biomechanics can be useful, despite if biomechanically driven, because creating input change is necessary to decrease pain, as is creating parasympathetic dominance. Creating more length, mobility, and stability around a joint stimulates proprioceptors, mechanoreceptors, and receptors sensitive to vibration (among others). These are all
afferent receptors and can provide temporary input change. Reinforcement through specific movement specifically designed to be at the threshold of an individual's control translates to non-threatening motor output. Changing biomechanics can help temporarily desensitize a region, presenting another opportunity to create neuroplastic changes that can be reinforced through specific movement, thoughts, and actions.

Touch and manual therapy are similar to biomechanics in that they all influence input. While overlapping and influencing each other, they are distinct categories unto themselves. Simply put, touch and manual therapy produce a cascade of physiological, mechanical, chemical, neurological, and cognitive processes that influence output and autonomic responses, among other processes.

Physical pain is often observable in movement, as most often people move around, instead of through, a painful body part. Over time, this movement pattern becomes ingrained in the system and acute issues often become chronic limitations long after the initial episode of pain and injured tissue has passed. Even when biomechanics isn't the primary dysfunction, from a mechanical standpoint, if there is asymmetry and if tissue doesn't fully lengthen, the lack of pressure differentials result in tissue that is unable to fully slide resulting in a nervous system that is not optimally engaged.

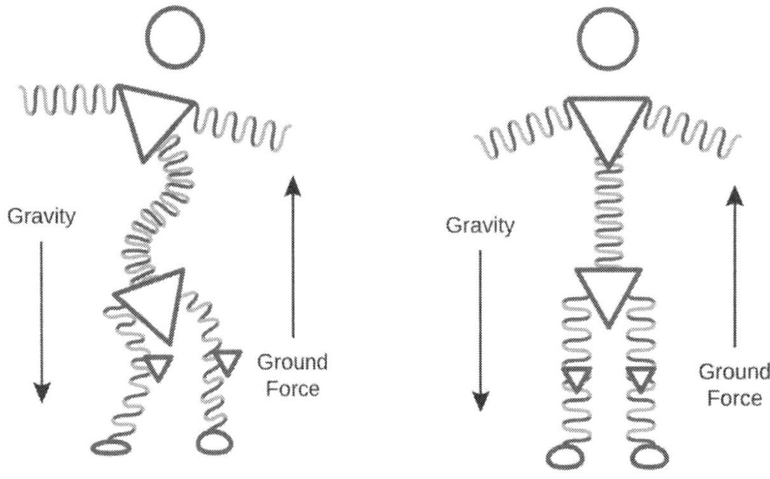

Asymmetries can be seen through movement because the body moves around and not through pain, The body needs to control gravity, ground forces, mass and momentum.

Both Geoffrey Bove and Robert Schleip made note of the fact most times the tissue being worked isn't being permanently changed, at least immediately. In other words, manual therapy likely isn't breaking down scar tissue, and, if anything, is improving the ability of tissue to glide and slide past each other by changing the viscosity of the extracellular matrix. What is more likely is that by improving tissue slide, a feed forward afferent response is created.

"The question becomes, is there mechanical or tissue change that is making the most impact on the area being treated, or is it that the brain suddenly has been given a better awareness, through the cerebellar and parietal feed forward and sensory mechanisms, to better move that body part in the future? If the brain knows better where and how to move a muscle or joint, if can effectively do so absent of pain."

This can potentially help to change output. Lengthening allows many receptors including proprioceptors, mechanoreceptors, exteroceptors, and interoceptors to relatively lengthen, and preserves the continuation of improved viscosity. Relative lengthening stimulates the nervous system because proprioceptors respond to length. This creates a more authentic load and improves output and will be discussed further in later parts. As researcher Dr. Geoffrey Bove describes, it is about the ability of the interfaces of tissue to slide past each other, and difficulty in doing so results in limitation in tissue extensibility, which will also be discussed in depth in later parts.

In conclusion, despite the mechanism of injury, the very nature of pain creates situations where people move around, instead of through, pain. This often results in asymmetrical tissue extensibility and changes to movement, which, over time, often result in functional biomechanical differences one side versus the other. Oftentimes, intervening via biomechanics is a great way to change input, even if temporarily. This illustrates a reason to have a thorough understanding of movement and biomechanics. Understanding integrated movement is a foundation to creating meaningful individual therapies and provides the basis to apply novel influence to the brain.

PART 2: REAL & RELATIVE MOTION

"Why is it so difficult for us to think in relative terms? Well, for the good reason that human nature loves absoluteness, and erroneously considers it as a state of higher knowledge." — **Felix Alba-Juez**

Learning Objective

The purpose of this chapter is to gain an understanding of the concepts involved in real and relative motions as experienced through movement. In this part, some qualities of integrated movement will be laid out, followed by the steps to identify 3D motion, and finishes with a discussion about potential consequences of the lack of full 3D Motion.

Introduction

Integrated movement is a topic studied since my path into physical therapy began over 20 years ago. It started with the Gray Institute as a recommendation from my father, who, as an Exercise Physiologist and personal trainer, also utilized their information. While diving deep into Applied Functional Science methodologies, my studies of integrated motion also included traditional and non-traditional PT approaches. I've always been one to try and find many different resources on one subject in order to synthesize the primary points of any topic and searching for real versus relative motion yielded few results. At the time I wrote my first book, the only resource I found that discussed real versus relative motion was found in Jean Pierre Barral's work about visceral manipulation. However, I have since found some other resources that discuss these concepts.

Texts discussing relative motion of tissue/joints include *Human Locomotion* by Tom Michaud, *Normal & Abnormal Function of the Foot* by Root, Orien, and Weed, along with *Visceral Manipulation* by Jean Pierre Barral. Without explicitly describing it as such, Barral briefly mentions relative motions while discussing how one organ moves past another at a faster rate.

"If a subject stands and bends forward at the waist, his liver will move forward, sliding over the duodenum and the hepatic flexure of the colon below. The liver and the hepatic flexure will both move inferiorly, but the liver more so, since it moves first and farthest with flexion. Thus, we can say that the liver slides anteroinferiorly over the duodenum and hepatic flexure, even if these other structures move in the same direction. Similar processes occur in the other viscera (page 4)."

While both segments are moving forward in space, the liver moves first and farther forward due to being closer to the starting point of the movement, hence describing relative movement of organs.

The body is INTERRELATED, and REACTS to gravity, ground reaction forces, mass and momentum, rather than parts acting independently. In *Human Locomotion*, Michaud has numerous references to relative motions, also without referring to them specifically in that manner. While Tom doesn't use the term 'real and relative motion' in his book, he does make several references that mirror this concept that will be mentioned throughout this book.

Qualities of Integrated Movement: Synchronous Dissociation

Human movement can be defined as a sequential dissociation of body segments. Sequence is important as it implies something moving faster and/or slower, or an order to what moves first and farthest. During gait and many activities, motion should be dissipated through the body by the time it gets to the eyes, to ensure a steady visual field, and means that one body region not moving enough forces another (above or below) to move too much. The ability to feel relative motion, and the ability for bones to move at different rates, is perhaps the most important concept to grasp when it comes to understanding 3D movement.

When assessing joint motion, an idea of what one bone does against the other in three planes of motion helps to create more specificity in intervention. The relative motion of one bone moving faster than the other results in relative lengthening of tissue past other tissue, stimulating proprioceptors and fully 'winding up' tissue in 3D. This wind up can contribute to a joint perceiving motion because stimulation of mechanoreceptors and other proprioceptors, interoceptors, and exteroceptors, send afferent information into the brain, helping to stimulate that region. When tissue can't fully wind up and lengthen, the asymmetries potentially lead to dysfunction because bones moving in the same direction at the same speed result in the joint not perceiving any relative motion and the brain not fully being stimulated, relative to that region.

Proper sequential dissociation of motion allows a full wind up of tissue because some areas move faster or slower. The ability of tissue to wind up and fully dissociate allows for combinations of joints/tissue to work together to control mass, momentum, gravity, and ground forces. When full wind up cannot occur, tissue doesn't go through its full excursion, or ability to get fully long to short, resulting in less blood and oxygen to the tissue. This perpetuates a movement pattern of some regions doing too much to make up for other regions above or below that aren't doing enough. While outright muscle strength is important, the ability to lengthen and fully dissociate allows for each part of the whole to do its share and not overwork one area. Overwork results in overuse and can perpetuate pain experiences, as overuse creates an inflammatory cycle, potentially contributing to peripheral sensitization and ultimately central sensitization.

Movement is asymmetrical and spiral in nature, not symmetrical and linear, traditionally taught in schools. The inherent nature of the body not only includes the movement system, but other systems. These inherent asymmetries include the lungs (3 left lobes and 2 right), one liver & spleen (as Barral speaks of), and asymmetrical hip flexor connections into the diaphragm. All of this asymmetry results in uneven distribution of

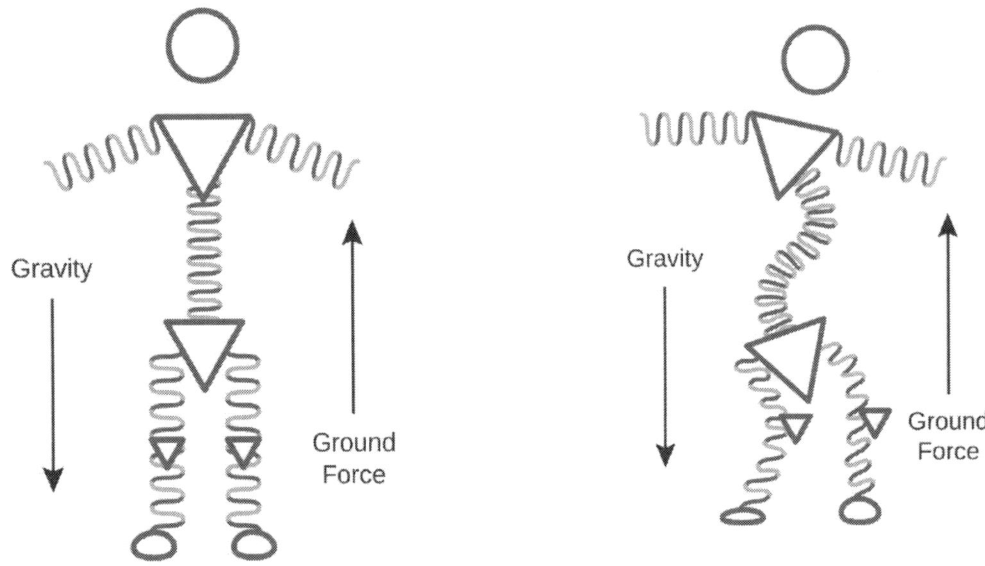

The spiral nature of movement is similar to a helix because gravity doesn't purely compress a helix, instead a helix escapes through rotation.

Forces throughout the system. Simply put, we are asymmetrical, and combined with brain dominance and habits grooved over time, asymmetries can be increased, which itself isn't an issue. However, when drastic asymmetries are observed, this can result in asymmetrical stress on tissues and potentially, pain. When excessive asymmetry causes dysfunction, which causes pain, differences should be considered as a potential source of dysfunction, and at the very least a place to create temporary afferent change.

The spiral nature of movement is similar to a helix because gravity doesn't purely compress a helix; instead a helix escapes through rotation. Rotation along the vertical axis of gravity creates compressive and tensional forces distributed through the body, allowing chains of joints/tissue to control forces presented. In a joint, oftentimes when one side is compressed, the other is tensioned. Segmentally, the middle region can compress while above and below tensions or vice versa. Alternating compression and tension allows for the proper amount of stability and mobility at each segment and can be felt when standing tall and reaching for something. Concurrently, when looked at three dimensionally, the spine and vertebrae also feel compression on one side and tension on the other while reaching. What's often felt is a stretch in the middle of the body (or core), and compression (or muscle engagement) above and below, or vice versa. While specific fascial lines aren't discussed in this text, understanding the connections assists in creating a workable framework to look at movement. Specifically, I ask myself what combinations of tissue would work together to control a painful motion.

The ability to fully lengthen and shorten while efficiently sequencing in and out of positions are other qualities of integrated movement. Sequencing into and out of a movement is relevant because when proper sequence doesn't occur, the result is often bones moving at the same speed, joints not registering any motion, and muscles creating rather and controlling force. Improper sequencing and lack of ability to eccentrically load means muscles need to create the same force as they would through a full eccentric load, and, over time, leads to overuse because eccentric load is far less energy expensive compared to concentric muscle action. Lack of lengthening combined with improper bone sequencing means often muscles around regions without proper bone dissociation have to concentrically work to synchronize the system as motion continues up/downward. Physiologically speaking, concentrically shortening instead of eccentrically loading and isometrically stabilizing, is an expensive strategy that is energy expensive and inefficient. My conjecture is when muscles have to concentrically work, particularly in the gait cycle, it is to resync an asynchronous system. Concentric muscle action through the gait cycle becomes problematic over time because it's energy expensive and produces a cascade of neurochemical events that drops the pH in tissue. This is a salient point that will be discussed in depth in later parts.

Muscles CAN produce force and during the gait cycle are far more efficient and effective when they first control and react to external forces. Lengthening creates an internal tissue tension that transmits forces through the body. Within this paradigm, it's possible to see how, from heel strike through foot flat, the quadriceps controls not only knee flexion, but abduction in the frontal plane and internal rotation in the transverse plane, or what we call knee valgus. Knee valgus is a normal physiological motion and not bad. Rather, not controlling knee valgus is bad.

Examples of isolated muscle function can be found in any number of books where muscles are named for their concentric action. I call this the seven ocean mentality to muscle function. The seven ocean mentality, like isolated muscle, is a man-made construct in that the quad, in isolation, or as one of the seven oceans, extends the knee. Yet, this is merely part of the equation because, in reality, the quadricep is hundreds of smaller muscles that we clump into four. Perhaps it should be called the 'quad stuff'. In isolation, the anterior thigh musculature (called the 'quads'), can extend the knee by creating a force, but most times they react to forces and work to control motion. In addition, the concept of concentric muscle action in isolation during activities, including during gait, is outdated.

A more realistic view of gait acknowledges a seamless coordination of eccentric load and isometric stabilization of multiple joints vs. the view that gait is created by individual muscles concentrically shortening. In other words, an inability to effectively eccentrically load and/or isometric stabilize can force the muscle to concentrically act, which is inefficient for reasons including increased energy production compared to eccentric and isometric (which is non-inflammatory) muscle action.

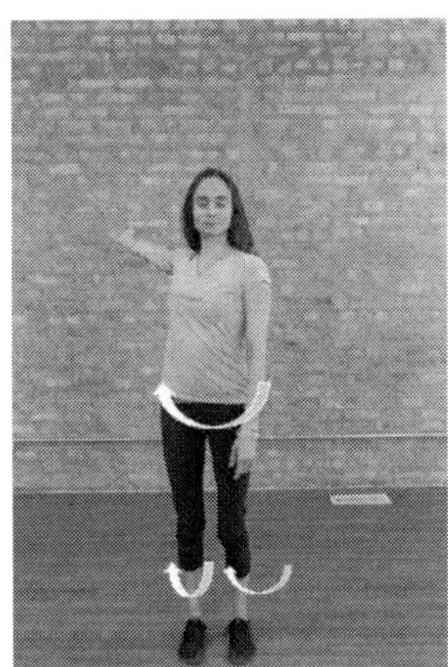

Driving the right hand in space to end range should create a subconscious reaction where both feet will rotate to the right in space, eliciting the left foot pronation and right supination at the feet and other reactions higher in the chain.

Qualities of Integrated Movement: Drivers

A large component to understanding 3D movement and using it as a tool for assessment and intervention, is the concept of a driver, defined as a way to create a reaction. Conceptualizing which bone should move faster and knowing how to create a reaction to see what happens at a specific region is part of the process. This section dives deeper into the specific qualities of drivers and why it makes them part of an integrated movement paradigm.

DRIVERS

As mentioned, a driver is a way to create a reaction. There are many different types of drivers in the body, including subconscious, biological, psychological, and sociological reactions, which continuously occur. AFS (Applied Functional Science) is defined as a combination of the physical, behavioral, and biological sciences, with drivers consistently subconsciously occurring in each system. Relative to movement, a driver is defined as using a body part to subconsciously create motion in another body part.

When the sequence into and out of the movement is understood, it can be assessed to see if it is happening, and if it is not then further investigation may be warranted.
A behavioral driver example is picking up a crying child who needs comforting or getting aggravated while driving because everyone else is a bad driver. The child crying elicited a behavioral reaction, as did the perceived bad drivers. In the driving example, getting cut off and aggravated releases the stress hormone cortisol. Cortisol stimulates sympathetic actions and represses parasympathetic response of the nervous system and perpetuates the experienced feelings. A full bladder is an example of a biological driver, as it creates a reaction to cease an activity to micturate.

Utilizing a body part to subconsciously create motions into another body part is a physical driver. For example, when standing with feet shoulder width apart and straight ahead, if the right hand is rotated right at shoulder height to its end range and the pelvis is allowed to also move, the expectation is the left foot will correspondingly pronate (flatten) and the right foot will supinate (higher arch). Driving the right hand in space creates a subconscious reaction where both feet will rotate to the right, eliciting the left foot pronation and right supination. If performed correctly and those motions don't occur, I'm going to assess further to try and find out where in the chain, motion may be blocked.

> ***Author's Note:***
> *The above driver is an assessment I often use in my clinic. The expectation is when the hand is reached to its end range in either direction and the pelvis can swing freely, there should be reactions from the feet to the cervical spine. Sometimes, the person will only move the arm and upper body with these reaches, in which case the instructions should be to let the pelvis follow the swinging arm. In addition, an 'eye' driver can be utilized during this same movement by having them look somewhere in space, winding up the tissue of the cervical spine. Looking forward in conjunction with the arm driver described above (as opposed to moving the head with the thoracic spine results in cervical rotation).*

Based on these examples and descriptions, including understanding that a joint can 'feel' the same motion in five different ways, knowing where a drive is coming from is helpful. The following section on the five ways a joint can feel the same motion is a section copied from my first text, *REAL Movement: Perspective on Integrated Motion & Motor Control:*

Remember that in the extremities, motion is named for how a distal bone moves on a fixed proximal bone. Yet, there are few times when one bone moves and another stays still. Instead bones move in the same or opposite direction, with one moving faster or slower than the one above or below. This is analogous to one train moving right out of the other train's window. For this to happen, one train has to move faster or slower than the other so that, from Train A's perspective, Train B is moving to the right.

The following pictures describe the combinations of movement that can result in Train B moving out of Train A's window to the right. As an analogy, Train A is the tibia, or distal bone, and Train B is the femur, or proximal bone, and the space between the two trains/bones is the 'knee joint'.

Recall that bones move, joints feel or sense the bone movement, and muscles react to the forces that create the bone motion; and if bones move in the same direction at the same speed, despite the bone motion, the joint won't sense any motion. If both trains move in the same direction at the same speed, Train B will never move out of train A's window to the right.

In Picture 1, the distal bone stays still, and the proximal bone moves right.

In Picture 2, the distal bone moves left on a fixed proximal, still resulting in Train B moving right from Train A's perspective.

In Picture 3, the distal bone moves one direction and the proximal bone moves in the opposite direction, resulting in Train B moving right from Train A's perspective.

In Picture 4, the distal bone moves in the direction, and the proximal bone moves in the direction faster, resulting in Train B moving to the right from Train A's perspective.

In Picture 5, Train A moves to the left faster than Train B. Both bones move in the same direction with the distal bone moving faster than the proximal, resulting in Train B moving right from Train A's perspective.

Picture 1. Train A stays still, and train B moves to the right, resulting in Train B moving out of Train A's window to the right.

Picture 2. Train A moves to the left, and Train B stays still, resulting in Train B moving out of Train A's window to the right.

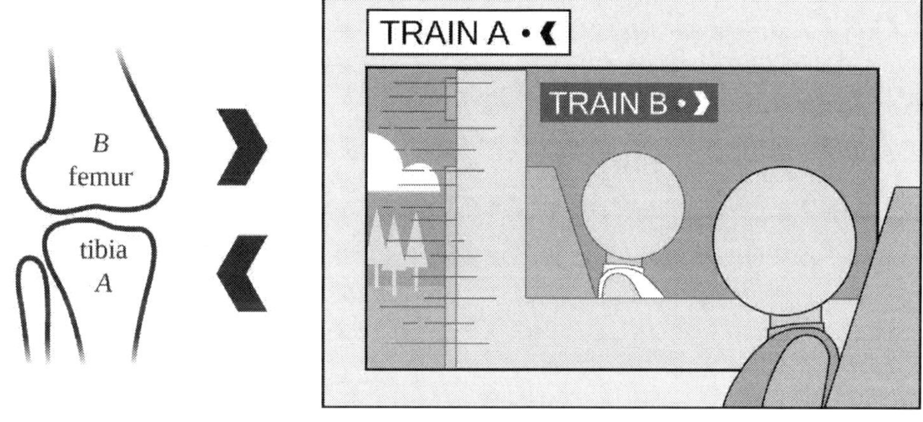

Picture 3. Train A moves to the left and Train B moves to the right, resulting in Train B moving out of Train A's window to the right.

Picture 4. Train A moves to the right, and Train B moves to the right faster than Train A, resulting in Train B moving out of Train A's window to the right.

Picture 5. Train A moves to the left faster than Train B, resulting in Train B moving out of Train A's window to the right.

TOP-DOWN VS. BOTTOM-UP DRIVER

When both bones that make up a joint move in the same direction and the top moves faster, it implies a top down driver. A ***top down driver implies*** that motion comes from above and the top bone moves farther and faster in the direction of movement relative to the bottom bone. The faster bone is always closer to the driver. The example of someone standing tall and rotating the right hand to the right at shoulder height to end range creates a top down motion into the joints below. This includes the feet and thoracic bones, meaning all the bones in the body moved and not one stayed still, however it doesn't mean they sequentially dissociated, as an understanding of integrated motion is necessary for that. Remember, bones move, joints feel (or perceive), and muscles react to motion; there aren't many instances when one bone moves, and another doesn't. Said differently, and a play on the previous sentence by my friend and clinical editor of this book, Dr. Mike Drzewiecki, "Bones provide structure and move, joints provide feedback and connection, muscles stabilize and can create motion, and the nervous system perceives, orchestrates, and fine tunes all of the above."

When bones move in the same direction and the bottom segment moves faster, it implies a ***bottom up driver*** because the bottom bone moves in the direction faster than the top bone. For example, using the same driver described above (right hand rotated right at shoulder height, or behind the body), if the eyes remain forward, the body (most of the cervical spine) *feels* left cervical rotation, even though the cervical spine segments are rotating right in space. If the head remains focused forward (look straight ahead), the cervical spine experiences left rotation despite the cervical segments rotating right. This is because the bottom bones move right faster than the top bones, and in the spine, motion is named for what the top does on a fixed bottom. In this instance, both bones are moving right with the bottom moving in the direction faster than the top. If the bottom bone is fixed and the above relationship remains the same between segments, the cervical spine feels left rotation. Although the cervical segments are rotating right in space, known as real bone motion (or osteokinematics), the joint perceives left cervical rotation due to the relative motion (or arthrokinematics). Right cervical segment rotation is considered the real bone motion, or osteokinematics. This example uses a right arm driver to create bottom up motion in the cervical segments and top down motion in the thoracic, lumbar, pelvic, hip, knee, and foot segments.

Both top down & bottom up during gait, depending on where

From heel strike through foot flat, the front leg in gait reacts to a bottom up driver because ground forces are lateral to the center of the subtalar joint. That is to say calcaneal eversion and foot flattening is given for free and the body should control these motions. This bottom up force creates a calcaneal eversion moment, allowing the talus to fall down and in at heel strike. The talus (rear foot) motion creates (drives) motion into the tibia, which creates motion into the femur. It is important to note while primarily a bottom up motion into the lower extremity, at heel strike there is top down drive into the forefoot. The forefoot and rearfoot both evert, however the rearfoot should do it faster and farther, therefore the forefoot experiences a relative inversion at heel strike while the rest of the lower extremity experiences a bottom up drive.

Bottom up motion occurs into the lower extremity at heel strike due to the center of gravity being medial to the calcaneus. This forces the tibia to also rotate inward towards midline, but not as far or as fast as the talus. Through this reaction, transverse plane tibial rotation should create femur rotation in the same direction, but not as far or as fast as the tibia. For example, when the left foot hits the ground, the left calcaneus everts for free, causing the talus to drop in towards middle. The talar motion towards midline causes the left tibia to rotate right towards midline, but not as far or as fast as the talus. The chain reaction forces the femur to follow in towards midline, also rotating right, however not as far or as fast as the tibia below. At least this should happen, and when it doesn't, potential issues may arise above or below the immobile region. Motion at heel strike is given for free that the body has to control and if one part isn't able to coordinate and synchronize movement effectively, the result is too much motion somewhere as compensation. The hypermobile region is typically the victim, or site of the injury while the criminal remains silent and can be found above or below.

Understanding specificity of 3D motion at a joint & through a movement

Often, a key to creating individualized programs is assessing 3D joint motion because comprehending what one bone should do against another in all three planes of motion creates an opportunity to check if it's happening, and if it's not, to ask why.

Rules to Identify joint motion

One example of synchronous motion can be seen when analyzing transverse triplane motion of the knee at heel strike. Following a systematic thought process is helpful. Breaking it down into answerable steps helps the process to identify 3D joint motion.

The **first step to define joint motion is** to answer what two bones make up the joint, because a joint is a space between bones. Understanding the arthrokinematics, or how one bone 3D moves against the other, is the objective. Relative to the knee, the two bones are the tibia and femur because the patella simply follows along for the ride.

The **second rule to identify 3D joint motion is** distinguishing if the bones move in the same or opposite direction in each plane during motion. For example, in gait, when the left foot hits the ground, the left tibia rotates internally, or to the right. It responds to the talus moving in and towards middle secondary to calcaneal eversion. The tibia responds to the talus moving, and the femur follows the tibia, but not as far or as fast because, when the foot hits the ground, motion is driven bottom up. If assessing the left knee at heel strike, both bones move right, from heel strike to foot flat.

When the bones making up the joint move in the same direction, **the third rule to identify 3D joint motion** is asked. Which bone is moving faster, the top or the bottom? Stated differently, knowing where the drive came from is important to answering rule three.

Recall that, in the extremities, motion is named for the distal bone moving on a fixed proximal bone despite this never happening. During motion, bones move in the same or opposite direction. If in the same direction, typically one bone should move faster or slower than the other, and so understanding what SHOULD happen is imperative. Bones could move in one direction and the joint could FEEL exactly the opposite, depending on sequence.

Author's Note

The rules laid out are simplified and not always complete and intended as the basic concepts that need to be mastered for conceptualizing 3D movement. For example, what is not discussed fully is the starting position of the bones, which sometimes is necessary. The Gray Institute is the authority for understanding three dimensional movement and assessment strategies for understanding real vs. relative joint mechanics. For further information on this in depth topic, please visit the Gray Institute.

THE BACK LEG IN GAIT EXPERIENCES PRIMARILY A TOP DOWN DRIVE, OR SHOULD BE

While the front foot is a bottom up driver into the system, the trail leg primarily experiences top down motion. When the right leg becomes the back leg during left leg swing phase, momentum of the left foot swinging forward causes the pelvis to rotate right with concurrent anterior translation. The action of left leg swing and pelvic translation causes the right femur to rotate right, just not as far or as fast as above. Right femur rotation causes right tibial rotation (but not as far or as fast), forcing talar abduction as it rides back atop the calcaneus, inverting in the frontal plane. Calcaneal inversion as a response to tibial external rotation should result in midfoot stiffening, necessary for effective and efficient toe off propulsion.

From mid-stance through heel lift, correct sequencing demonstrates that right femoral rotation (external rotation of bone) causes right tibia rotation (external rotation of bone), creating relative right knee *internal* rotation. That is to say, stance leg bones externally rotate due to the left leg swinging, and as a result, the right knee joint experiences internal rotation, right up to the point of heel lift.

This is contrary to what many descriptions entail because they illustrate external rotation through this entire phase. However, according to this thought process, external rotation should only occur from heel lift through toe off as a result of the momentum of the swing leg combined with ground forces inverting the calcaneus causing tibial external rotation that is faster than the femur. The feeling of external rotation is 'felt' at the knee joint at this phase because the tibia externally rotates faster than the femur. If literature that describes extremity motion is applied to this situation, the knee feels external rotation because the mind's eye sees the top bone moves externally slower than the bottom bone, which means fixing the top makes the bottom move outward, relative to the top.

KEY POINT

Motion in the extremities is named for the distal bone moving on a fixed proximal bone. Motion in the spine is named for the proximal bone moving on a fixed distal bone.

This can be seen by applying the steps to naming joint motion described above. The knee feels more internal rotation while the bones are externally rotating when the calcaneus is on the ground, because motion in the extremities is described relative to the distal bone moving on a fixed proximal bone. Recall that bones move, joints feel, muscles react, and the nervous system responds, regulates, and refines movement. If two bones move in the same direction, also described as real bone external rotation, one most likely will move faster.

In the situation described above, the proximal stance leg bone moves externally faster than the distal bone because it Is driven from the swinging leg that creates pelvic motion causing the femur to move accordingly. This occurs despite both bones externally rotating. As a result, the knee should feel internal rotation at the back phase of gait until the heel raises.

Upon heel raise, at the end of the stance phase, the knee should experience external rotation due to the calcaneal inversion at heel lift that causes tibial external rotation at a faster rate than the femur. This bottom up drive into the knee results in faster tibial motion into external rotation compared to the femur and creates the perception of stance knee external rotation from heel lift through toe off, into swing phase. Knee external rotation should be perceived through swing until heel strike, when the cycle begins again.

Knee Motion from midstance until heel lift:

1. What two bones?:

   Tibia and femur

2. Same direction or opposite direction?:

   Same direction, motion is being driven from the opposite leg swinging.

3. Which bone is moving faster, the top or bottom?:

   Top is moving faster in the direction because it's being driven from the opposite leg swinging.

Therefore, the knee feels internal rotation because both bones are moving in the same direction, but the top is moving faster than the bottom.

Describing motion at a joint

- Joint:

  -space between bones

  0. What is bone starting position?

  – 1. What 2 bones make up joint?

  – 2. Are bones moving in same or opposite direction in each plane?

  - Think clock!

  – 3. Top faster than bottom? Bottom faster than top?

Cant just look at body part. Ie hip or knee
ITS ALL RELATIVE!!!

20

KEY POINT

Understanding why someone has pain or dysfunction is not easy. We all strive to answer that question to the best of our ability. Often times, the reasons why are beyond our capacity and scope to help. Therefore, having other medical professionals to refer to is important. Nobody is an island unto themselves. Having a team of medical professionals outside your immediate scope is beneficial to the patient. My team includes one or two non-surgical doctors, one or two surgeons, DC and Osteopath, a physical therapist, two massage therapists, and a podiatrist, in addition to personal trainers. Not being able to answer "why" is a huge personal driver to be the best clinician I can.

What happens when relative motions don't happen?

In my experience, often injury occurs when forces are presented that the body can't handle, typically having difficulty controlling some combination of gravity, ground reactive forces, mass, and/or momentum. Most often, the difficulty occurs at the point when the body should transition a load into an unload. In other words, injury occurs when the body should begin the sequence out of the movement while it is still getting loaded into the movement.

With knee pain, understanding and assessing correct bone sequence into and out of motion is helpful because often dysfunction occurs from lack of sequencing. It's possible the knee experiences pain as a result of the tibia not achieving full bottom up rotation at this phase, creating faster femoral external rotation vs. the contralateral side. In this case, if the femur moves externally faster than the tibia, based on rules of naming motion, dictate the knee would feel external rotation at a point in time when it should feel internal. While not always the case, if it's not compared to the other side and taken into account, how is it known?

Therefore, understanding sequencing and knowing how to logically assess movement, regardless of the lack of empirical evidence surrounding Transformational Zones (TZ-as described by the Gray Institute) is important in creating logical movement progressions. Yet, assessing the specific mechanics at the joint isn't always necessary, and while helpful when it is, there isn't much research surrounding it, which in certain cases can prove a challenge. However, there is substantial knowledge on joint capacities associated with the gait cycle and assessing and treating capacities as a primary strategy is more reproducible. While knowledge of TZs is helpful and a personal go to, treating capacities simplifies things, and is discussed more in future parts.

Through understanding 3D joint motion, specific reactions can be created for different situations, including analyzing specific capacities of a task, such as gait. Gait is a good example because most people do it and there is a substantial amount of empirical evidence supporting joint capacities during activity. If a movement is understood, it can then be assessed to see if what should happen, does. When compared to the opposite side, if a body part is restricted and unable to fully lengthen or *dissociate,* the result is often a segment above or below moving at the same speed.

Clinical Concept: I recall learning in an orthotics course called Orthotic Chain Reaction to think fore foot first for pain below the knee and rear foot for pains above the knee. Obviously, there are exceptions to the rule, as there are times when the foot isn't the driver of dysfunction, yet it is often a good place to start.

Understanding proper sequencing is necessary for a joint to feel the proper 3D motion, creating an opportunity to see if it is happening symmetrically in the body. When it isn't and there's pain, I find it is common for the two bones making up a joint to move in the correct direction with incorrect sequencing compared to the non-painful side (but not always). Incorrect sequencing, where the bone above or below is moving too fast or not fast enough, can create a situation where a joint feels the opposite motion of what it should be feeling at a particular time for a specific task.

Dissociation of segments is often required for fluid movement, and when there isn't, (particularly in pain situations where one joint is different in motion compared to contralateral), an opportunity for improvement arises. If two bones move at the same speed in the same direction, the joint won't perceive any motion, limiting tissue and receptor lengthening. Limited lengthening (loading) means there is a limited ability to absorb forces and decelerate motion, potentially creating situations that require increased concentric action. In other words, the ability to sequentially lengthen, absorb forces, and decelerate motion, creates situations that allow the joint to register movement and improves proprioception and muscle activation.

Said differently, at heel strike, the tibia and femur should move towards midline with the tibia moving faster. This creates an internal rotation moment at the knee. Often, I've found those with patellofemoral knee pain experienced during heel strike>foot flat, (runners, jumpers, lungers, walkers, or stair steppers) is due to the tibia not rotating inwards at the rate it should relative to the femur. The lack of proper sequence often results in the femur moving inwards faster, creating an external rotation moment at the knee. This typically coincides with the patella smacking the lateral femoral condyle, where we often blame the dysfunctional VMO (vastus-medialis oblique, or inside quad muscles). Yet looking within an integrated lens, it's seen the tibia not moving inward faster than the femur, causes the femur to move faster and results in the patella smacking into the lateral condyle, causing 'patellofemoral pain" and knee external rotation. In short, it's not the VMO's fault when the knee hurts. The tibia and femur should move towards midline at this phase, with the tibia moving faster and farther, resulting in knee internal rotation at the First Transformational Zone. However, often for whatever reason, the tibia doesn't move inward as fast as the femur, creating a knee external rotation moment at the wrong time. This can easily occur with a limitation in the foot that reduces calcaneal eversion or the talus from dropping in towards the middle, or because of too much forefoot motion.

Another example is anterior knee pain when stepping down. In my experience, the pain is often driven from too much anterior shearing and translation forces of the femur while translating anteriorly on the tibial plateau. This can happen for any number of reasons including too much transverse plane rotation from the lack of dissociation at the foot and/or hip. These people also often exhibit a knee instead of hip dominant strategy to bending. Knee dominant squatting increases femoral shearing forces, therefore, therapeutically improving transverse plane motion improves real bone rotation and reduces translation. Improving motion needs to occur in conjunction with teaching correct movement patterns, which, in this case, would include hip dominant strategies. Of course, the question clinically becomes why is the femur (or tibia) translating rather than rotating, which many times is from lack of foot dissociation during the first phase of movement? In other words, lack of motion in a joint(s) in the foot can result in lack of dissociation into the lower extremity. Therefore, it is important to check foot mechanics on anyone with knee pain.

A step down can highlight asymmetries in the lower extremity, and can be helpful for those in pain, particularly in the first phase of the gait cycle. The foot, knee, hip, and pelvic control can all be easily assessed via this movement.

These concepts hold true throughout the body, including the shoulder complex, particularly with 'impingement syndromes' of the rotator cuff. Experience dictates during shoulder flexion/scaption/abduction moments, there is a 'scapular rhythm' that consists of two degrees of humerus motion for every one degree of motion at the scapula. In other words, the humerus needs to move farther and faster compared to the scapula, however, sometimes, the scapula and humerus do not sequentially dissociate. In these instances, the result is often the scapula and humerus moving at the same speed, altering joint mechanics that often results in angry shoulder tissue. Like most body parts, assessing which bone is moving farther and faster can be accomplished simply by placing the hands on the two bones making up the joint and driving motion into it, combined with knowing what should happen.

Shoulder complex capacities will be discussed in the capacities part of the book, and while palpation skills shouldn't ever be solely relied upon for intervention, developing a sense of touch can be helpful. In addition, having thorough assessment skills to differentiate the driver of the uncomfortable sensation in the shoulder creates more specificity. Sometimes the sensation will be capsular/joint limited, other times it will be muscle or soft tissue, or even peripheral nerve irritation; having that understanding allows for the most specific intervention.

Chapter Conclusion

Before moving forward with this book, it is important to understand the fundamentals in this chapter, because integrated movement provides the foundation for how I apply the rest of the information discussed throughout later parts. Having knowledge of the different types of drivers and how to assess them not only helps determine the 3D mechanics of any motion while allowing the most individualized intervention. We also discussed the concepts of sequential dissociation, and that limitation in a region can create compensation in other areas.

Additional Reading Suggestions

- Gray, G. *Functional Video Digest Series. Vol 3.4 Functional Manual Reaction- The Foot and Ankle, Vol. 3.8 Proprioceptors.*
- Gray, G. Tiberio, D, video blogs on www.GrayInstitute.com
- Rolf, Ida P., and Rosemary Feitis. *Rolfing and Physical Reality*
- Vernon Brooks: The Neural Basis for Motor Control
- Cook, G. *Movement Functional Movement Systems: Screening, Assessment, Corrective Strategies*
- Barral, J. P., and Pierre Mercier. *Visceral Manipulation.*
- Root, Orien, Weed; *Normal and Abnormal Function of the Foot*
- Michaud, Thomas; *Human Locomotion*
- Wolf, Adam; *REAL Movement: Perspective on Integrated Motion & Motor Control*
- *Robert Schliep Website: www.somatics.de*

PART 3: CAPACITIES: THE GAIT CYCLE

"Always walk through life as if you have something new to learn, and you will."

— Vernon Howard

Introduction

The concept of treating capacities instead of anatomy was put into words for me by Dr. David George, founder of FNOR. It immediately made sense to me, as I was already treating in this paradigm without describing it as such. This part will discuss why we treat capacities and will focus on gait, while the next part (Part 4), will discuss other movement related capacities. These parts will also further introduce why to consider a brain-based approach, including understanding the role of the cerebellum and vestibulo-ocular systems in all movement.

Capacities include everyday activities that are grounded in empirical evidence and include gait, squatting, reaching, and sit<>stand, to name a few. Treating capacities is similar in concept to Transformation Zones, which provides a helpful thought process to understand sequencing into and out of movement, yet I've observed difficulty in practitioners truly understanding and utilizing AFS strategies effectively due to the depth of knowledge required for effective utilization. Treating capacities provides an easy framework because it anchors to established metrics and is validated by empirical evidence such as gait. Capacities are less abstract than TZs, which are helpful when more specificity about a specific joint motion is required, particularly when comparing one side to the other (an N of 1).

While gait can be simplified to first and second transformational zones as discussed by the Gray Institute, I've found measuring specific angles of joints during the gait cycle is more reproducible and will be expanded upon in this part. Maintaining the ability to keep specific body parts aligned through specific movements is necessary. It's my observation the inability to do so results in increased movement often in either the knee, low back, neck, or shoulder or neck, depending on the movement.

Spectrums, Thresholds, and Capacities

Movement is a spectrum that can be progressed based on specific individual thresholds with one end housing integration, and at the other, isolation. With two steps in the middle, the four step progression laid out in later parts allows for the ability to work at a threshold, which is important to making changes. Working below or above a threshold results in little positive neurological adaptation, which is often a primary goal of therapies, and a reason to have various ways to monitor a threshold. Intermediate steps allow for a progressive<>regressive strategy based on the individual. In other words, if the threshold is exceeded or never met in the first place, the desired neurological response is difficult to achieve. Pain science emphasizes graded exposure, or progressing slowly with any new biological, physiological, or sociological stimulus. Too much (or not enough) stimulus won't have the desired results, which often include stimulating specific regions of the brain in order to create neuroplastic changes.

Integrated movement patterns that aren't clean or controlled should be regressed, otherwise it reinforces poor movement. In other words, when a joint/tissue is unable to handle an integrated load, regressive strategies are necessary for the region to learn and accept the load. This includes possible isolated movements if the body is unable to effectively control loading forces (including gravity, ground force, mass, or momentum). Once isolative movements are controlled, they can be progressed with emphasis on ensuring that correct relationships are maintained through movement applied with appropriate intensity.

Extrapolating current research provides many insights and few definitives. Insights include recognizing pain produces a latency or delay in timing to the painful region. Pain is an output and in chronic situations results in "cortical smudging" or decreased representation in the somatosensory cortex to the painful region. Therefore, strategies to improve brain representation to the painful region are necessary. This is best accomplished when working at (without exceeding) an individual threshold. Exceeding a threshold is easy, and once passed, difficult to step back or unwind during that session. Similarly, it is just as easy to never work at the individual threshold and consequently never make the desired (or rapid) changes. Driving intense multimodal input into specific parts of the brain can create improved representation to that body part, which often takes a specific amount of stressor to stimulate and maintain representation. The brain needs novelty when learning new tasks. Said differently, too much stress applied too early can easily overstress a system that is already compromised and stuck in a perpetual cycle, just as not enough stress at a threshold won't make the desired changes.

Key Point

There are many ways to assess thresholds, which will be discussed in later parts, however a quick reference is if the breath is held with the activity, or position is difficult to maintain, you're close.

The ability to understand where someone is on an integrated<> isolated movement spectrum combined with understanding their threshold allows for a truly individualized program. This will be discussed in depth in a later part. Pain is complicated, multifactorial, and an output. This means non-threatening input, even if short lasting, can help to change output. These inputs can be repeatedly performed in order to long term potentiate new behaviors. Inputs include touch, vibration, heat/cold, two point discrimination, vision, movement, and self-talk, among others. In my experience, repeated mindful inputs combined with education about WHY these inputs are important can help create parasympathetic dominance, behavior change, and new patterns necessary to improve a desired outcome.

Working at Thresholds, They Are Required for Change

Input takes on many forms and examples include vibration, heat, pressure, proprioception, vision, hearing, cognitive function, and self-talk. Clinically, I've observed commonalities of people in pain. Generally speaking, they tend to demonstrate a pattern of sympathetic dominance (fight or flight). Those in pain also often have neurogenic inhibition that results in cortical smudging, or less representation in the somatosensory cortex. Pain forces people to move around, instead of through, painful areas and is easily observable. Over time, moving around instead of through pain results in adaptations in the composition of soft tissue, resulting in asymmetrical lengthening and load distribution. Therefore, creating parasympathetic dominance, improving brain representation to a painful region while improving tissue quality, are all important aspects of working with those in pain.

Time and application of load and force is required to change soft tissue, positive or negative. Mechanical load stimulates a chemical process that influences fiber alignment, direction, and ability of tissue to maintain glide, while concurrently influencing neuroplasticity. Said differently, and to quote Dr. Andreo Spina, founder of Functional Range Conditioning, "force is the language of the cells". Neuroplastic changes consistently occur, reinforcing old pathways or creating and improving new pathways. Therefore, the application of thoughtful and meaningful mechanical load must be considered, particularly for those with pain or injury. Appropriate load is necessary for stimulating the nervous system and working at an individual threshold and is also necessary to create soft tissue changes. For example, when a hamstring is injured, the result (and expectation), is that myofibroblastic activity will lay down tissue that is less elastic and more collagenous in nature. This is a good thing but can also be a bad thing if there's too much or it's too multidirectional in nature. Therefore, applying external loads into tissue, including muscle contractions of various intensities, along with manual therapy, is warranted because the external application of mechanical load 'tells' the cells to lay down new tissue in along the applied lines of force. In other words, an external application of force is required to mediate a chemical response in tissue.

According to Merriam-Webster, a threshold is defined as "the magnitude or intensity that must be exceeded for a certain reaction, phenomenon, result, or condition, to occur or be manifested".

A ***physical threshold*** can be thought of as the point when performing a clean, fluid, and rhythmical motion without compensation is difficult. This threshold coincides with a loss of form through a movement.

A ***biological threshold*** includes nerve polarization action potentials for contraction or relaxation (depending on the mechanism), and also reflex systems of the body. Reflex systems include bladder, muscle, and pressure receptors. In addition, the gate-threshold pain theory explains that a certain level of noxious stimulus is required for the 'gate' to open and the brain to perceive a threat. In simplified terms, over time, the gate can get 'stuck' open due to a series of chemical and biological process. These processes essentially merge the various input pathways to the point of brain confusion. This is something that occurs in chronic pain experiences and should be addressed through various modalities to help create input differentiation.

A ***behavioral threshold*** is defined as "the point at which a stimulus is of sufficient intensity to begin to produce an effect" on behavior, positive or negative. For example, concentration has a threshold, and from my understanding, after fifty-ish minutes, there's a point of diminishing returns. For that reason, my sessions are scheduled on a 45 minute structure, with emphasis on learning a new task being kept to the first half of a session, with reinforcement through the remainder (although when appropriate, patients often stay longer).

Understanding an integrated to isolated movement spectrum can allow the most specificity and ways to create lasting change. This is best accomplished by working at the threshold of the nervous system, which requires consistent bouts of focused, intense, and mindful activity over time.

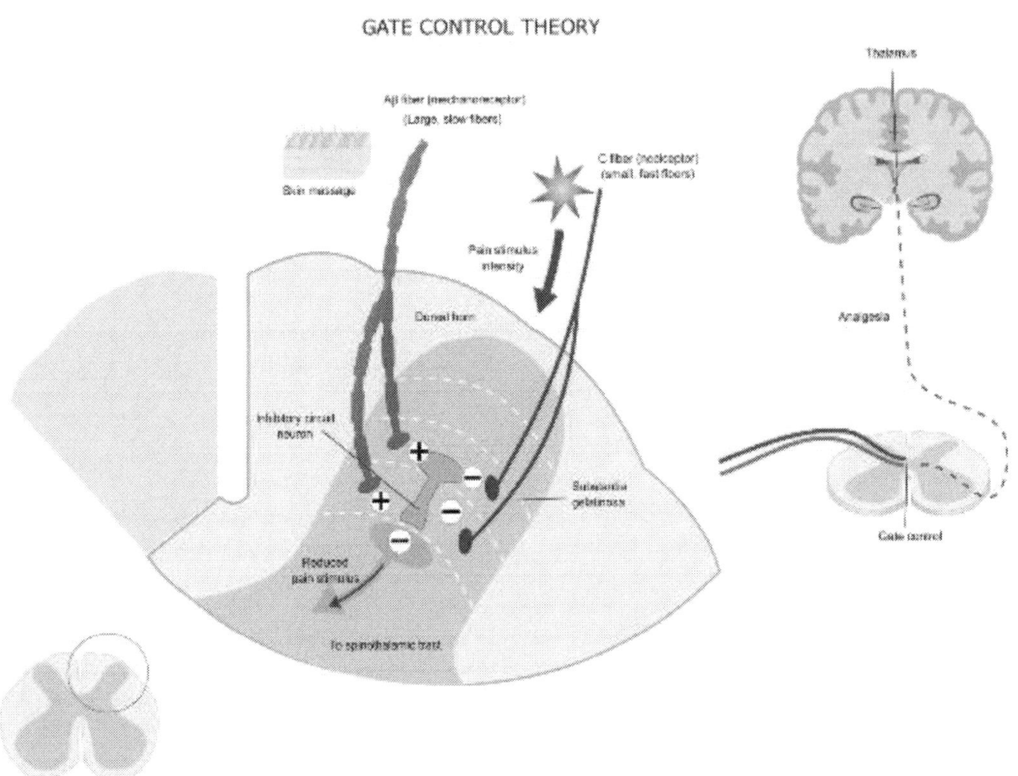

The gate-threshold pain theory explains that a certain level of noxious stimulus is required for the 'gate' to open and the brain to perceive threat and will be discussed more in depth in later chapters.

Soft Tissue, Tensegrity, and Capacities

Soft tissue should stabilize joints through isometric contraction more than produce joint forces through concentric activity. This is discussed at length by Dr. Tom Michaud in his book *Human Locomotion.* He notes, "As demonstrated by Biewener and Daley, the proximal muscles of the hip and knee tend to have long parallel fascicles with little tendon elasticity, while the distal muscles of the foot and leg tend to have short, pennate fascicles with long, flexible tendons (106)." He goes on to state, "The short fibers present in the distal muscles allow them to generate force extremely economically by contracting either isometrically or with low shortening velocities. Energy is stored in their stretched tendons, with little work being done by their short pennate fibers (107)." When viewed from this lens, it's evident the role of isometric contraction in stability and energy transference through soft tissue is important. Understanding that muscles with long tendons are force reducers and muscles with short tendons are force producers (or should be) is helpful.

Clinically, isometric activity is a powerful strategy to find more representation in the somatosensory cortex and should also dynamically occur during gait to stabilize joints. Concentric muscle activity is inefficient and not the desired strategy to utilize, particularly during gait. Instead, tendon lengthening combined with sustained isometric contractions result in efficient force production. Michaud goes onto say, “In order for tendons to store energy effectively, they must be stretched through very specific ranges, since excessive stretching could produce injury, while too small a range would limit energy storage; e.g., a rubber band stretched through a small range of motion would not return significant energy, and an overstretched rubber band would break (108)”. In other words, when muscles are required to concentrically produce force without an efficient eccentric load or isometric stabilization, the result is often overworking and muscle irritation, along with the associated inflammatory processes.

Early in my career I didn’t grasp the concept of multi-joint muscles lengthening to control forces while one joint muscles should stabilize. Rather than follow a logical thought process of mastering isometrics followed by eccentric work, my focus would often be on concentric muscle activation. This is what was taught in school and what I observed as ‘go-to’ movements for many clinicians. However, concentric actions spur inflammatory processes and are metabolically more demanding compared to isometrics (and eccentrics), which often isn’t considered.
Initially, I also found it challenging to conceptualize muscle fiber length doesn’t change during most movement including gait. Instead, muscles isometrically stabilize while tendons eccentrically lengthen. Michaud states, “Although counterintuitive, muscle fiber lengths present during midstance remain relatively unchanged while their corresponding tendons stretch and rebound back through significant ranges, comparable to the spring on a pogo-stick. This relationship allows tendon elasticity to perform most of the work while muscle action occurs isometrically”. He goes on to state, “Eccentric contraction followed by near isometric contraction, allowing for the storage of energy, is not unique to the gastrocnemius/soleus, since it occurs in almost every other shock absorbing muscle in the body (i.e. tibialis anterior and vastus lateralis)”. Put differently, eccentric and isometric actions combined are more effective and efficient compared to concentric muscle action. This is because concentric muscle action during activity can easily result in overuse due to the associated metabolic demands. Overuse causes a predictable neurochemical process that can certainly lead to dysfunction and pain.

During normal activities increased tissue oxygen and glucose demand leads to relative hypoxia and is exacerbated by low endurance. Limited eccentric lengthening reduces pressure change in the tissue vs. what is around it, reducing pressure differences. This results in less blood and oxygen flowing through tissue. When combined with soft tissue degeneration and poor tissue compliance, the result is mechanical irritation that primes sensory nerves and causes inflammatory metabolite dumping, specifically of CGRP, or Calcitonin gene-related peptide & Substance P, which are amino acid neurotransmitters produced in neurons. They have functions with vasodilation and transmission of pain. It is suggested that "substance P and CGRP are involved in the development and maintenance of neuropathic pain." Substrate P is pH lowering and creates acidic tissue that sensitizes peripheral nerves, reduces power and isometric force, and contributes to fatigue. It also creates a situation of sub-optimal range functioning that perpetuates a cycle.

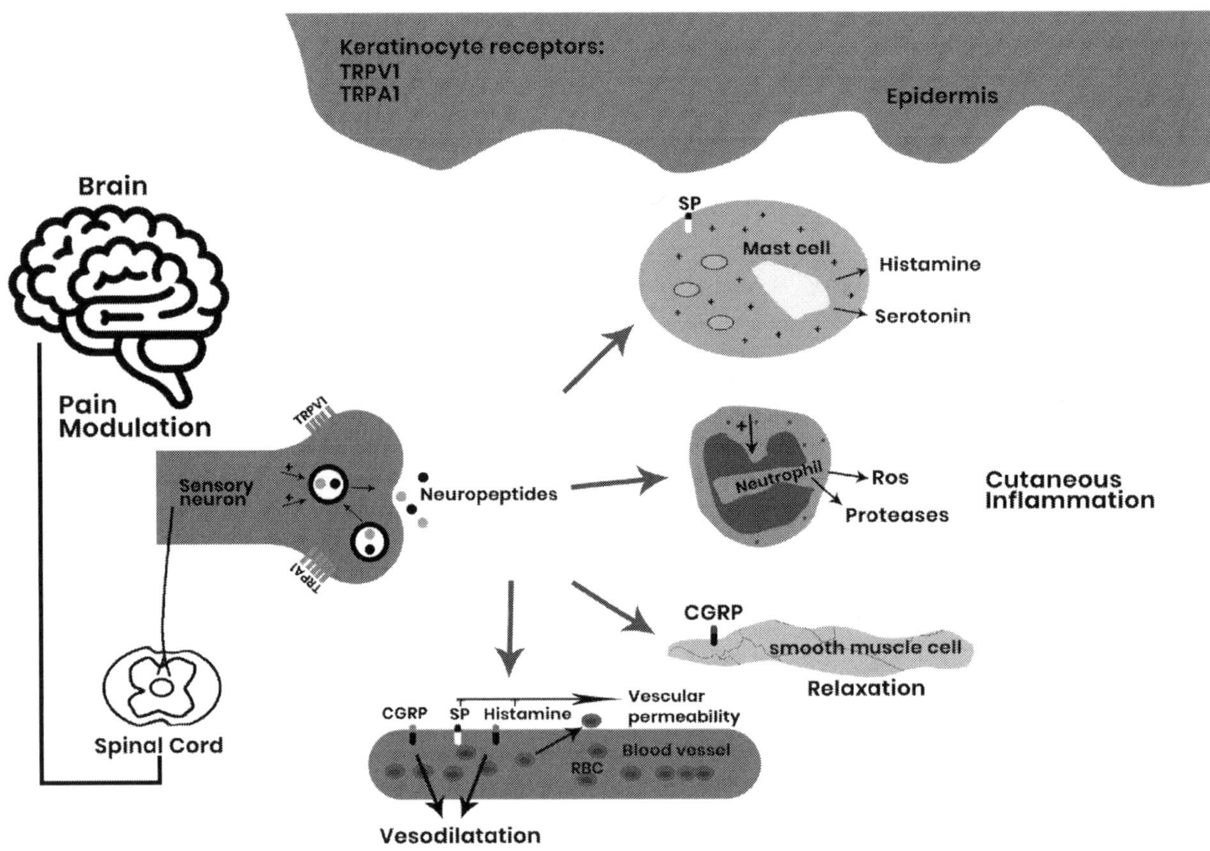

During normal activities increased tissue oxygen and glucose demand leads to relative hypoxia and is exacerbated by low endurance. Limited eccentric lengthening reduces pressure change in the tissue vs. what is around it, reducing pressure differences. This results in less blood and oxygen flowing through tissue. When combined with soft tissue degeneration and poor tissue compliance, the result is mechanical irritation that primes sensory nerves and causes inflammatory metabolite dumping, specifically of CGRP.

Tensegrity

The concept of tensegrity was popularized in 1961 by engineer Buckminster Fuller, although the concept has been around much longer. Tensegrity is the property certain structures possess of maintaining their integrity as a result of continuous tensile integrity, rather than continuous compressive integrity (Pienta & Coffey, 1991).

Tensegrity-based structures are composed of a series of continuous tension resistant components, such as myofascia, and a discontinuous series of compression resistant elements, such as bones, and describe structures that stabilize themselves mechanically by balancing local compression with continuous tension

Tensegrity structures are pre-stressed and require continuous transmission of internal tensions to maintain stability, analogous to the resting tone the central nervous system (CNS) keeps in muscle. An important concept is the idea of alternating compression and tension relationships that exist in the body.

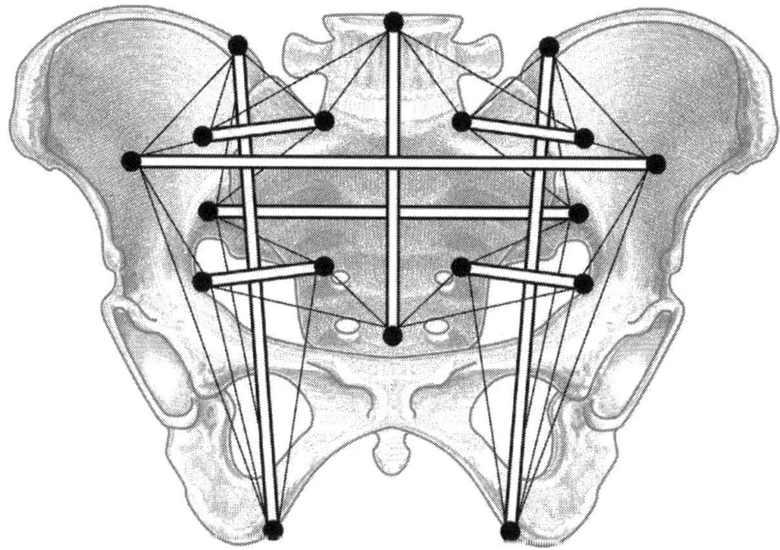

Alternating compression and tension can be found throughout the body and is a concept that can be applied in manual and movement therapies.

Compression tension relationships are seen throughout the body and everywhere in nature, and are important because together they work to distribute forces across a larger surface. Buckminster Fuller was an architect and futurist and described this relationship as Tensegrity, which is the combining of the words tension and integrity, which is seen throughout the soft tissue continuum. Often times, a dysfunctional joint demonstrates compression on one side and more tension on the other (either front to back or one side to another), or above to below. Tensegrity allows for stability and mobility at each segment.

In my experience, this tension/compression relationship can be felt by the practitioner as an abrupt or sudden tension in one spot instead of a uniform tension throughout the entire tissue, and also as compression via closing angle joint restrictions. If tissue or joints can't go through full range of motion (ROM), there won't be as much excursion, defined here as the ability to get fully long to short (and by the dictionary as moving through a path or on an angle). In these cases, there won't be as much pressure difference in the tissue vs. what's around it. Pressure differentials are important for pumping fluid throughout the body. Less pressure change means less pressure difference in tissue, less blood pumped through the soft tissue, and therefore less oxygen getting to the tissue creating a chemical reaction that lowers the pH. Decreased pH results in peripheral nerves being bathed and enveloped in acidic tissue, easily aggravating the superficial mechanoreceptors that respond through mechanical, temperature, and chemical stimulus.

Chemical irritation creates neurogenic inflammation and peripherally sensitizes the nerve, which if left untreated, can progress over time to central sensitization. Mechanically, the inability to glide cross links the tissue to the layers around it, resulting in less tissue hydration, which is important for allowing tissue interfaces to slide past each other. This lack of slide and cascade of cross-linking perpetuates less hydration of tissue and chemical leads to a palpable tissue densification. Dr. Geoffrey Bove eloquently describes how it is all about improving the ability of tissue interfaces to slide past each other, and that issues can arise when tissue can't. Densification results in a lack of slide, felt as increased and abrupt tension. Therefore, restoring intra-tissue slide/glide can be beneficial, and most easily accomplished through tensegrity principles applied to bodywork and also in mobility, defined as the ability to lengthen under load and control and range motions.

For more information on tensegrity and its relationship to the body, movement, and bodywork, please reference the mobility part of this book.

Author's Note

My definition of mobility is the ability to utilize end range motion and lengthening under load, while flexibility is passively hanging at end-range. It is different than mobility, and until recently I didn't appreciate the chemical side of mechanoreceptors, and it can't be discounted. My FNOR (Functional Neuro-Orthopedic Rehab) coursework really illustrated this point, and turned me on to Neuro-gel, which is a product that creates alkaline responses in the mechanoreceptors and can be used diagnostically. FNOR, provided me the framework to do something specifically for neurogenic inflammation and the multistep process associated with it, and has also improved outcomes.

Capacities During Gait

Treating capacities rather than anatomy provides a framework to look at the system rather than individual body parts. Gait is a good starting point for analyzing capacities because it is consistent across most populations with much empirical evidence. While there are numerous books discussing gait mechanics, the primary references used in this text relative to gait are *Human Locomotion* by chiropractor Tom Michaud, and *Normal & Abnormal Function of the Foot,* by podiatrists Root, Orien, and Weed.

Both references discuss various aspects of the gait cycle in great detail, including specific joint motions, positions, and muscle function. They provide fantastic references about the intricacies of the gait cycle and are recommended readings for anyone interested in learning more about the foot and gait. While this text won't cover in depth specifics of gait, it will touch upon the basics and what has proven clinically useful on a regular basis. I particularly recommend everyone pick up Michaud's book because it is chock full of relevant information that will improve your overall understanding of the specifics of gait.

Author's Note

I'm grateful to Tom Michaud for his guidance and permission to use his pictures and quotes from Human Locomotion.

Gait Cycle

One complete gait cycle begins the moment the foot contacts the ground and ends when the same foot hits the ground again, consisting of stance and swing phases. As expected, stance phase is when the lower extremity is in contact with the ground, while swing phase is when the lower extremity swings through the air in preparation for the next impact. Gait is undoubtedly one of the more repetitive activities in life, which highlights the importance of using it as an insight into the nervous system and as an assessment tool. As discussed previously, motion should be dissipated through the system before it gets to the eyes. This means if motion isn't gotten somewhere (one joint) it's going to be achieved somewhere else, typically a joint above or below. Michaud states, "In order to create metabolically efficient gait, individuals must learn to translate their center of mass through space along a path requiring the least expenditure of energy" (Ch 3, p 88). Efficiency is critical, which is great when there's motion and control, however when one (or both) is lacking, the path of least resistance isn't always beneficial.

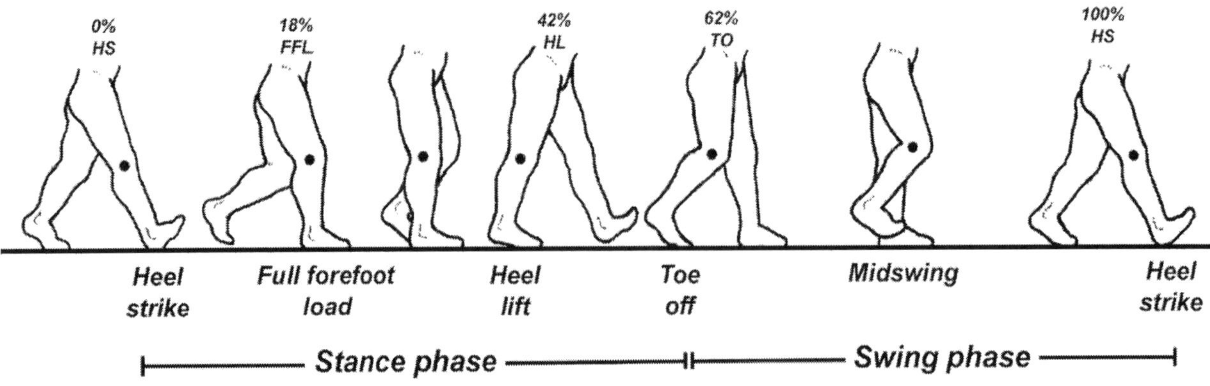

Michaud states "In order to create metabolically efficient gait, individuals must learn to translate their center of mass through space along a path requiring the least expenditure of energy"

"Nearly the entire nervous system is utilized in a normal gait cycle including contributions from the cortex (premotor, supplementary motor, temporoparietal junction, occipital lobe), the basal ganglia, the limbic system, the cerebellum, the corticospinal, reticulospinal, rubrospinal, and spinocerebellar tracts, segmental spinal cord areas (Central Pattern Generators – CPGs), and peripheral sensory nerves in the skin. More specific details about how these systems work together, and the specific roles they play, can be found in *Neurophysiology of Gait: From the Spinal Cord to the Frontal Lobe* by Takakusaki, 2013".

Generally speaking, the cerebellum is responsible for coordinating movement and has afferent connections from both ascending sensory and descending motor pathways. It compares information and alters motor plans based on balance, coordination, and load tolerance via efferent pathways in order to make a movement coordinated. "Recent studies indicate that cerebellar processing intervenes in locomotion by providing advance information on subsequent step events, suggesting how such motor prediction can be obtained per the sequencing hypothesis of cerebellar function. In nearly all cerebellar functional domains — from motor to cognition — cerebellar symptoms can be attributed to impairments in recognizing repeated sequence patterns. Only recognition of a previously experienced pattern allows a prediction to be made and thus effective feed-forward control to be instigated. (Pisotta, Iolanda, and Molinari, Marco, 2014)". In other words, sub-clinical cerebellar issues can impact the gait cycle and cause compensatory patterns.

"Likewise, the corticoreticulospinal system is responsible for the execution of anticipated postural adaptations (APAs) which create stabilization prior to any movement. This is exceedingly important in gait when the variables of the gait cycle and environment are complicated and ever changing, especially with increased speed of gait. These APAs are a hard wired and subconscious excitation that allows us to reflexively carry out tasks accurately without thought of exactly where or how the limb needs to be positioned to best accept the load of each step."

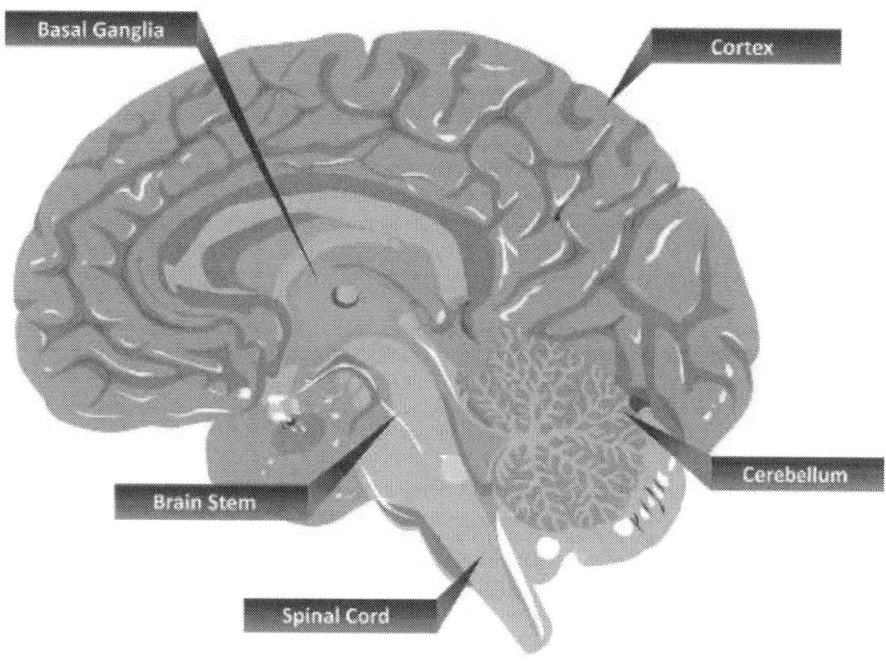

The corticoreticulospinal system is responsible for the execution of anticipated postural adaptations (APA's) which create stabilization prior to any movement.

Information allows the cerebellum to make a prediction with regard to the sensory consequences of motor commands, allowing the musculoskeletal system to prepare to successfully execute a movement. "During movement, predicted sensations are then compared with the actual incoming sensations. If there is a positive match, the pattern is maintained for the next movement. The lack of a match is associated with an alert signal that is sent back to the motor cortical and subcortical areas, which activates feedback movement corrections and calibration of the feed forward model (Shadmehr et al., 2010)".

Assessing cerebellar integration independent of gait is a good idea when working with any population, especially in someone with uncoordinated or altered gait patterns, keeping in mind there is no way to isolate out any system. There are simple and quick tests to assess that can easily be integrated into a general movement assessment. With subclinical cerebellar dysfunction, such as with difficulty with rapid alternating movements on one side of the body in upper and lower body, motor rehabilitation can attempt to refine the target and the goals for therapy accordingly. Creating programs that may stimulate specific regions of the brain, including the cerebellum, are warranted in order to drive the most input to the brain and assist it to eventually 'predict' a situation not threatening to the nervous system. Understanding the cerebellum plays a role in this process, as well as gait, is helpful, especially in identifying when integration disorders of the cerebellum may influence movement and gait.

Clinical Concept

Since learning more about cerebellar and vestibular integration, and specifically the role in subclinical vestibular and cerebellar populations, I've been surprised with how many people actually demonstrate integration difficulty. When looked for through simple neurological exams, and understanding the specifics of different systems, it can be observed how subclinical integration disorders are present and not diagnosed. Signs of cerebellar integration disorders can include mildly ataxic gait, clumsiness, mis-stepping, and floppy or decreased tone gait patterns, among others. Other signs often seen include a unilateral loss of associated arm swing, which can point at frontal lobe or mesencephalic demise. Or a toe out gait absent of structural deformity, which may point to reticulospinal inefficiencies. Often these symptoms can be exacerbated with 'dual tasking', for example walking and counting by twos starting with three or saying the alphabet backwards (something that makes the cognitive brain use cognition in order to not help integrate the discrepancies in systems). With integration dysfunction, the gait pattern deficiencies often get worse with dual tasking. When observed, further investigation by standardized neurological exams are warranted, including what is considered a 'bedside' neurological exam. A unilateral loss of associated arm swing is often the very first sign of potential Parkinson's Disease up to twenty years prior to initiation of other symptoms such as tremor.

"When assessing gait, it is important to recognize why we walk or run. Many clinicians miss this thought almost inherently because of the unconscious motivational drivers of gait. Two areas of the brain are responsible for any initiation of gait, frontal lobe cognitive drive, and limbic system emotional drive. These systems work in tandem, while in certain situations one system may be more active than the other. The scenario plays out as follows: "I need to get where I am currently to where I want to be to achieve a goal." Now, that goal may be to walk from one end of the office to the other, to speak with a co-worker. This is more of a cognitive driver than an emotional driver, while there are still emotional undertones to every decision.

In another scenario, the goal may be running from one location to another, to get away from an angry dog who is about to attack. The limbic system is much more active in this scenario, while there are still cognitive factors of recognizing the consequences of not acting quickly in this situation. When you break down the reasons for initiation of gait in any scenario throughout the patient's daily life, it can be looked at through this lens, 'What is the goal that is being achieved and does the patient have the ability to complete his/her goal appropriately with the current gait cycle?'

In a more complicated patient population, such as stroke patients, they may not be able to perform any of the gait cycle to get from point A to point B regardless of motivation. Whereas, in a highly functioning population, such as a professional athlete, s/he may not be able to complete a symmetrical glute drive regardless of motivation.

In each scenario, the motivating factors may not come into play with their individualized treatment, or it may be the biggest piece, to them achieving their goals."

Stance Phase Motions

Stance phase gait can be broken down into three phases: initial contact, midstance, and propulsive phase, recognizing each can be further broken down. Relative to capacities, measuring joint angles during key phases of gait (or any functional activity) provides a place to start and can identify what requires further investigation. Michaud states, "In order to prepare itself for the sudden application of ground reactive force associated with contacting the ground, the body aligns itself during the swing phase so every joint is in an ideal position to dampen these forces. At the moment heel strike occurs, the spine is in a neutral position; the hip is flexed 30'; the knee is almost fully extended, the ankle is slightly dorsiflexed; the subtalar joint is slightly supinated; and the midtarsal joint is fully pronated about its oblique axis and supinated (inverted about its longitudinal axis). The muscles stabilizing these joints are in their midline positions, (maximizing their length/tension relationship) and many of them are pre-tensed in anticipation of impact forces. In fact, switching from soft to hard surfaces produces immediate increases in anticipatory muscle activity prior to heel strike as pre-activation improves the ability to absorb shock" (Chapter 3, P. 97).

"This is a primary example of APA activation to place the limb in the most optimal position to appropriately handle the upcoming ground forces."

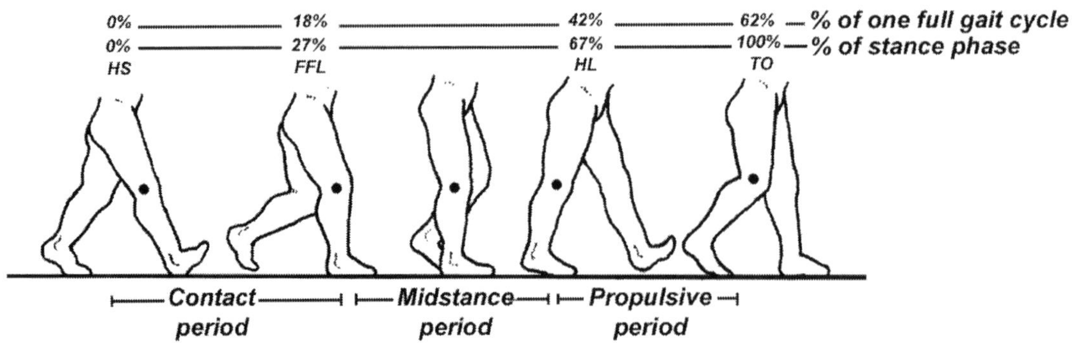

The stance phase takes up 60% of the gait cycle and can be broken down into four phases, heel strike, foot flat, heel lift, and toe off. Courtesy of Tom Michaud and figure 3.2 in Human Locomotion.

Initial Contact Phase

Gary Gray said, "when the foot hits the ground everything changes". This is not only the title of a course, but very descriptive of how proper foot motion sets up the system for success. Foot issues easily can wreak havoc above, and so ensuring proper foot function is important. At heel strike, the ankle should be at 0' DF-PF in preparation to go through approximately 10' of plantar flexion. Relative to contact phase, Root et al, states, "Indirect shock absorption by knee flexion is also dependent upon subtalar joint pronation… At heel strike, the knee is extended, but it must flex rapidly to absorb the shock associated with heel strike (20' according to Michaud). Pronation of the subtalar joint and lower extremity occurs at heel strike that the body must control. Adduction of the talus associated with pronation causes the tibia to internally rotate faster and farther than the femur, as the entire lower extremity rotated internally at heel strike. Therefore, adequate shock absorption cannot occur at heel strike unless subtalar joint pronation can occur. Secondly, muscle function is influenced by subtalar joint pronation. Inability of the subtalar joint to pronate at heel strike causes abnormal muscle function which stops knee flexion, (Ch 6, P.151-152)." In other words, the subtalar joint is an important region to help dissipate forces and also to create transverse motion proximally via frontal plane calcaneal eversion at heel strike. The talus can be thought of as a torque converter, taking frontal plane motion from the calcaneus at heel strike and creating transverse motion as the talus concurrently moves towards middle. The STJ has a major influence on the function of the joints and tissue immediately around it. Improper STJ joint motion influences gluteus function, because if the foot doesn't do what it should when it should, the glutes will not either.

Key Concept

Note the descriptions of relative motions without naming it as such, by Root et al., "adduction of the talus associated with pronation causes the tibia to internally rotate faster and farther than the femur, as the entire lower extremity rotated internally at heel strike." Recall the best description of human motion is a synchronous dissociation of body segments. Bone dissociation, or something moving faster or slower than what's above/below, is necessary for the joint to perceive motion. Therefore, ensuring the proper sequence in the motion is important, highlighting the necessity of observation through eyes, hands, and video. Movement happens so fast and being able to look at it on video can help to understand dysfunction.

The ability of soft tissue to absorb and dissipate forces is critical to efficient gait. A main shock absorber is the quadriceps and its ability to resist knee flexion from initial contact into midstance. Due to ground reaction forces being fairly low with walking, the knee should flex approximately 20 degrees through this phase, yet often people move through contact into midstance with their knees fully extended, or never reaching the 20' necessary for efficient load. As Michaud describes, "While a stiff knee gait is metabolically efficient because it lessens strain on the quadriceps, it significantly increases stress on the gluteus medius muscle, which eccentrically fires to lower the contralateral pelvis. The gluteus medius muscle, however, has a limited ability to absorb impact force, and as shock absorption requirements increase with the transition to running, the degree of knee flexion increases in a linear manner..." (Chapter 3, P. 99-100). This illustrates the importance of eccentric load in the role of shock absorption and efficient gait. When proper knee flexion isn't obtained, it's important to find out if it is a mobility or stability-centric problem, recognizing it probably going to be both, depending on where in the body. It is possible a tight foot or hip can contribute to less knee flexion, just as it may be from lack of strength of the quadricep, gluteus complex, or somewhere else along the kinetic chain.

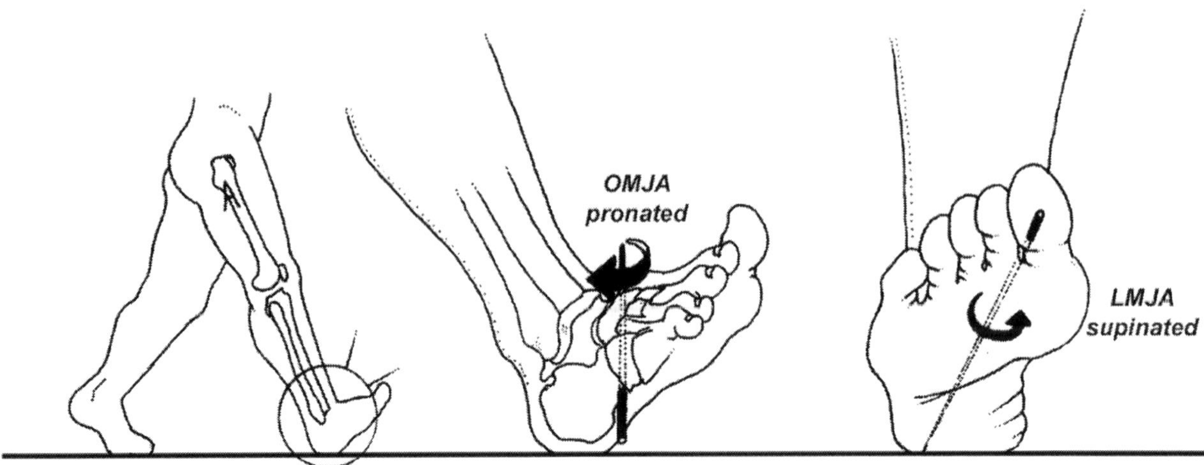

Ideal lower extremity joint positions present at heel strike. OMJA, oblique midtarsal joint axis, LMJA, longitudinal midtarsal joint axis. Picture courtesy of Tom Michaud in Human Locomotion Figure 3.14.

In addition to going through approximately 20 degrees of knee flexion after heel strike, the hip should also be properly positioned in order to accept and control greater loads. At heel strike, the hip should be flexed approximately 20 degrees, depending on the literature. 20' of hip flexion allows for better distribution of pressure throughout the acetabulum when the hip is flexed. Due to forces with walking being relatively small, the gluteus medius works to control these forces by eccentrically contracting to control the contralateral pelvis from dropping. As Michaud describes, "Forces not dampened at the pelvis travel into the spine. In the transverse plane, the lumbar spine rotates approximately 3' in each direction and these forces are dampened by the spinal rotators. In the frontal plane, the contralateral pelvis drops approximately while the spine laterally flexes less than 1' in each direction" (Ch 3, P. 104)". This emphasizes the importance of the gluteus complex, particularly the gluteus medius, in controlling the contact through midstance phases of gait. The ability of the hip and knee regions to control this capacity is important to optimal function. Clinically, I've found that many of the people I treat, regardless of diagnosis, have difficulty controlling the pelvis in at least the frontal plane.

"As Gary Gray stated above, "When the foot hits the ground, everything changes", and this has to be taken into account by the nervous system. Skin afferents play a major role in sending initial information to the higher levels of the brain to allow for near immediate adjustments to the foot, ankle, hip, and at all times, core and upper extremity. This particularly occurs when the initial contact with the surface is different than the anticipated contact. Think of what happens when you step on a small rock that was not picked up by peripheral vision while walking down the sidewalk. Immediate afferent signals must be transmitted to adjust load on that foot to avoid minor or major injury."

Midstance

Merton Root describes, "Midstance period begins at full forefoot load and ends at heel lift, when walking, it's the longest period, occupying 40% of the stance phase. While walking, the knee should go through approximately 20 degrees of knee flexion as the body absorbs contact phase forces and enters into midstance. As midstance begins, the knee begins moving through extension, which is necessary in order to elevate the body over the foot when it reaches its highest point during mid-midstance." As previously discussed, the inability of the knee to achieve 20 degrees of knee flexion can often result in tissue irritation along the line of tissue that lengthens together at this phase of gait. In addition, the knee should go through 20 degrees of knee extension, to the point that at midstance the knee is at 0 degrees.

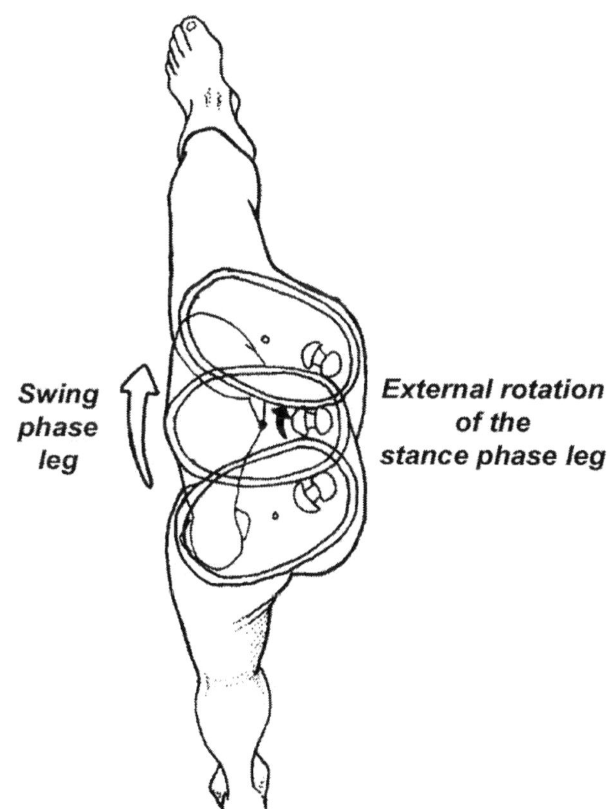

The forward motion of the swing phase leg creates a top down motion in the back phase of gait, creating relative motions into the stance leg and supinating the subtalar joint. In Figure 3.33 in Human Locomotion (picture at left), Michaud says the adductors play an important role in "producing external rotation in the stance leg....and act as an effective lever arm capable of translating forward momentum of the swing leg into external rotation of the stance leg femur". Note that the external rotation referred to of the stance femur is the real bone motion, not relative joint motion, while he also describes the phenomena of drivers because the swing leg creates stance leg motion.

Midstance: Frontal Plane Control

While there are numerous data points to analyze during gait, possibly the most easily observable (especially when being recorded) is frontal plane pelvic motion at midstance. At midstance, the stance leg hip should adduct no more than 3-5'. There's often more, increasing shearing forces at the low back, hip, or knee, with compensation seen anywhere from the toes to the thoracic spine. This will often coincide with a failure in a single leg test such as a step down, as lack of control and proper motion on one side compared to the other will be observed. In these cases, single leg activities should be performed with caution and within controlled ranges until proper strength and control is demonstrated. This is consistent with the developmental principle of stability before mobility and two legged activities before single leg activities.

Strategies for improving strength should include both one and two joint muscles, recognizing their actions are different. Generally, one joint muscles are force producers and stabilizers, while multi-joint muscles should function as force reducers. Issues arise when multiple joint muscles are forced to perform the strength actions of the single joint (intrinsic) muscles. What's interesting is proximal lower extremity muscles of the hip and knee tend to have long parallel fascicles with little tendon elasticity, while distal muscles of the foot and leg have short fascicles with long, flexible tendons (Michaud Ch 3, P. 106-107). This is clinically relevant while designing a movement program, specifically by ensuring proximal joints will be progressed to more dynamic activities as warranted. These include movements that drive specific motion into regions based on individual needs. Integrated programs for the foot and leg can include progressive isometric activities that provide higher level and more authentic loads that are comparable to specific functional activities. The concept of progressive isometric activities is referenced in depth in the isolated<>integrated spectrum discussion found in later parts.

This movement mimics midstance in the stance leg by positioning the body to have 3-5 degrees of hip adduction while driving motion top down motion into the body via the arm reaches.

Michaud states, "The short fibers present in the distal muscles allow them to generate force extremely economically by contracting either isometrically or with low shortening velocities. Energy is stored in their stretched tendons, with little work being done by their short pennate fibers. Although counterintuitive, muscle fiber lengths present during midstance remain relatively unchanged while their corresponding tendons stretch and rebound back through significant ranges, comparable to the spring on a pogo-stick. This relationship allows tendon elasticity to perform most of the work while muscle action occurs isometrically." What this means is that eccentric load and isometric stabilization through this phase of gait is efficient and lessens the risk of overuse and shearing occurring at joints and in tissue. It also means if the pelvis isn't controlled in the frontal plane, muscles of the lateral hip may work to stabilize via concentric muscle action, which is less efficient.

The previous passage illustrates the importance of the isometric contraction during movement. If muscle can't maintain isometric consistency then concentric action is required, potentially leading to overuse, because "in order for tendons to store energy effectively, they must be stretched through very specific ranges, since excessive stretching could produce injury while too small a range would limit energy storage; i.e. a rubber band stretched through a small range of motion would not return significant energy and an overstretched rubber band would break." Simply put, if tissue can't efficiently lengthen and control load, then muscle is required to concentrically work more than optimally, resulting in increased energy production. This extra energy production leads to acidic responses and often a neurogenic inflammation cycle that is regularly mistaken for pathoanatomical/joint pain.

Author's Note

While referencing Normal and Abnormal Function of the Foot, in preparation for writing this text, I was pleased to find even more terminology that references relative motion. On page 132, chapter 6, he writes, "In the sagittal plane, the hip joint extends during the contact and midstance periods. Early in propulsion, the hip begins to flex, and continues to flex throughout the propulsive period. In a transverse plane, the pelvis and thigh internally rotate throughout the contact period. The thigh internally rotates farther and faster than the pelvis, thus producing internal rotation at the hip joint." It's important to note this relative motion occurs at the hip at both phases of gait. In the front foot, there is a bottom up drive into the lower extremity, while the back phase is a top down drive due to the opposite swing leg creating motion into the stance leg. Due to the rules of naming motion, the hip experiences a relative internal rotation at both phases.

"Central Pattern Generators (CPGs) play an integral role in gait and other patterned movements of the body. Primarily, CPGs are located in the spinal cord, and create a reflexive sequence of patterns that allow for smooth transition neurologically during the gait cycle."

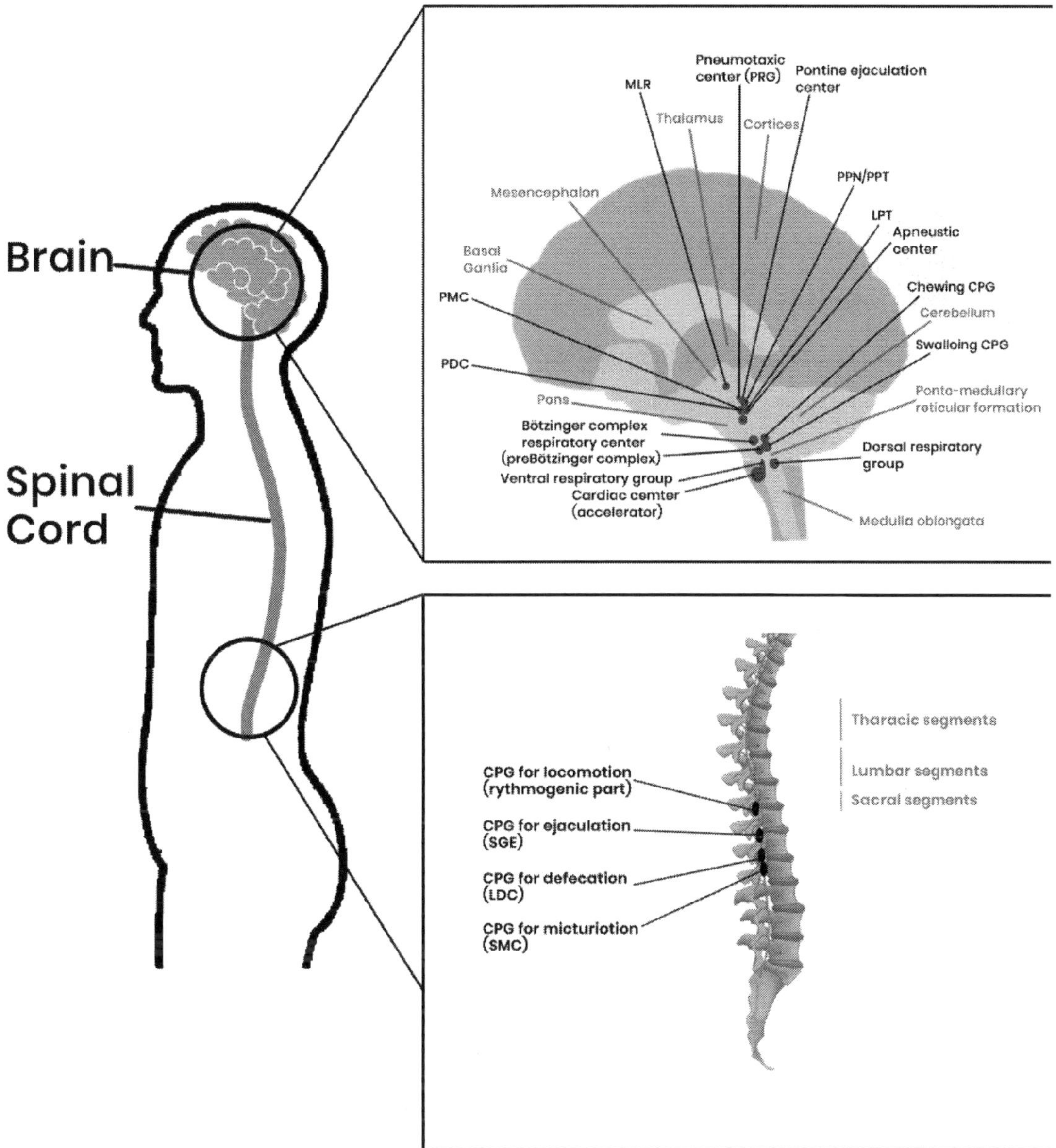

Central Pattern Generators (CPG's) play an integral role in gait movement and are primarily located in the spinal cord. CPG's create a reflexive sequence of patterns that allow for smooth transition neurologically during the gait cycle.

"Because this is a cycle, there is no starting point nor ending point, but during stance, phase skin afferents on the bottom of the foot cause excitation of extensor muscle tone that further exacerbates extensor activation of the ipsilateral limb in aid to propulsion forward."

Toe off – Propulsion

The propulsive phase begins with heel lift and ends with toe off. Occupying about 33% of stance phase, here, the foot is required to transition from a mobile adaptor into a rigid lever in preparation for propulsion. This is accomplished from top-down (due to the opposite swing leg) and bottom-up drivers, as well as from the ability of the system to isometrically stabilize and eccentrically lengthen. Michaud states, "It is metabolically expensive for muscles to generate force when tensing either concentrically or eccentrically and isometric contractions are significantly more efficient because they produce large forces with little metabolic expense… By converting the gradual eccentric contraction present during midstance into an "isometric impulse" that allows the Achilles tendon to store and return energy at just the right moment, isometric contraction of the gastrocnemius allows the body to take advantage of the elastic energy associated with stretching the gastrocnemius tendon". In this passage, Michaud provides another example of the importance of isometric activity in the gait cycle.

Key Concept

Eccentric contraction along with isometric contraction allows the storage of energy and is not unique to the gastrocnemius/soleus and occurs in most shock-absorbing muscles in the body, including the quads, tibialis anterior, and others. Think shock absorption with long tendon muscles.

During Propulsion, momentum continues to carry the body forward in preparation for swing phase. Like other regions, ensuring capacities of joints to obtain proper position at the right time is important. This phase can be broken down even further, into terminal stance and pre swing. Terminal stance is the point when the heel is still on the ground, prior to it lifting, while pre swing is the time from heel lift through toe off/propulsion. At terminal stance, the hip should be in approximately 20 degrees of hip extension in the sagittal plane, while the knee should be at 0 degrees with 5-10 degrees of ankle dorsiflexion.

Clinical Concept

During swing, when the swing leg tibia is vertical (perpendicular to the ground), the stance heel should still be on the ground. Often times at this point, the stance heel is already lifted, possibly indicating a tight heel cord and potentially indicating a dysfunction somewhere along the kinetic chain.

Michaud states, "Once the heel has left the ground, a considerable amount of stress is transferred directly into the forefoot. To protect the forefoot from the extreme ground-reactive forces associated with propulsion, stimulation of cutaneous receptors in the skin (i.e. Meissner's corpuscles) cause the digital flexors to tense reflexively, producing a strong plantar flexion force at the toes that significantly reduces pressure beneath the metatarsal heads (Ch 3, P. 112)." If the plantar flexors and intrinsic muscles of the foot are weak, lack endurance, or joints in the foot are limited in mobility, altered motion and increased demand to specific tissues will likely occur. He goes on to say, "To improve muscular efficiency, the gastrocnemius fires almost isometrically during the latter half of stance phase, allowing the Achilles tendon to store and return energy".

"As toe off is happening, the skin afferents are creating stabilization of the metatarsals as stated above. Cyclical flexion of the ipsilateral hip cannot take place until the extensor muscles are unloaded immediately upon toe off. The skin afferents create a signal that causes flexion of the ipsilateral leg joints while simultaneously exciting extensor muscles of the contralateral leg. This transition happens in the central pattern generators of the spinal cord with higher level coordination from the cerebral cortex, cerebellum, and brain stem via the corticospinal, raphe spinal, coerulospinal, inhibitory reticulospinal, and excitatory reticulospinal tracts."

It is interesting to note that stance leg subtalar supination during the second half of stance phase is accomplished from the forward motion of the swinging lower extremity, known as top down motion in AFS vernacular. Michaud describes how, "the forward momentum of the swing phase leg externally rotates the pelvis, which then externally rotates the weight-bearing leg. Since the leg and talus behave as a closed kinetic chain during midstance, external rotation of the weight bearing leg causes the talus to abduct, which in turn supinates the subtalar joint. This motion helps to stabilize the tarsal by decreasing parallelism of the midtarsal joint axes (Ch 3, P 109)." Without explicitly saying such, Michaud is describing top down motion into the back leg in gait. The swing leg causes motion into the pelvis, creating motion in the stance leg rotating in the direction of the pelvis, but not as far or as fast. This causes motion below in the same direction, but not as far or fast. He goes on to describe more relative motions during the gait cycle by stating, "By the end of midstance period, the ankle is dorsiflexed 10'. Forward momentum of the body coupled with simultaneous knee extension throughout mid stance allows ground-reactive forces applied beneath the forefoot to dorsiflex the ankle, the subtalar joint is moving towards it's neutral position and the midtarsal joint is fully pronated about both axes... (Ch 3, P 110)".

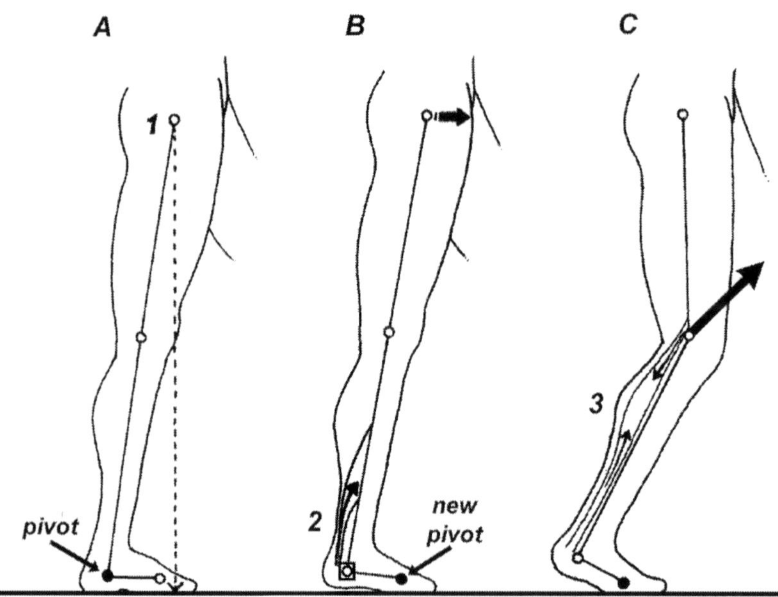

As Michaud states, "Heel lift results from the combined actions of the forward momentum of body mass (1), muscular deceleration of ankle dorsiflexion (2), and active flexion of the knee produced by gastrocnemius contraction (3). Note that in panel A, the pivot point for motion is the ankle joint, while soleus contraction in panel B locks the ankle (square) and creates a new pivot point at the forefoot (black circle in B and C). Picture and description courtesy of Michaud and is figure 3.37 in Human Locomotion.

At the time of pre-swing, or as the toe is coming off the ground upon completion of propulsion, the hip should experience approximately 0 of flexion, while the knee should be flexed about 40 degrees with 20 degrees of ankle plantarflexion. Misalignment is often indicative of compensation somewhere in the system. If breakdown occurs at this phase, improving joint capacities for this phase of gait is necessary. This very well may include strengthening of the intrinsic muscles of the foot as well as the peroneus longus and brevis. Both these muscles assist in transferring the weight to the medial aspect of the foot and first ray. Michaud states, "The improved ability of the peroneus longus to function as a first ray plantarflexor is extremely important during the propulsive period, because the increased height of the medial longitudinal arch coupled with that normal parabolic curve of the metatarsal heads necessitates the first ray actively plantarflex in order to maintain ground contact." In other words, intrinsic foot muscle strength is important for proper foot function and efficient gait, and lack of strength can cause issues.

Midstance through propulsion: relative motions of LE

Merton Root notes, "Locking of the forefoot against the rearfoot around the longitudinal axis is necessary for normal propulsion. Deformities that maintain the foot in a pronated position, forefoot valgus deformity, and mild plantarflexed first ray deformity, all prevent normal locking of the forefoot around the longitudinal axis of the midtarsal joint prior to propulsion (Ch 6, P 140)." What's interesting is Root describes relative motions during gait, specifically in the lower extremity and the screw home mechanism. He describes the knee during stance as, "In the transverse plane, the leg (tibia) internally rotates farther and faster than the thigh during the contact period, thus producing internal rotation at the knee joint. During the midstance and propulsive periods, the tibia externally rotates with the femur (author's note: the femur does it faster until heel lift). Momentarily before heel lift, and again just prior to toe off, the tibia externally rotates farther and faster than the femur; external rotation of the tibia then occurs at the knee joint."

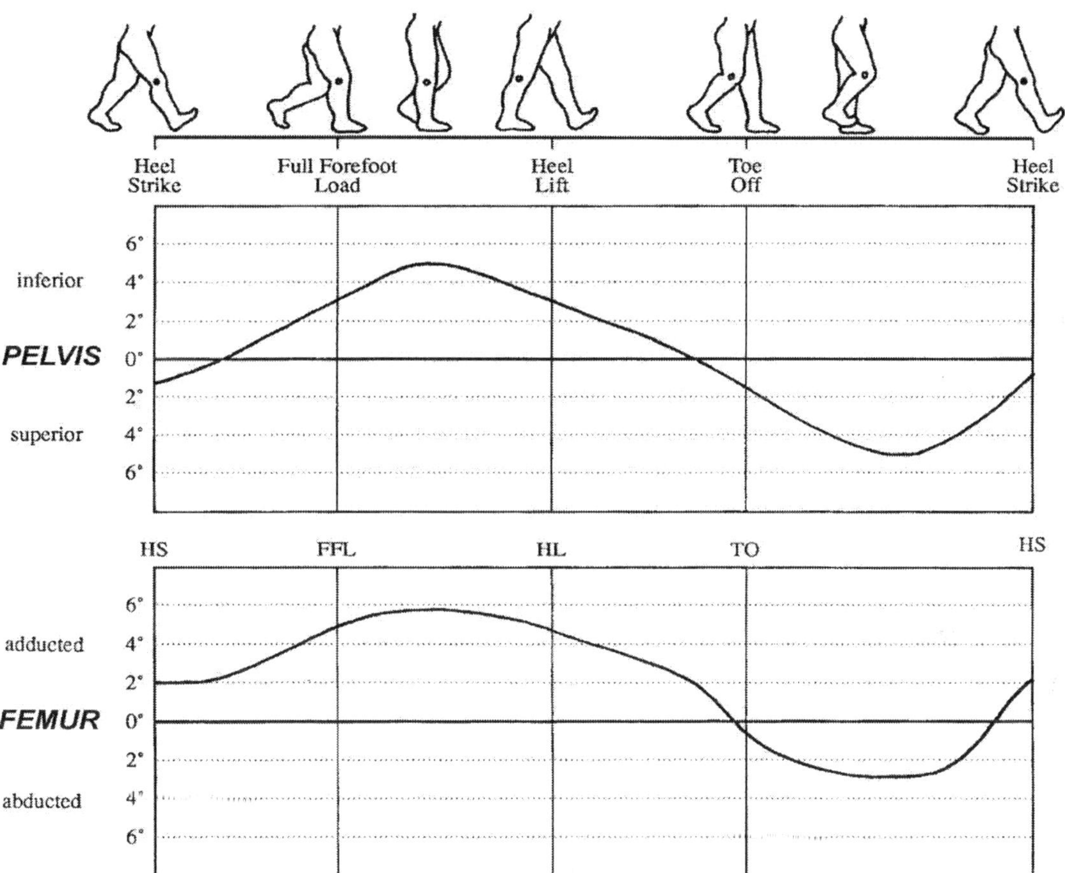

Midstance control during the gait cycle is important. The picture above highlights the frontal plane motion of the hip bones. Notice that at midstance, the pelvic obtains 5' of hip adduction. Numerous potential issues arise if the hip has too much midstance motion. Picture curtsey of Tom Michaud and is picture 3.51 in Human Locomotion.

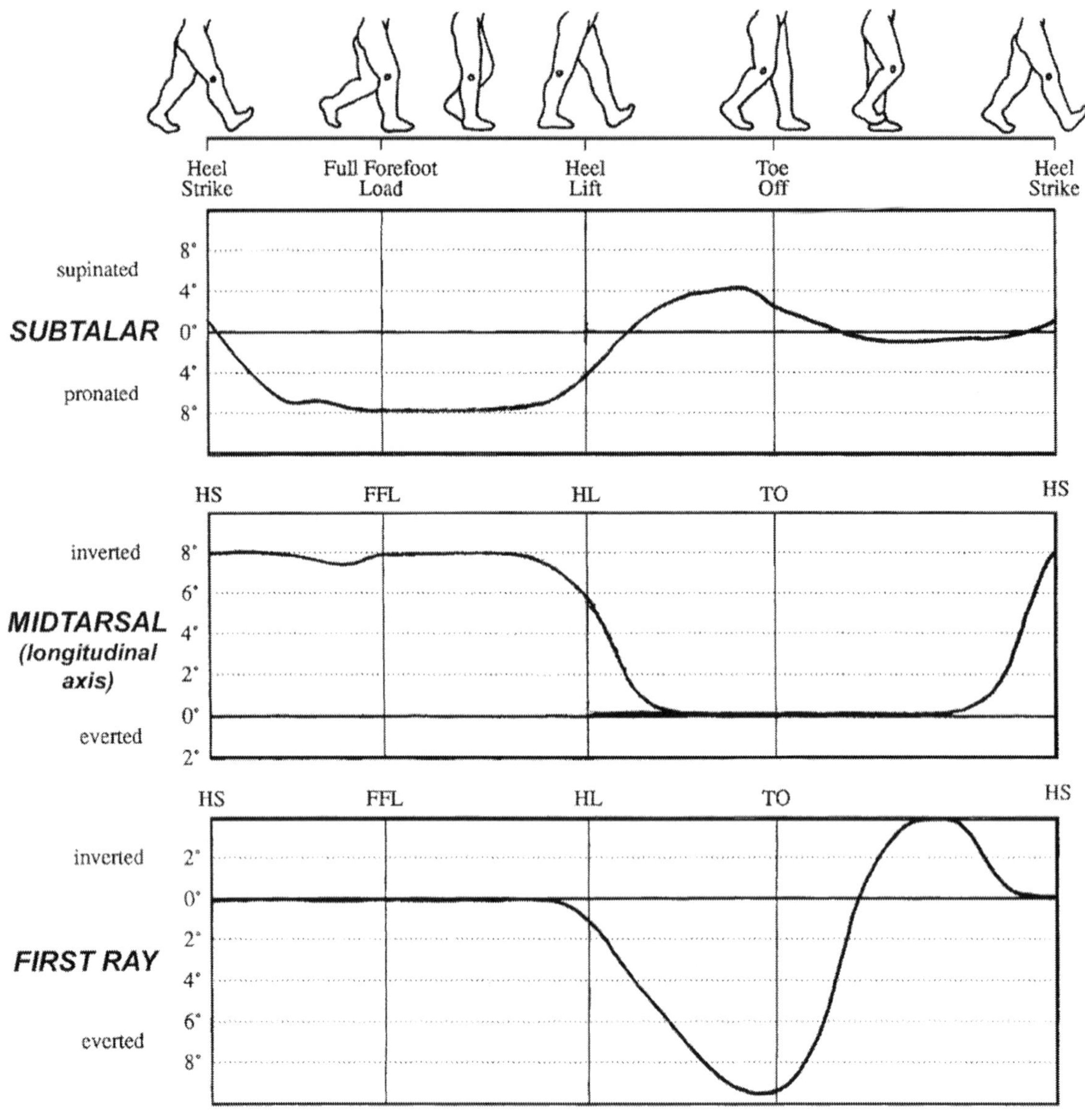

Author's Note

It is exciting to see these descriptions in texts such as these. It also highlights the importance of rereading information and books long after they're initially read. I didn't pick that information up the first time around. New information will be highlighted with each read. Said differently, save your books and articles and reread them after a period of time.

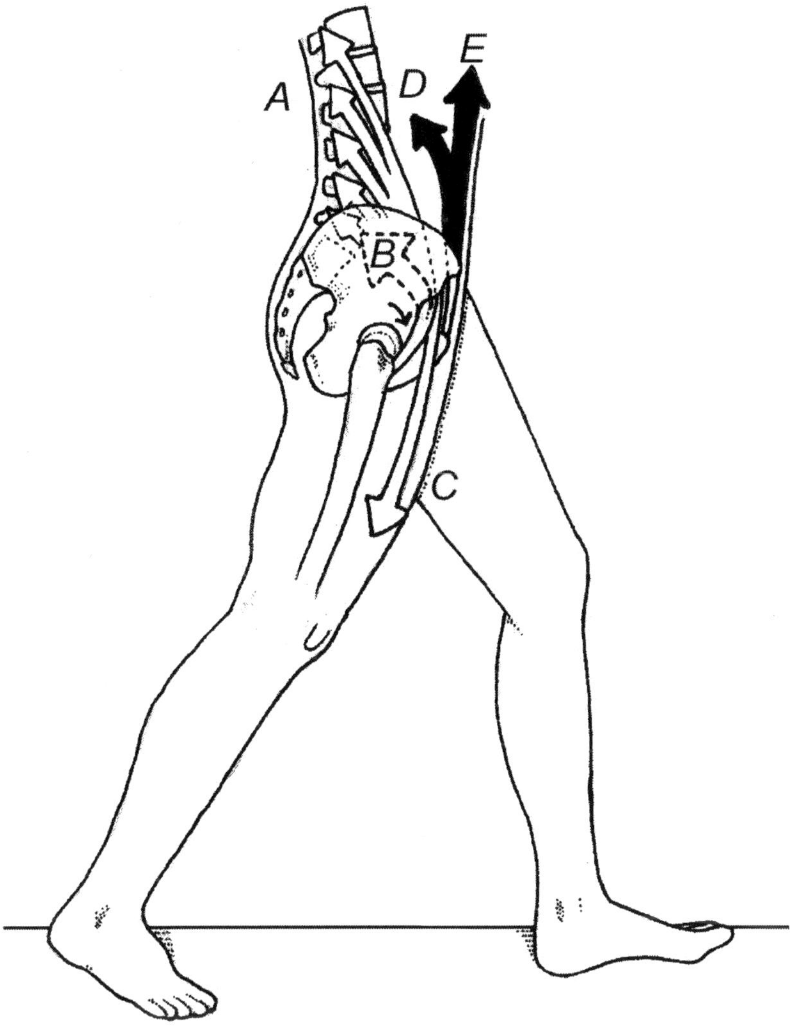

The above picture and description are courtesy of Tom Michaud, and found in Human Locomotion, Figure 3.46. During the late propulsive period, tension created in the psoas (A), iliacus (B), and rectus femoris (C), extend the lumbar spine and tilt the pelvis forward (black arrow above acetabulum).

Swing Phase Motions

Swing phase is relatively simple compared to stance phase, which begins at toe off and ends at heel strike. The primary action in swing phase is clearing the foot and positioning the joints so muscles are prepared to dampen impact forces at heel strike. As Michaud states, "By far, the most important kinematic factor responsible for producing ground clearance is flexion of the knee. In fact, if for any reason the knee is unable to adequately flex during midswing, the metabolic cost of locomotion skyrockets, because the individual is forced to circumduct the stiff swing phase lower extremity by excessively abducting both the stance and swing phase hips. By the time midswing has occurred, the hip and knee are flexed 30 and 50-60 degrees respectively; the ankle is dorsiflexed to a near neutral position;

the subtalar and midtarsal joints are pronated (the midtarsal joint is pronated about both axes); and the first ray is dorsiflexed and inverted (Ch 3, P 118)." Swing phase prepares the body for stance. If a joint doesn't have proper motion to properly clear the ground and be set for heel strike, the eccentric capabilities of the system will be compromised. Clinically, it's important to recognize the swing leg is impacted by stance leg function, and vice versa.

Clinical Correlation

Clinically, there are numerous situations when one side effects the other's ability to properly load or unload. One example is Achilles pain in the stance leg being linked to a tight swinging leg adductor. When the adductor can't fully dissociate and the soft tissue tension is taken up in the swing leg, it can easily cause the pelvis to rotate towards the stance leg prematurely. This can compromise the eccentric loading ability of the stance leg calf and create a situation where the stance leg calf has to concentrically produce force secondary to lack of ability to eccentric load and isometric stabilize. This can lead to a situation where the peripheral nerves get irritated due to the increased energy demands of concentric muscle action, considered as neurogenic inflammation. Please note, this topic is covered more in depth in the pain part. At this point, recognize that tissue far away from the site of pain can play into a dysfunction. Keeping an open mind to look for potential links will allow the ability to consider the potential for limitations up and down the kinetic chain. Credit to Dr. David Tiberio for the nugget of information about the 80pprox./opposite adductor relationship.

Conclusion

Understanding the gait cycle has proven endlessly useful in working with anyone who ambulates. A gait assessment doesn't require complicated equipment and simply takes practice and knowing what to look for.

Additional Readings:

Can be found at end of Part 4.

PART 4: TREATING CAPACITIES: MOVEMENT THRESHOLDS

This part is divided into a discussion about ensuring how the positioning of various body parts through motion can be maintained. It will begin with higher level integration, specifically how the vestibular system plays into controlling movement, and describing how the various components of it work together to help govern movement. After discussing some specifics of the brain, it will continue top down, first discussing the cervical spine, then the shoulder complex, and also the costo-pelvic region. Having various ways to assess these regions is a large part of creating individualized interventions. While out of the scope of this text, simple assessments will be discussed in order to reinforce various thought processes.

Author's Note:

I considered separating this chapter into two chapters, one on the brain, and one on 'musculoskeletal dysfunction". However, after reflection, I decided to keep it as one longer chapter, in the spirit of not separating the brain from the body.

The point of any exam is to drive thresholds of numerous systems in various ways and observe the point when each system demonstrates instability. One strategy to assess is to take away stability and observe any compensation. Sway or decreased movement are signs of instability, as are 'breaking' form at the cervico-thoracic or thoracolumbar junctions. These regions are common areas for breakdown in form during exercise, with the CT and TL junctions being 'dumping points' for an asynchronous system. Knowledge of how, what, and when to load or unload specific systems creates more specificity and reproducible results. Assessing the stability of a system can be accomplished easily with logical and progressive thought processes. For example, in standing with feet together, if sway increases with closed eyes (Romberg test), the body is demonstrating instability, and the threshold is reached. In this case, further assessment of the vestibular and cerebellar systems may be warranted because removing stability (the eyes), resulted in instability. When this happens, the exercise should be dialed back because a threshold has been found. In other words, regressing exercise may be a good strategy when at a threshold. Another strategy may include finding ways to influence the eyes while decreasing the influence of the system (sitting?), before progressing by 'layering' an eye exercise with a standing position movement. Recognizing that a threshold is an opportunity to either intervene, assess further, or dial back the activity.

From a musculoskeletal perspective, there are numerous ways to globally or locally assess the shoulder complex. One way to check stability is to lay supine on the ground holding a dumbbell up towards the ceiling over the shoulder. Once the weight is stabilized, the eyes are closed to observe, as sway of the weight increases. If sway does increase, it is fair to say the visual system assists in stabilizing the weight. In other words, removing the vestibular system (laying down), and visual system (eyes closed), created a situation where the proprioceptive system (muscle spindles), worked solely to stabilize the weight. When a weight is stable with eyes open and not with eyes closed, emphasis can be placed on the proprioceptive system to stabilize. The idea is to layer progressive input until the point when instability is flashed at which point intervention or further assessment is warranted. Special thanks to Dr. David Traster, DC, and Dr. Stuart Fife, PT, for the thought processes described in the previous two paragraphs.

"In addition, when it is recognized that, with eyes open, the patient or athlete is more stable, it is important to teach how to use this to their advantage. For example, in powerlifting or CrossFit type athletes, it is readily seen that giving the athlete a specific point to hold his/her gaze, typically in the midline, and eyes neutral position, will increase lift stability, and therefore, the ability to lift more weight efficiently. Although anecdotally, it has been seen that an athlete will max out on a lift with their own technique, then when given a specific point to maintain gaze through the lift, they are able to increase their PR (Personal Record), often times at significantly higher weight than just previously attempted.

With that being said, if the clinician is adept at recognizing optimal points of gaze stability, a point that is not in midline may be even more effective to the particular athlete. If the eyes are taken away from the midline, it is important to know what spinal reflexes are going to be elicited by having the athlete hold her/his eyes in a position other than neutral, especially when lifting heavy weight. Eyes held in a gaze outside of neutral can be extremely effective if the spinal reflexes are recognized, or detrimental to the athlete if not taken into account."

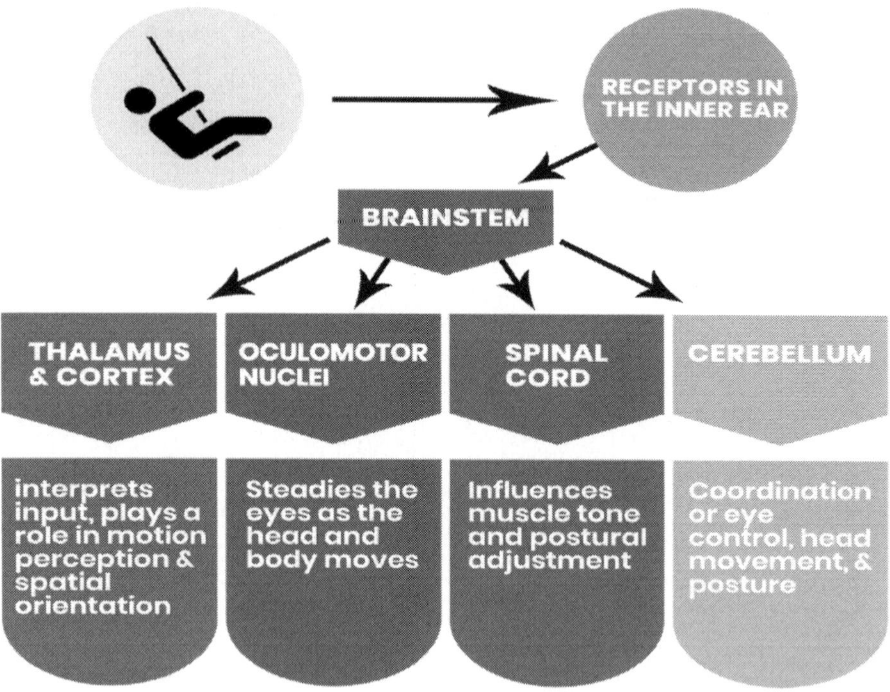

Understanding the vestibular system's influence in movement, and how to assess, is a necessary part of a brain-based approach to treatment.

Clinical Concept: Remove stability and observe the system response.

When instability increases with removal of the visual system, further assessment of the vestibular and cerebellar systems may be warranted. With non-clinically presenting (subclinical) vestibular issues, individuals can be positioned into various head positions that bias certain vestibular semi-circular canals to observe what outcome measurements change. The head positions associated with each vestibular canal are as follows: Right rotation – Right horizontal canal; Left rotation – Left horizontal canal; Extension and right rotation – Right posterior canal; Extension and left rotation – Left posterior canal; Flexion and right rotation – Left anterior canal; Flexion and left rotation – Right anterior canal. If the outcome changes (and they do not demonstrate BPPV), the vestibular canals may be playing into the dysfunction, and specific correction may be warranted. Outcome measurements can include muscle testing as well as other neurological exams including comparing rapid alternating movements (RAM), which measures the integrity of the ipsilateral cerebellum and contralateral frontal lobe. In subclinical dysfunction, often rapid alternating movements will be limited completely on one side of the body when compared to the other. For example, if RAM was limited in the left shoulder (IR/ER), elbow (pronate/supinate), fingers (finger to thumb), heel/knee tap, and toe tap, cerebellar integration on the left may be dysfunctional. NOTE: Without the understanding of the central mechanisms at play for dizziness, it is NOT recommended to perform these activities on a dizzy or clinically observed vestibular issue.

In the above examples, when RAM is lacking on the left side of the body, brain-based strategies should be focused on providing input into the left side of the body. This could include complex movement (to drive the cerebellum), isometric holds, and/or joint manipulation to the left side of the body. It is also not uncommon to see left RAM dysfunction and pain in multiple joints on the right side of the body. This type of pattern with pain on the right side of the body and dysrhythmic movements on the left is due to the axis of pain inhibition coming from the right side of the brain, which is ipsilateral in nature. In many situations, the practitioner would look at the painful side of the body and focus on treating that side, when in fact, performing complex exercises and providing stimulus on the opposite side of pain (the side of rapid movement dysfunction) may have a better outcome. This is a very difficult concept for practitioners to grasp, especially in the current environment of zeroing in on the area of pain. In this case, brain-based strategies would target the left side of the body, including complex/complicated type movements on the left and muscle/sensory stimulation on the left to reduce pain on the right side of the body.

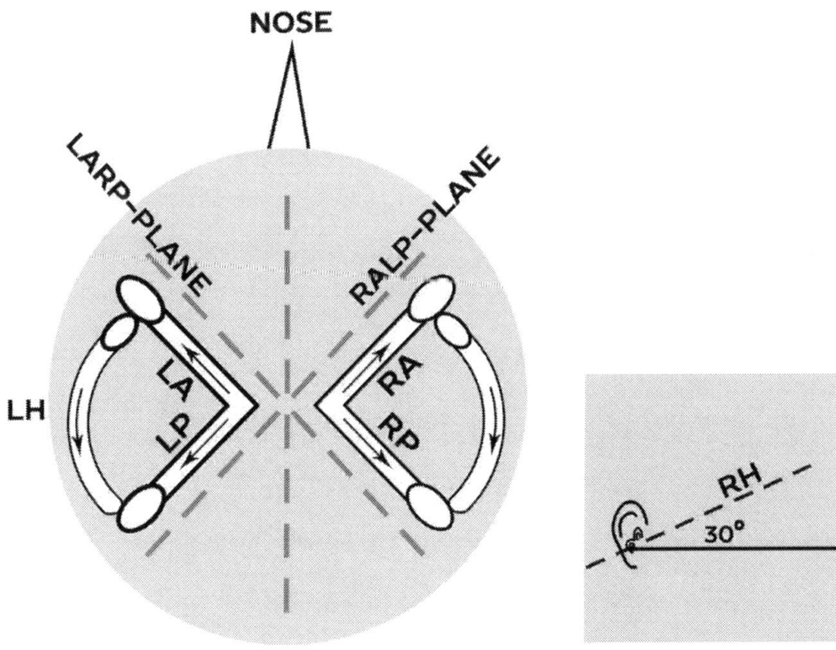

(picture on previous page) The head positions that are associated with each vestibular canal are as follows: Right rotation – Right horizontal canal; Left rotation – Left horizontal canal; Extension and right rotation – Right posterior canal; Extension and left rotation – Left posterior canal; Flexion and right rotation – Left anterior canal; Flexion and left rotation – Right anterior canal. RALP plane refers to right anterior, left posterior plane, while the LARP plane refers to the left anterior and right posterior plane.

One way of looking at dynamic vestibular function is to test at the Vestibular Ocular Reflex (VOR) in every vestibular canal plane looking for errors in the ability to maintain forward gaze with various head thrusts. A modified Romberg balance test, where the patient's balance is tested with a neutral head position in addition to testing with their head in a static angular position associated with each vestibular canal; right horizontal, left horizontal, right anterior, left anterior, right posterior, and left posterior. Assessing for errors in response of the vestibular system such as loss of balance, sway patterns, cantilever responses, accessory muscle recruitment, and general affect should occur. This will give an idea of the integration of each of the peripheral canals with the central mechanisms that govern function of those associated canals.

When there are errors picked up in assessment, treating the dysfunctional areas of the vestibular system becomes a priority, however as discussed in this book, the vestibular system can be used when functioning properly to enhance treatment. When the vestibular system is intact and appropriate, use vestibular based therapies in order to have an effect on other areas of the nervous system and body.

For example, someone with an acute chronic low back pain and has an anterior head carriage, anteriorly rotated glenohumeral joints bilaterally, and utilizes accessory muscles rather than diaphragmatic breathing. He may have low back pain, and that will be addressed, but it is greatly important to assess the rest of his central nervous system including his eye movements and vestibular system function to see if there are central biases or abnormalities that could be contributing to poor postural control and chronic low back pain. Perhaps it is found that his upward eye movements are slightly insufficient both in fast (saccades) and slow (pursuit) movements, and his visual optokinetic movements are also slightly decreased going upwards (this will be discussed more in depth in later parts). It could be this patient has an abnormal perceived posterior center of pressure. In other words, the patient's brain/vestibular system perceives a posterior center of pressure and that he is always leaning back slightly. If this is the case, postural muscles will have an increased tone on the anterior side. Often this will lead to hypertonic pecs and hypertonic hip flexor muscles.

Clinical Correlation:

Clinically, this is something I often have found with those in chronic pain. Since checking via my Btracks plate, the finding described above is something to be considered and is seen relatively often in practice. Said differently, many people with spine pain 'feel' like they're going to fall backwards, which forces their nervous system to feel comfortable leaning forward, resulting in the 'bad posture' often seen with those in pain. In this case, his poor posture isn't peripheral in nature, rather it's central. This can be seen with the Btracks Cervical Challenge Test because there are more perturbations with cervical extension compared to less perturbations with cervical flexion.

"In this situation, layering central treatments with peripheral treatments will greatly enhance the outcome. For this particular patient I would consider downward head thrusts while he looks forward at a gaze fixation point. Activation of the anterior canals of the vestibular system will activate postural mechanisms to shift the perceived posterior center of pressure to a more anterior position. This will improve the upward eye movements, having an effect on the central mechanisms that drive these eye movements. It may also offload the tone of the anterior muscles including the pecs and hip flexor muscles, relaxing the strain on the low back. Following anterior canal activation exercises peripheral treatment modalities would also be addressed. By bringing in a central and reflexive (vestibular ocular reflex) treatment, the outcomes will be faster and will have a better chance of lasting longer."

In the two pictures on the left, the head positions correspond to the right posterior canal & left anterior canal. (LARP plane). Notice when in the right posterior canal, the eyes are down to the left, while in the left anterior canal, the eyes are up to the left. The two pictures on the right correspond to the right anterior canal and left posterior canal (RALP plane). Notice when in the right anterior canal, the eyes are up to the right, while in the left posterior canal, the eyes are down to the right. With this in mind, the specific canals of the vestibular system can also be stimulated with those corresponding eye positions. The LARP and RALP planes have a push/pull relationship, in that when one is activated its counterpart will be inhibited.

The two pictures on the left represent the right horizontal canal and the left horizontal canals, which demonstrate a push<>pull relationship. Notice that with right cervical rotation, the eyes are in the left part of the orbit, and with left cervical rotation the eyes are in the right. With this in mind, the specific canals of the vestibular system can also be stimulated with those corresponding eye positions. The two pictures on the right demonstrate a Romberg and Tandem Romberg with eyes open (it is recommended to also test with eyes closed).

Basic Vestibulocerebellar Capacities and Midline Stability

Integrating new material into practice can be challenging, regardless of how useful the information is. Recently, my education has focused on learning more about cerebellar and vestibular pathways. I have learned that subclinical integration issues can be seen by evaluating these systems and testing them against each other. Before learning more about the cerebellum and vestibular systems role in movement, I never thought to check to see how they function. However, since learning more about, and assessing for, contributing signs of movement dysfunction, I've been amazed at the amount of people who demonstrate these deficiencies.

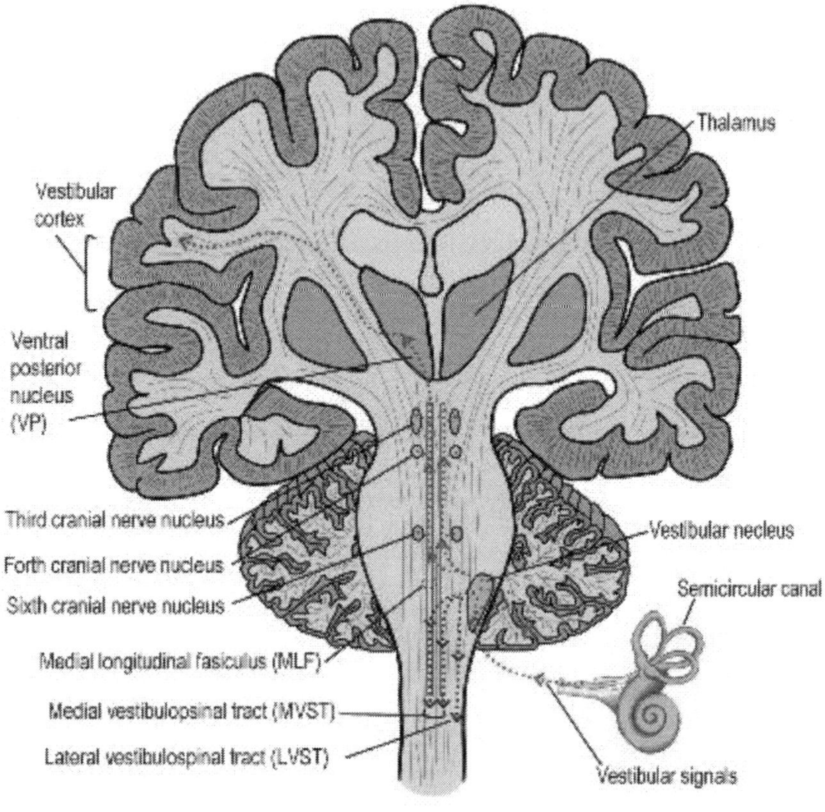

Input from the eyes, ears, and spine, converge in the central vestibular system, the cerebellum, and in the mesencephalon.

When neurological tests are understood, specific systems can be stimulated to observe the result. Similar to a physical driver that creates a reaction into another body part, a 'neurological' driver with specificity should create an expected result; and when it doesn't happen, further investigation is required. Understanding even the general function of the proprioceptive and vestibulocerebellar systems has proven extremely valuable in my outpatient clinical practice. Musculoskeletal dysfunction is easily driven from a hierarchically higher system such as the vestibulo-ocular and cerebellar systems. Integrating quick neurological screens to observe general capacities of these systems doesn't take long and helps to create a clearer picture of the individual. A clearer picture means more specificity in interventions and often quicker results.

The vestibulo-ocular and cerebellar systems are all midline in the brain. Therefore, ensuring midline stability is necessary. It is a concept I've always known about and has taken on a new meaning since learning about these regions. A brain-based approach to midline stability should include at least a basic understanding of brain structures and their function. The book, *Functional Neurology for Practitioners of Manual Therapy,* by Randy Beck, describes the Carrick Institute term of the "SEE Principle" (spine, eyes, ears), which can be applied across all movement disciplines.

Beck states, "...convergence of spine, ear, and eye afferents in the vestibulocerebellar system and mesencephalon will have a more direct effect and the relationship between dysfunction in these areas and autonomic asymmetry can be readily observed" (102). In other words, input from the eyes, ears, and spine, converge in the central vestibular system, the cerebellum, and in a part of the brainstem called the mesencephalon. Therefore, basic assessments for functions of these regions is beneficial.

Since integrating the SEE principle, I've observed many people with bilateral joint pain, or have multiple sites of pain, particularly on the same side of the body, also have dysfunction in the spine, eye, and/or ear systems. Beck goes on to say that, "a vestibular induced symptom may be in fact be due to vestibular hypofunction on the contralateral side and vice versa. Dysmetric eye movements and some signs associated with autonomic function are not classed as being due to hypo or hyper function as individual bedside tests may not be adequate to confirm this relationship. All clinical signs and symptoms help establish the diagnosis or clinical impression" (102).

The previous passages refer specifically to applying neurology and clinical presentations of the pathologies. However subclinical presentations do occur and affect the musculoskeletal system. A current challenge, personally, is knowing I am seeing something in one of these systems, but often not knowing exactly what. It reminds me of when I was learning integrated movement. There are many examples, including differentiating if an eye isn't converging vs. the contralateral side, or if it's already converged and can't anymore (which is what's seen with a convergence spasm), which would look like it can't go in (instead of already position inward). In these situations, my strategy is to keep it simple, and safely drive as much input to the specific system as possible. Recognizing when visual fixation is challenged (as seen when postural sway increases during visual fixation upon fixation), or the cerebellar function is impaired (difficulty with rapid alternating movement in an extremity), provides information necessary to drive safe input to these systems. When sway increases with fixation, simple fixation exercises (i.e. Horizontal sinusoidal VOR movements, often termed No-No's for how they appear when being performed), can be integrated into the MSK rehab routine, just as a non-linear complicated movement (figure 8 of the hand or foot), can be added to an exercise addressing soft tissue to drive more cerebellar function when appropriate. In other words, it doesn't make sense to work extremities and complicated multi joint muscles that require control when the vestibulo-ocular or cerebellar systems are involved in the dysfunction. In addition, if no change has occurred within four sessions, I refer out, which is always my rule in clinical practice. In this case, to someone specializing in functional neurology (including the clinician 'neuro' editing this book, Dr. Mike Drzewiecki).

For example, it is common for someone to present to clinic having bilateral pain in the same joints, perhaps the shoulders, knees, or hips. Prior to learning about the specifics of the brain, my approach was to concentrate on general 'core' instability. My focus was on improving control of joints and motion in key regions of the body including the foot, hip, and thoracic spine. It often was a correct approach without brain specificity. Now, through assessing vestibulo-ocular and cerebellar systems in an effort to better understand how they may be influencing movement, more specificity can be created, yielding quicker results. Only through detailed assessments can specificity in intervention be applied. Utilizing the SEE Principle, the visual, vestibular, and cerebellar systems can be assessed for overall general function without getting into specific mechanisms as to why there's dysfunction, which is beyond the scope of this text.

Clinical Concept

In practice, I work under the rule "if you're not getting better in four, you're out the door". What this means is there should be change (positive or negative) after 4-5 sessions and when there is not, it's time to refer to another medical professional. This rule holds true for coming up against the limits of knowledge around a particular topic, meaning drive safe input, and as long as there's progression, then the direction of treatment is appropriate. However, if no change is made AND limits of intervention are reached, considering referring out even sooner is warranted.

"An important concept for both new and seasoned clinicians who want to integrate any new approach to their practice, but very importantly for implementation of brain-based therapies, is to comply with the following steps:

1) Learn how to use a test appropriately. What is normal? What is abnormal? What is subclinical, and is there a grading system to appropriately describe the severity of the pathology? (i.e. Modified Romberg or Finger tap test.)

2) Learn exactly what parts of the brain the test is intended on assessing, (contralateral frontal lobe).

3) Perform whatever therapy you are going to do for the particular injury or presentation of the patient. (Instrument assisted myofascial release of the quadriceps.)

4) Re-test immediately after the therapy. (i.e. Modified Romberg or Finger tap test.)

5) If the test improves, the therapy is appropriate for the individual's nervous system.

6) If the test degrades, the therapy was not appropriate for the patient, regardless of how appropriate you think the therapy should have been based on your current paradigm.

Be humble, knowing that many times a therapy may make sense from a patient presentation and textbook theory, but may not be correct for the individual. This does not mean giving up on all therapy is appropriate, rather it means another way must be found to rehab the injury and nervous system. It is important to remember that providing input to a body part and the nervous system is not responding in a positive manner can cause more harm than good. For new practitioners, or for veterans who are learning new brain-based tools, this will be very frustrating and possibly hard to integrate into a treatment paradigm. Be patient, keeping these concepts in mind will ensure faster and better results once you, as the clinician, become more proficient in your skills."

The concept of treating capacities places emphasis on driving safe input through a layered approach that works at the threshold of the individual. It is common to observe difficulty with rapid alternating movement on one side of the body in numerous regions through multiple tests. Even at a basic level, this information can be used to create a program focusing on simple rapid alternating movements while concurrently driving input to specific brain regions.

Midline Stability

From a musculoskeletal perspective, midline stability can be thought of as stability of the proximal joints. For me this includes spine before extremities, hips before knee (and often feet), and shoulders before elbows, as this works midline out to the periphery. In addition, representation of body parts in the brain is also arranged midline to periphery; with the spine, vestibulo-ocular, and cerebellar system, being most midline. (Please note, this is extremely simplified, and it is recommended for you to learn more about these systems.) When these systems are understood, they can be assessed and interventions to target them can be applied. There are simple tests to assess midline function, including rapid alternating movements and finger to nose, both ipsilateral cerebellar and opposite frontal lobe dominant activities. Interventions for the deficiencies found in the exams can easily be layered into a movement program geared towards improving functionality of the system.

Incorporating simple assessments that check specific regions of the brain can also help to create the most individualized program possible. For example, if visual fixation is poor with someone with shoulder pain, starting with movements that stimulate and improve axial based positions compared to scapular retractions. This is because hierarchically, midline posture control, including midline gaze activities, stimulates regions of the brain important for midline and core stability, specifically the eyes and spine. It is neurologically more demanding to stabilize midline. Midline stability is necessary in order for scapular muscles to pull from, and therefore should occur prior to improving peripheral regions.

Creating brain change requires safe intense input, therefore utilizing large muscle groups more central to the midline helps to drive more input to the central mechanisms. In other words, most people compensate in the cervical spine or at the thoracolumbar junction. Ensuring these relationships can be maintained through movement is important to minimizing positions that can aggravate soft tissue. Hierarchically, establishing a proper cervical retraction and maintaining a costo-pelvic relationship prior to assigning more complicated movements (such as single leg activities) creates the greatest chance of cementing a desired neurological change.

Hierarchically, higher level sensory integration should occur prior to strength and balance of the musculoskeletal system because focusing on perception deficits, even if sub-clinical, provides a better neurological environment for musculoskeletal integration. Sensory integration can include cerebellar and vestibular activities, which can be performed in conjunction with musculoskeletal activation, and should be performed prior to more complicated single leg activities. Sensory integration can also incorporate proprioceptive activities including two-point discrimination, which has found to be diminished in painful regions when compared to the non-affected side. Improving two-point discrimination theoretically can help to lower the threat levels in painful populations due to having more awareness of the region. Evidence demonstrates manual interventions can improve two-point discrimination. In addition, ensuring that all movements are performed appropriately and within controlled ranges, including hip hinges and cervical retraction, is imperative. Remember, to teach a new behavior, the intervention must be focused, intense, mindful, and repeated.

Generally speaking, squats and retractions aren't introduced in my practice until overall proprioceptive, perceptive, and endurance based activities are improved. Once form and proper technique is demonstrated in double leg activities, including hip hinge and body weight squatting, the movement will be progressed to ensure the greatest chance for desired neurological changes. This strategy is consistent with AFS

(Applied Functional Science) which teaches to start with success instead of failure. In this case, starting with double leg activities will ensure more success, which can be appropriately layered with concurrent neurological interventions. This will be more successful compared to starting with more demanding activities that increase chances of non-desired neuroplastic changes.

Specifics of the Cerebral Cortex:

"More notable lesions in the cortex are cerebrovascular accidents (stroke) with signs and symptoms that are more exaggerated than what will be laid out in this section. The following is meant to give an idea of how to assess the cortex from a functional standpoint, rather than a frank lesion standpoint such as a tumor or a stroke. It should provide ideas on how and what to assess from a brain function and also how to also treat musculoskeletal dysfunctions with other body dysfunction.

Along with subconscious cortical activity, the various lobes of the brain can be assessed through specific tests. For example, the finger tap test for the frontal lobe, graphesthesia for the parietal lobe, auditory awareness for the temporal lobe, and visual confrontation for the occipital lobe. Of course, with each of these tests there are many other areas of the brain to consider if abnormalities are recognized. For this reason, it's important to choose a variety of tests for each area of the brain, which helps to guide examination and helps to rule in or out specific syndromes.

Frontal Lobe:

The frontal lobe governs motor programming and executive function. Assessing the frontal lobe requires assessment of both motor and cognitive function, both with specific tests such as the Cambridge Brain Sciences online cognitive tests as well as real time cognitive abilities including affect, conversation, eye contact, mood, perseveration, and motivation. In addition, most times specific tests such as finger tap, gait pattern, go-no-go tasks, and Luria sequencing tasks are also looked at. These are assessed in isolation as well as with a simultaneous dual task such as reciting every letter of the alphabet out loud while performing the test to provide insight about how they perform while under cognitive load. Oftentimes there will be a breakdown in motor planning and execution during the dual task. In cases where the motor program improves, it is a sign that the patient should be pushed cognitively during other exercises.

The eye movements associated with the frontal lobe, specifically the frontal eye fields, are saccades and anti-saccades. Saccades are fast eye movements, moving the eyes from point A to point B quickly. A leftward saccade is generated from the right frontal lobe and vice versa. Treatments for the frontal lobe could include sequencing tasks, memory tasks, saccade and anti-saccade tasks, and go-no-go activities.

These can be performed in isolation or in combination with other movement exercises. For example, a patient with poor anterior dominant posture, low back pain, and shoulder pain with abnormal frontal lobe tests could be given go-no-go activities with overhead reaching while balancing on a foam pad.

Parietal Lobe:

The parietal lobe is responsible for the majority of sensory integration. The primary sensory cortex is located in the parietal lobe which contains the sensory homunculus, the map of the body. Errors in the parietal lobe can result in minor symptoms such as always bumping into objects with one side of the body, sensory abnormalities, body dysmorphia, and even dystonia. Most commonly, abnormalities in the parietal lobe will cause sensory abnormalities. This can be differentiated based on sensory loss or sensory aberration patterns.

If the sensory abnormalities cannot be described by a peripheral nerve, dermatome, or spinal cord pattern, it is likely either the brainstem, thalamus, or cortex. Looking at other objective findings, brainstem and thalamus can be ruled out. If so, then it is likely the parietal cortex causing problems. Another sign of parietal lobe dysfunction is errors in the smooth pursuit mechanism. A smooth pursuit is a slower eye movement than the faster saccadic eye movement that is initiated by the frontal lobe. A smooth pursuit is utilized when following an object as it moves in space. This is precisely why the parietal lobe must be intact to maintain a smooth pursuit. The parietal lobe encodes the conscious awareness of where the object is in space and allows the eyes to maintain focus on the object. This movement is driven primarily by the ipsilateral parietal lobe.

For instance, tracking an object moving from the left visual field to the right visual field is initiated and maintained by the right parietal lobe. A breakdown in this smooth pursuit mechanism should be considered an ipsilateral parietal lobe issue until it is ruled out by looking at other potential areas of dysfunction which could cause this error. As with any eye movement, it is not as simple as to say that the abnormality is always from just one area of the brain. There are many other nuclei, peripheral nerves, and eye muscles that could cause an error but the specific breakdown of those neuro pathways are beyond the discussion of this book.

Other tests that I perform when assessing the parietal lobe include graphesthesia, pinprick, light touch, deep touch, temperature, baragnosis, two-point discrimination, and point localization. In serious conditions, such as stroke, all of these tests will be abnormal. In other conditions, such as concussion or chronic pain, some of these tests may be normal while others are abnormal.

This gives a good opportunity to utilize the normal tests as treatments to aid in progress of the abnormal tests. For example, if graphesthesia is abnormal but light touch is normal, then graphesthesia training using light tough would be a warranted approach. If deep touch is more appropriate, then deep touch graphesthesia training would be best. As described earlier, if the patient has chronic and persistent knee pain, it is likely that the sensory map of the knee will be altered. Warming up with graphesthesia training over the area of pain prior to performing any other therapeutic approach directly to the knee will produce a better likelihood of positive outcomes."

Clinical Correlation:

As with anything else, utilizing the test, treat, re-test method is great here. For example, the patient with the bad knee, assess graphesthesia over the area of pain, assess the knee for dysfunction (along with everything else in the kinetic chain), and assess the pursuit mechanism in the contralateral direction of the knee (to assess the affected parietal lobe). If the pursuit mechanism is broken, graphesthesia is difficult, and the knee hurts, use graphesthesia training and treat the knee then reassess the pursuit. If the pursuit improves, something positive for the parietal lobe occurred. Likewise, you could go the other way and train the pursuit by providing passive Halmagyi head thrusts towards the side of the painful knee (to drive the eyes contralaterally) several times, then reassess graphesthesia. If it improves, there are now many ways to access the parietal lobe and layer knee therapy. These are all examples of various avenues that could be taken. Understanding the anatomy and connections of the neuroaxis can be amazingly beneficial for your patients.

Temporal Lobe:

This is probably the least involved area when assessing and treating the cortex. It doesn't mean that it is not important, just that there are fewer ways to directly access it. The temporal lobe is primarily concerned with integration of sound, speech, understanding of language, memory, mood, and vision. Sound is contralateral to the ear where the sound stimulus is provided. Noise into the left ear is processed in the right temporal lobe. Outside of sound, the visual pathways from the superior portion of the contralateral temporal field and ipsilateral nasal field travel through the temporal lobe. (The visual radiations from the inferior portion of the contralateral temporal field and ipsilateral nasal field travel through the parietal lobe).

In cases of cerebrovascular accidents in the temporal lobe, vision will be completely lost in these fields. With non-structural lesions (functional lesions) vision could be distorted or just not as crisp in these fields. Most patients won't notice this unless they are specifically tested for vision in these fields."

One test for the temporal lobe is sound localization. With the sound localization test, the patient closes his/her eyes and points to or grabs the sound of snapped fingers or a clicked pen. It is very easy to see accuracy of sound localization with this test. There should be an allowance of minor error, as sound is not as perfect as visual localization but the patient should be within about one inch of the sound. Again, the left field is integrated in the right temporal lobe. All four quadrants should be tested and noted. Comparing sound and visual point localization is a good tool to assess various areas of the brain including the parietal lobe, temporal lobe, superior and inferior colliculus of the midbrain. Because all of these are connected, treatment through point and sound localization will improve the connections of all of these areas. The superior colliculus is associated with visual localization, while the inferior colliculus is associated with sound localization and is not as accurate as the superior colliculus because it does not contain the grid map of its counterpart. Rather, the inferior colliculus borrows the map of the superior colliculus to send the information to the temporal lobe. Thus, the allowance for minor localization errors.

Clinical Correlation:

One treatment for the temporal lobe can consist of sound localization training, where the patient tries to touch where a sound is coming from, if they are inaccurate, opening their eyes to see where the sound was originated can help restore those maps. Although this seems like a negligible deficit, imagine being in a closed tin room with many sounds echoing around you. After several minutes it would be disorienting and most likely would start to create irritation and activation of the sympathetic nervous system. The equivalent happens when the brain cannot process which direction sound is coming from. Patients will often describe this as "being easily distracted or overwhelmed when in a crowded environment with many sounds, especially if trying to listen to a conversation."

Occipital Lobe:

The occipital lobe is home of the visual cortex, and nearly the entire occipital lobe is concerned with integration and understanding of visual information. The parietal and temporal visual radiations converge at the posterior occipital lobe. Lesions in this area will cause visual disturbance in a full hemifield distribution contralateral to the side of the affected occipital lobe. A simple test to measure function of the occipital lobe is the visual confrontation test. This is performed by bringing moving fingers or a colored card from around the patient's head in their peripheral vision and having them verbalize when they first see the object. Measuring the degrees at which they stated that the object appeared will give an idea of which occipital lobe may be affected and to what severity. If there is a deficit in both the superior and inferior hemifield, it is likely an occipital lobe or optic chiasm issue, whereas deficit in the superior field or inferior field only can be localized to the temporal lobe or parietal lobe respectively.

Cervical Position & Retraction

Ensuring proper cervical position is maintained during movement is important. Often compensation can be observed in the cervical spine with challenging movements. People aren't normally aware of when their threshold is approached; observing which region of the body is 'dumped' into is a good strategy to identify unstable regions. In the cervical spine, the compensation with difficulty movements is often cervical protraction. Proper cervical retraction without upper cervical flexion (which is a common compensation), is necessary because the horizontal canal is angled by up to 20 degrees. If the head is in a compensated and maximally flexed position, which occurs with upper cervical flexion, the horizontal canals aren't properly stimulated (which occurs with a proper cervical retraction), and the vestibular system is forced to work harder to compensate. Once proper cervical spine relationships can be maintained, a hip hinge is introduced, emphasizing proper costo-pelvic alignment.

"The question must be asked. Is the cervical malposition a primary or secondary issue? In other words, is there a peripheral cervical pathology, such as soft tissue injury, that is causing an abnormal positioning of the cervical spine or is the malposition a result of faulty central mechanisms, the vestibular system being a common culprit.

It is also important to note that as a result of improper cervical positioning, the vestibular system will cause muscular compensations in postural muscles based on the alignment of the head relative to gravity. The compensations become chronic when certain vestibular canals are stimulated more often than others. Because the semicircular canals work in a push-pull relationship, when one canal is stimulated, the opposing canal is inhibited. (For example, right anterior canal activation causes left posterior canal inhibition.) When this happens over an extended period of time. The central projections from the effected canals change, thus creating habits of improper postural control. These muscular compensations can easily become the starting point for chronic abnormal movement patterns, increased risk of injury, causes of pain, and increased risk for degenerative pathologies".

Clinical Concept

Achieving and maintaining proper head position is critical, and when it is lost during movement, there will be compensation. This slightly retracted cervical spine and head should be the starting point when walking. I like the 'rocking chair' analogy for cervical retraction, where the head moves back/forward on the frontal axis, rather than flexing the cervical spine on the axis.

Ensuring Proper Scapular Complex Positioning

Scapular positioning must be maintained during overhead activities for risk of shoulder issues. Performing repetitive activities with altered scapular mechanics increases the risk of injury or soft tissue irritation. When scapular impairments are observed, emphasis should be on setting the shoulder girdle in neutral range and beginning the work to control upward rotation and posterior tilt. Often, compensation with overhead activity will be seen as scapular elevation using the pec minor and upper trap rather than upward rotation and posterior tilt, which is often quite challenging with dysfunction. When altered mechanics are demonstrated, emphasis should be placed on proper form in a controlled (and limited) range. In addition, differentiating capsular vs. soft tissue limitation is necessary. Generally speaking, if there's closing angle pinch, think capsule, and if the restriction is on the opening angle, think soft tissue (although there are exceptions to this rule).

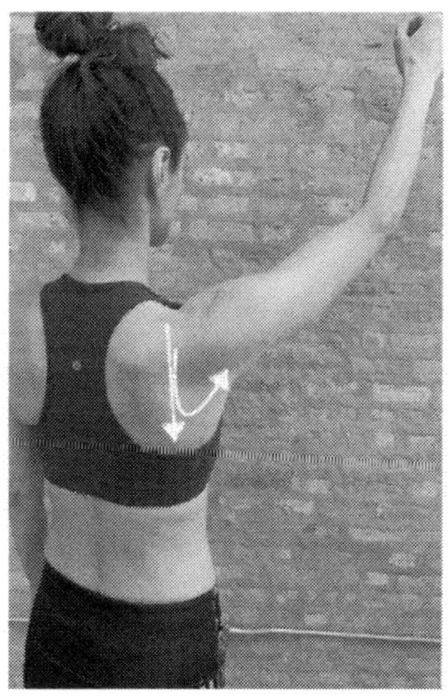

With shoulder pain, consider upward translation via the coupling of the pec minor & upper trap (picture A) as compensation for posterior tilt and downward translation (picture B) via the lower/mid trap and serratus anterior.

Ensuring proper scapular complex positioning during dynamic motion is an important component to shoulder health. The scapula has to move between a bipedal context where it retracts and downwardly rotates on the thorax into an upwardly rotated and protracted position during overhead activities including throwing and reaching. Strategies to assess and work within the individual ability to control these motions is important to correcting dysfunction and preventing injury. The serratus anterior, along with the lower trap, should ideally work to couple a motion and provide a stable base that 'anchors' the scapula. When the scapula is properly anchored for overhead activities, utilizing the serratus anterior and low trap, the humerus can easily move on the scapula. Yet, with upper trap and pec minor dominance with scapular motion, scapular positioning is altered, and shoulder dysfunction can occur.

Clinical Concept

With shoulder pathology, consider the coupling of the pec minor and upper trap as compensation for the lower/mid trap and serratus anterior.

"Often times, anterior positioning of the glenohumeral joint and weakness of scapular stabilizers can be from poor posture, as an environmental result, but also have to be thought of as a disorder of the frontal lobe. As the brain grows in infancy, posterior muscle tone increases allowing for strengthening of the postural muscles that cause upright positioning, or the opposite of fetal positioning. As the brain declines, often the frontal lobe as seen in degenerative brain disorders, the posterior postural muscles weaken causing a camptocormic posturing. This posture is a result of weakness of the posterior upper chain and a tightening of the anterior upper chain, specifically the pectoral muscles, as well as a shifting center of pressure that moves more posteriorly.

Clinically, it is important to remember this concept, not only for patients dealing with late life cognitive decline, but also for those who struggle with subclinical frontal lobe disorders such as learning disabilities, ADHD, autism, and others of this sort. Patients who present with shoulder injuries or neck pain often have these comorbidities, although they may not believe it is important to bring up to a physical medicine clinician. On the contrary, implementation of front lobe exercises in conjunction with traditional scapular stabilizing physical exercises will speed time to recovery and put the patient in a position physically and neurologically where s/he is less likely to experience reinjury."

In his book *Corrective Exercise Solutions to Common Hip and Shoulder Dysfunction*, Dr. Evan Osar describes the thoracoscapular muscles as follows, "The serratus anterior and pectoralis minor are the only muscles attaching directly from the scapula to the thorax… While no muscle works in isolation, the serratus anterior may be the muscle most responsible for scapular stabilization, whereas the pectoralis minor may be the muscle most responsible for the anteriorly tilted scapulae and resultant forward shoulder posture… The serratus anterior is most responsible for stabilizing the scapulae on the thorax. Additionally, it assists in overhead motion by upwardly rotating and abducting the scapulae. The lower fibers have the important function of anchoring the lower aspect to the thorax as the scapula upwardly rotates. Weakness in these fibers results in scapular elevation as the arm goes overhead and scapular winging as the arm returns from an overhead position. With the upper limb fixed, the serratus anterior can also assist trunk motion" (79-80).

He goes onto describe attributes of the pec minor, including, "it is responsible for stabilizing the scapula; however, when overactive and unchecked by the lower trapezius and serratus anterior, it anteriorly tilts the scapulae, contributing to the forward shoulder position. Additionally, the pectoralis minor is an accessory muscle of respiration. In the presence of poor diaphragmatic breathing the pectoralis minor becomes overactive as it attempts to elevate the rib cage… dysfunctional breathing has been clinically found to be the most common cause of hypertonicity of the pectoralis minor as well as the scalenes and sternocleidomastoids."

Ensuring Proper Thoracic Spine Motion

The thoracic spine is a complex region of the body that literally has books written about it, and so while we won't go deep into the specific anatomy, physiology, neurology and mechanics of this region outside of what's already in the text, a brief conversation is warranted. Regardless of how the 'core' is defined, the thoracic spine is a crossroads of the body because all fascial lines pass through it. In addition, any concurrent arm and leg motion likely requires 3-dimensional thoracic motion in order to transfer top down and bottom up forces. Due to the numerous muscle and bony attachments into the thoracic spine, it's often a region with a large opportunity for improvement, particularly around breathing and movement mechanics, especially with those that have neck or low back pain. In addition, as Mike mentioned, there are Central Pattern Generators also found in the thoracic region.

Authors Note:

It's recommended to independently learn about the thoracic spine, including breathing mechanics.

Along with the foot and hip, the thoracic spine is often one of the 'criminals' of movement, meaning its lack of motion easily creates 'victims' as often witnessed by dysfunction above or below the t-spine. Dysfunction includes pain or the inability to maintain the capacity of the cervical spine, shoulder, or costopelvic region. Said differently, not enough motion in the thoracic spine can easily lead to too much motion of the neck, shoulder, low back, and even the knee and below, which are interestingly, the areas people tend to complain about having pain in.

Limitations in the thoracic spine can be caused for all sorts of reasons, including emotional. In his book Body & Mature Behavior: A Study of Anxiety, Sex, Gravitation, and Learning, Moshe Feldenkrais describes the following: "According to my own observation, all individuals classified as introverted have some habitual extensor rigidity. Either the head or the hip joints are therefore leaning abnormally forward; turning the body is achieved by detour or roundabout means and not in the simplest direct way. Extroverts on the other hand have amore erect standing posture and gait." (page 127). He goes on to say "…there are somatic changes that give an indirect observable account of such reactions (emotions). This is particularly so in the case of anxiety states where the extensor inhibition is most marked....people with anxiety seem to be incapable of full extension (page 140)". What this means is that in this case the input of anxiety creates situations where the output is movement dysfunction and emotion (more anxiety), including what he (in the 1940's) referred to as 'rigidity' and inhibition, which seem to be almost interchangeable terms for him. This creates a situation where the body is positioned, often subconsciously, into a protective state, eventually creating and feeding into the forward head position and inhibitions. Therefore, treating the entire, integrated person instead of just the tissue is necessary.

Feldenkrais goes on to say "Repeated emotional upheavals condition the child to adopt an attitude which brings a sense of safety and enables him to abate anxiety. We have seen that such passive safety is brought about by flexor contraction and extensor inhibition (due to anxiety provoking posturing?)……in the long run this becomes habitual and remains unnoticed. The whole character is, however, affected. The partially inhibited extensors become weak, the hip joint flexes and the head leans forward." This passage illustrates the importance of recognizing the whole person while working with those in pain. I like how Feldenkrais discusses how emotion can affect positioning, which in turn effects structure. Therefore, when working with structure, concurrently integrating psychological components into rehab is warranted. In other words, poor posture can be our bodies search for comfort against gravity, possibly as a result of physical or psychological injury, or possibly because of weakness and lack of awareness of positioning. Either way, simultaneously improvement of motion in this region (via movement and manual therapy) while bringing awareness to positioning and the act of being in a specific position can help to create better long term change to the region compared to simply providing an exercise to the region with limited motion.

Authors Note

While behavior change is mentioned throughout the book, it's not in the scope of this text. It's recommended to read independently on behavior change, cognition and neuroplasticity, and specific drills will not be mentioned in this text. Also, Moshe Feldenkrais was an amazingly interesting person and I encourage you to learn about him.

Without getting into too many specifics, having various strategies to assess and intervene upon the thoracic region is important, including breathing, side bending, rotation, and the combination of side bending and rotation. According to Osteopathic literature, combinations of side bending and rotation is referred to as Type 1 (neutral) and Type 2 (non-neutral) spinal mechanics, which is also part of Fryette's Law's of spinal motion. Type 1 spinal mechanics is defined as when the side bending and rotation are in opposite directions, while Type 2 spinal mechanics are defined as side bending and rotation in the same direction, or "two-gether". According to Lisa DeStefano, DO in her book Greenman's Principles of Manual Medicine", "Neutral mechanics, or its synonym type I mechanics, results in coupled movement of side bending and rotation to opposite sides." She goes onto say "Nonneutral mechanical coupling, or its synonym type II mechanics, results when side bending and rotation of vertebrae occur to the same side."

When put into the context of gait, it can be seen that the thoracic spine (or most of it) demonstrates neutral, or Type 1 mechanics, and can best be seen by understanding the motion's that occur from heel strike into foot flat. When the right foot hits the ground, along with the pelvis rotating to the left in the transverse plane, in the frontal plane the left side of the pelvis should drop towards the ground, creating right hip adduction. In the frontal plane, right hip adduction creates right lumbar side bending and a reactive left thoracic side bend, all in order to keep the head and eyes level with the horizon. As this occurs, the left hand moves forward in space, counter rotating the shoulders to the right relative to the hips. The 'coiling' nature of gait and 'out of sync' nature of the pelvis to the shoulders means the thoracic spine rotates to the right as it side bends left, or Type 1 motion. It's also important to note that most often, swing sport athletes require both type 1 and type 2 motions, depending on which phase of the rotational motion (serve/swing/throw).

Clinical Correlation:

Ensuring thoracic mobility, particularly into Type 2 motion is a powerful strategy to improve thoracic mobility. It's also important to note that the motion is a continuum and that the transitional regions for lumbar into thoracic and thoracic into lumbar will vary between type 1 and 2 depending on the anatomy and movement.

Creating thoracic mobility is often a key component of improving overall movement and capacities while concurrently stabilizing the core by improving breathing. Without getting into specifics, checking the thoracic spine's ability to go through type 1 and 2 motions is something assessed with virtually everyone. This can be done isolated and integrated, passive and active, and all should be in order to correlate the most 'bang for the buck'. Thoracic-centric movements will be briefly discussed in Part 9 of this book.

Costo-Pelvic Relationship

The inability to maintain a proper costo-pelvic relationship during movement is another sign of a biomechanical leak. Evidence supports that difficulty in maintaining costo-pelvic positioning through movement leads to compromise in tissue somewhere along the chain. I've often found the costo-pelvic region (thoracolumbar junction) moves too much in compensation for what doesn't move enough. With limitation, compensation often occurs at either the cervico-thoracic or thoraco-lumbar junction as evidenced in difficulty maintaining these relationships during motion.

Integrated motion emphasizes the need for proper pelvic and thoracic motion. The inability to maintain proper alignment and relationship between the pelvis and the rib cage also aligns with the teachings of AFS (Applied Functional Science), which emphasizes the need for proper motion at the hip and thoracic spine. Difficulty in keeping the rib cage aligned over the pelvis can easily contribute to pain elsewhere, particularly at the knee, hip, shoulder, or spine.

The gluteus muscles directly stabilize the pelvis and knee during gait. They are the largest in the body and consequently have a lot of 'real-estate' in the somatosensory cortex. Glute complex strength is important to maintain the proper costo-pelvic relationship. The ability to maintain the relationship between the ribcage and pelvis, as well as of the head during movement, should be an early goal of treatment. Movement should be distributed symmetrically throughout the spine during motion rather than some regions doing all the moving. Difficulty in maintaining proper costo-pelvic alignment during movement should be regressed to the point it can be controlled. Emphasis should be placed maintaining a long spine through movement rather than flexing and rotating, particularly during transition movements (sit>stand, rolling, etc.).

"In line with the idea of posterior muscle tone being a direct result of cerebral cortex thickening as the brain grows, the glutes are critical postural and movement muscles that must be activated to initiate walking in infants. Likewise, glute heavy exercises and coupling of brain-based activities with glute isometric holds and glute strengthening can have a profound impact on the health of the cerebral cortex."

Hip Hinge

A hip hinge can be difficult to teach. Emphasizing controlled ranges is important, as is proper form and awareness of compensations during movement. In addition, staying in pain free uncompensated ranges that are controlled provides the best chances for success. Compensation is often seen towards the bottom of the motion when transitioning from the eccentric (loading), into the concentric (exploding). Clinically, when hip joint motion is taken up, compensatory movement will be observed, often at the costo-pelvic region. This is often described as a "butt wink", or posterior pelvic tilt. In addition, the full ROM before compensation should be correlated to an on table hip assessment to understand if the limitation is soft tissue or joint related. Once identified, ensuring therapeutic movement takes place in a range that preserves proper hip and spine relationship should be drilled. In addition, special emphasis should be taken on educating on the awareness of position during transitions such as sit<>stand and lifting; particularly in situations that require movement outside "neutral".

A posterior tilt (or other compensations) at end ranges of a squat is a common compensation found in this movement pattern. The compensation can take on many forms, as seen above. Picture 1 demonstrates an ideal position, as seen in the 'parallel lines' between the tibias and spine. When coaching a squat, the verbal cue of

keeping the spine and shins parallel is a good visual. Pictures 2-5 demonstrate various compensations that may occur as a result of lack of either foot, hip, or thoracic spine motion (or a combination therein).

Once a hip hinge has been well grooved, it can be progressed to higher level sit to stand activities that emphasize maintaining the pelvic, scapular, cranial relationship. Emphasis should be placed on performing in ranges without compensation, looking for breaking at the thoraco-lumbar or cervical-thoracic junction. To accomplish this, sitting position must be raised in order to maintain the proper alignment of the hips. This is because those with limited hip ROM often compensate by flexion of the spine with sitting.

A Hip Hinge can be challenging to teach, when someone can't perform this movement. The compensation often looks the same and includes an inability to ensure a 'long spine'. However numerous potential reasons for the compensation should be considered, including active and passive hip motions.

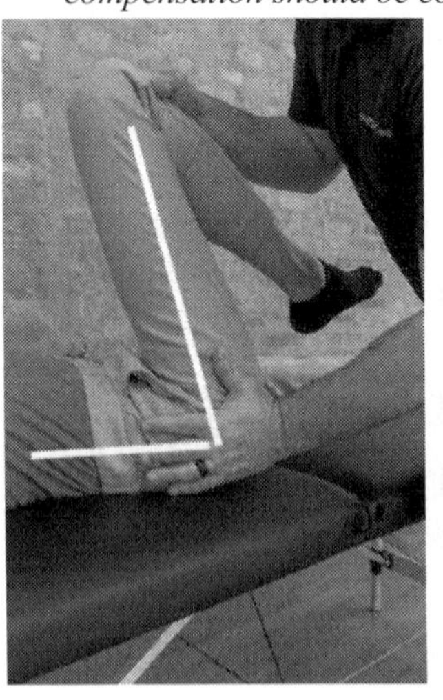

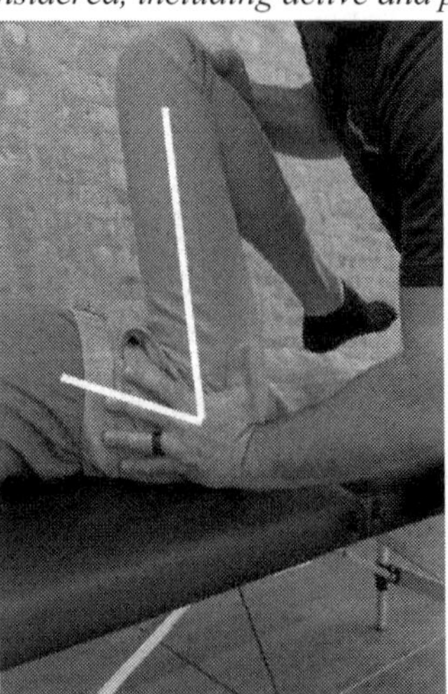

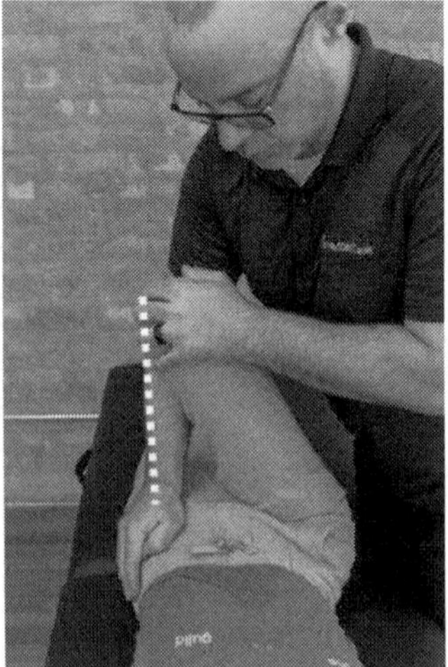

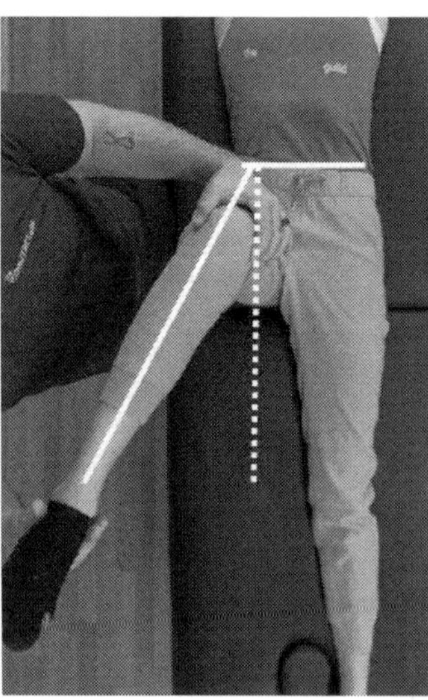

When compensation is observed at the hip, understanding if joint or soft tissue is limited (or both) directs the next steps of intervention. Passively flexing the hip and taking note of when the lumbar spine begins moving will often correlate with a simultaneous restriction being felt in the closing angle. Hip angle should be noted, becoming the place to begin reeducation. The picture 1 on the left represents femur motion, taking note of when the pelvis starts to move. Picture 2 illustrates a potential compensation with an anterior tilt of the pelvis. Another compensation might be a posterior tilt of the pelvis. Picture 3 illustrates how far the femur, when flexed to 90', should be able to adduct prior to pelvic compensation, which should be over the opposite ASIS. Picture 4 illustrates the amount of passive femur on pelvis internal rotation that should be available in the hip, which is approximately 35 degrees.

Clinical Note

Hip hinging can be quite difficult for some people and ensuring it can be performed correctly is imperative. Not everyone learns in the same way and so having numerous ways to accomplish a hip hinge is helpful. Verbal cues like 'pretend to go to the bathroom in a public toilet' tend to be a useful extrinsic cue to create proper form. It provides the person with the idea of sticking the pelvis back. This movement is performed with a long spine, instead of the flexed spine associated with a knee dominant strategy of squatting. It is virtually impossible to perform a knee dominant squat with a neutral spine or a proper costopelvic or cervical relationship. Another strategy to accomplish a proper hip hinge is to stand against the wall with toes and nose against the wall with hands below chest height on the wall. The cue is to 'lower yourself towards the ground and don't let your knees hit the wall while keeping your nose against the wall'. Like the first example, squatting with toes and nose against the wall provides the kinesthetic feedback necessary to teach the proper position and motion. With both suggestions, maintaining a long spine during movement is important.

Hip Hinge Progression: Squat

The hip hinge is a foundational movement that can be observed in the youngest ambulators, yet, in most of the population is lost by the time of adulthood. Everyone at one point had the ability to perform it correctly, as evidenced by children deep squatting without effort. Sitting and not utilizing existing ranges are ways people lose the ability to perform a squat appropriately. The spine shouldn't have much relative movement between segments during a hip hinge. In other words, the hips and spine should be independent in their motion, however observable interdependence will be observed with compensation. While slight spine movements with a hip hinge are expected, spine movement should be minimal and occur in response to pelvic motion rather than driven from the spine into the pelvis.

Ensuring hip hinging can be maintained throughout a sit<>stand is important. This motion links the pelvis to the body, helping to create stability of the system. Dr. Andreo Spina, creator of Functional Range Conditioning (FRC), illustrates the importance of joint independence instead of interdependence, which is highlighted with a hip hinge. A hip hinge is the foundation of a squat, step up/down, and involved with many reaching movements. A long spine should be maintained with sit<>stand, and progressions shouldn't occur until it can be accomplished. Once a hip-hinge is properly demonstrated repeatedly, progressions and variances emphasizing controlled range can occur.

Movement Capacities: Step Down Test

A step down is a great way to assess stance leg eccentric control. It can be correlated with loading and early phases of gait, as well as midstance in the frontal plane. It is a dynamic activity that should only be performed once proper strength and control has been demonstrated. When there is similarly poor control bilaterally, centrally mediated dysfunctions should be considered and dealt with before progressions occur.

Compensation in a step down can be observed at the knee and hip, as well as distant regions including the shoulder complex and cervical spine. It is also an effective strategy to assess and train knee control from contact to midstance. Michaud states, (ch3, p121), "The quadriceps pretense during late swing phase and demonstrate peak activity during the early contact period, when they eccentrically contract to decelerate knee flexion. These muscles continue to contract until the center of mass passes in front of the knee." The quadriceps muscles are by far the body's most important shock absorbers, and activity in these muscles increases as the degree of knee flexion increases. In other words, the step down is a great way to mimic the actions of contact and midstance phases and is a movement that, in itself, can be regressed and progressed. An effective hip hinge is necessary to properly execute a step down and is important to master before progressing.

Single leg activities including single leg balancing and squats can be regressed by toe touch support of the other foot. Toe touch support provides enough stability to allow the system to stabilize. If the body doesn't feel stable during movement it is harder to create proper movement patterns that are stable. Toe touching is a way to work at the threshold that can be taught to the patient.

Breathing

Proper breathing mechanics are amazingly important, and easily influences the entire musculoskeletal and nervous system. There are literally books written on this subject alone, and with that in mind, breathing is not discussed in this text. However, it is HIGHLY recommended to study more on breathing.

Conclusion

Movement dysfunction can include compensation from the top-down, neurologically via a brain lobe 'opportunity for improvement', or top down musculoskeletally via 'forward head'. It can also include compensation bottom up, neurologically via an opportunity to improve the afferent information the brain takes in, and musculoskeletally from an altered costo-pelvic relationship resulting in the same forward head position. Therefore, ensuring that musculoskeletal relationships and brain optimization of reactions is occurring because to minimize compromising positions that contribute to pain and dysfunction is beneficial. Dr. David George, DC, illustrates the costo-pelvic and cervical spine are two regions that 'flash instability' through movement. Therefore, ensuring these relationships are maintained throughout any progression is paramount, just as maintaining gaze stability is important, both of which can prove challenging for the patient.

Simply put, treating capacities instead of anatomy makes it easier to look at the entire integrated system, rather than focusing on a specific body part. The concept of the site of the injury isn't the cause of the injury, is consistent with enhancing capacities and ensuring the body can maintain fundamental positions. Everything exists on a spectrum, and sometimes treating the anatomy or specific body part is warranted and justified. However, it is important to recognize, when working in isolation, and make sure to integrate it into the higher level system when appropriate. Treating capacities rather than anatomy allows for easier integration into a bio-psycho-social construct. When properly done, differences in the ability to control motion one side vs. the other, combined with education and awareness of those differences, creates easy goals and awareness about the changes that are being worked to achieve.

Additional Readings

- Michaud, Tom; Human Locomotion

- Root, Orien, Weed: Normal & Abnormal Function of the Foot

- Shadmehr, Reza, Maurice A. Smith, and John W. Krakauer. Forthcoming. Error correction, sensory prediction, and adaptation in motor control. Annual Review of Neuroscience 33.

- Cerebellar contribution to feedforward control of locomotion; Pisotta I., Molinari M.(2014) *Frontiers in Human Neuroscience*, 8 (JUNE) , art. No. 475
Functional Neurology for Practitioners of Manual Therapy, by Randy Beck

- Chinkulprasert C, , Vachalathiti R, , Powers CM. and Patellofemoral joint forces and stress during forward step-up, lateral step-up, and forward step-down exercises. J Orthop Sports Phys Ther. 2011; 41: 241– 248. http://dx.doi.org/10.2519/jospt.2011.3408

- Lee, Seo & Kim, Jin-Hyuk. (2007). Involvement of substance P and calcitonin gene-related peptide in development and maintenance of neuropathic pain from spinal nerve injury model of rat. Neuroscience research. 58. 245-9. 10.1016/j.neures.2007.03.004.

- Takakusaki, K. (2013), Neurophysiology of gait: From the spinal cord to the frontal lobe. Mov Disord., 28: 1483-1491. Doi:10.1002/mds.25669

  Pisotta I, Molinari M. Cerebellar contribution to feedforward control of locomotion. *Front Hum Neurosci*. 2014;8:475. Published 2014 Jun 25. Doi:10.3389/fnhum.2014.00475

- Feldenkrais, Moshe; Body & Mature Behaviour: A Study of Anxiety, Sex, Gravitation and Learning

- www.fnor.net

PART 5: WORKING WITH PEOPLE IN PAIN

"...Findings clearly support the theoretical concept that pain is a specific sensation subserved by specific neural elements that are morphologically and physiologically distinct, comparable to vision, audition, and discriminative touch."

-Dr. Bud Craig, author of *How Do You Feel? An Interoceptive Moment with Your Neurobiological Self (chapter 3, page 68).*

Introduction to the Chapter

This chapter was one of the tougher to write for a few reasons, specifically, there is so much information on the topic. Initially, my first book was intended to talk about pain, but I didn't have the confidence to include it. However, over the years, my process has been synthesized to the point where it is logical, based on the individual, and anchored in evidence. Simply put, pain is an output, and so we work to change the input. This chapter will initially lay out some commonalities I have observed while working with those in pain before talking about the specific processes of pain and why neuroplasticity is so important. It will then discuss more specifically how body maps are lost, followed by a discussion about some of the receptor types found in the skin. The chapter will end talking about pain and neurogenic inflammation, along with why behavior change is so important to change pain experiences.

Common characteristics of those in pain

Clinically, I've observed many in pain demonstrate similar qualities, including anxiety around their pain, possessing behavior(s) that contributes to the pain experience, while being sympathetically dominant instead of parasympathetic in nature. The sympathetic nervous system is the automatic part of the nervous system, responsible for decreased smooth muscle tone and contractility, and increased heart rate experienced with anxiety. In a sympathetic state, it is difficult to learn new tasks compared to a parasympathetic state. The parasympathetic system slows heart rate and increases intestinal and gland activity, while relaxing sphincter muscles in the gastrointestinal tract. Simply put, a parasympathetic dominant state is desirable for learning new tasks because the body is more ready to 'restore and regrow' instead of 'protect and defend'. Early interventions should focus on creating parasympathetic dominance in order to create behavior change. Anxiety around pain manifests in many aspects of life and gets in the way of daily requirements, regardless of if a physical, behavioral, or biological driver of pain.

Clinical Concept

Patients with chronic pain have often seen multiple practitioners and have received contradictory information, leading to even more frustration. Clinically, it shouldn't take two weeks for progressions to be seen when performing an activity. When little change in the perception of pain or increased function hasn't occurred, in my opinion, something is being missed. For example, people often present in clinic with a list of exercises they've been prescribed, such as a stretch or strengthen activity. While the stretch may temporarily relieve pain (due to an analgesic effect?) over time, little difference is experienced in overall sensation. In these situations, the possibility exists stretching that tissue isn't the answer, or that something needs to be stabilized. Or perhaps it was the correct activity not performed at the appropriate intensity, but it shouldn't take weeks to see a difference. When dealing with the nervous system and brain, changes will be seen quickly.

I have also observed that often, people aren't aware of anxieties or how they potentially contribute to dysfunction and a painful experience. In other words, people aren't aware of the characteristics they demonstrate that potentially contribute to pain, let alone know how to change it. Therefore, one role of a movement practitioner is to bring forth an awareness of contributing pain behaviors and what to do about it. A primary early objective should focus on reducing pain and increasing awareness about how a specific behavior contributes to pain. This should coincide with education about pain being an output and strategies to safely change input. There are many inputs including pressure, temperature, vibration, thoughts, and emotions, just to name a few.

Pain produces neurogenic inhibition, or a delay in the timing of the nervous system to a region. People also move around pain rather than through it. Neurogenic inhibition and motor control explain why stretching or rubbing an area for more than a couple weeks isn't an effective strategy. It is quite possible the tissue being stretched or rubbed/rolled with a foam roll or trigger point ball is already down regulated. If so, stretching/rubbing can perpetuate the nervous system down regulation, which will be discussed more in depth in later parts.

My observation is many in pain demonstrate sympathetic dominance, and so, early intervention should revolve around parasympathetic stimulation. Too much stress too early, can easily result in the continuation of a negative feedback loop. Pain is an output, and so early interventions should be non-threatening, geared towards changing input and in stimulating parasympathetic response. In clinic, non-threatening movement (free of gross compensation) is one go-to, to stimulate the parasympathetic system, along with simple breathing activities in a quiet warm space (including the full spectrum infrared sauna in my clinic, The Movement Guild). Compensations with movement include rushed activity, holding breath with motion, or lack of fluidity and smoothness that's grossly different from one side to the other.

There will also be an assessable difference in sensorial experience, one side to the other. Part of your 'job' becomes being able to find the subtle differences in the way the body maps both sensory input and motor output. Sensory input can be obtained by tests including cranial nerve assessments, two-point discrimination, sharp/dull, point localization and more. Motor output can be assessed via muscle testing (discussed in later parts), muscle force production ability via a dynamometer, or Kaiser equipment demonstrating force production (and also used at The Movement Guild). Other assessments include a gait assessment, which comes from an understanding of the various phases and capacities of motion during gait. The important point to remember is pain is going to result in differences one side to the other that can be assessed, intervened upon, and reassessed. While beyond the scope of this text, simply understanding the assessment leads to a direction of treatment and more specificity of intervention

Neuroplasticity, Body Maps, and Pain

Neuroplasticity implies a mechanism whereby the physical anatomy and physiological workings of our nervous system happen, both in normal and pathological conditions. Under normal conditions, the process of neuroplasticity works in harmony within the brain to regulate our learning, emotions, thinking, and controls through a multilayered neurophysiological feedback system. However, neuroplastic changes can also be negative, which occurs in chronic pain situations including fibromyalgia, complex regional pain syndromes, and neuropathic pain.

While often difficult to learn a new habit, it is possible to teach an old dog new tricks. In his article, Albert Ray defines *Neuroplasticity* as "the mechanism by which the brain encodes experience, learns new behaviors, and is the mechanism by which a damaged brain relearns lost behavior in response to rehabilitation/stimulus". These maps are profoundly plastic, capable of significant reorganization in response to damage, experience, or practice, and are formed early in life. Body maps mature and are refined with experience and continue to change throughout life and are flexible to continually update specific representation of the body. There are many types of body maps including head and neck centered maps, trunk centered, eye centered, arm and shoulder centered, hand, and also whole body centered maps, to name a few. When these maps effectively work together it should create a seamless understanding of where you are in the world and how you relate to it. (Note: this previous sentence was taken from a lecture by Dr. Traster I attended on Brain Based Solutions.)

Pain immediately changes brain chemistry, and over time diminishes brain maps. This can be observed by lack of two point localization, two point extinction, and hypertonicity of the muscle or hyporeflexia of the region, among other ways. Diminished and limited maps result in limited proprioceptive awareness, as evidenced by the lack of two point discrimination in the thoracolumbar fascia of those who have pain versus those without pain. Simply put, people in pain often lose awareness of where they are in space because their body maps become altered resulting in decreased neural connections and less somatosensory representation of the painful region. Cerebellar integration also contributes to diminished maps and can be seen in many ways including rapid alternating movements and coordination difficulties.

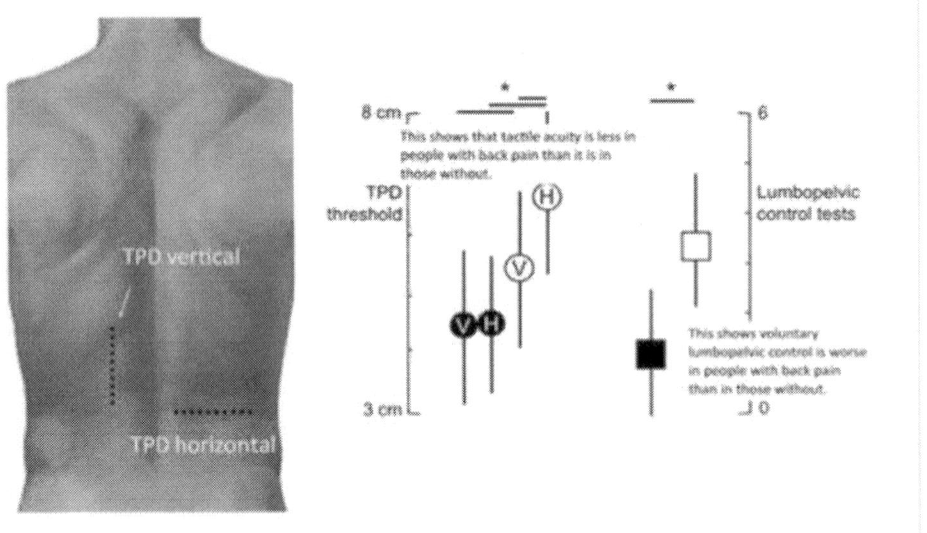

Pain results in less somatosensory cortex representation to the painful body part, which can be 'seen' when mapping the sensory system, including two point discrimination. The above picture highlights those with thoracolumbar pain register two points instead of one at a larger distance. (Wand, et al)

My experience demonstrates those in pain tend to also display a sympathetic dominance of the autonomic nervous system. This can perpetuate their cycle and makes it more difficult to retain new information. Chronic pain means chronic protective states which easily leads to undesirable predictions and highlights the importance of creating parasympathetic dominance. Parasympathetic stimulation is necessary to teach a new behavior and remap the brain toward the new task. It's a reason that early sessions should focus on input change, including self-talk and mindfulness strategies in order to down regulate. Being observant of emotions surrounding pain allows the person to identify the beginnings of when sympathetic cascade begins. Mindfulness surrounding bodily sensations can help repattern the brain to not let sympathetic dominance occur because biological drivers aren't always the cause of pain. There are often psychological or sociological factors that contribute to a pain experience. Mindfulness practices that focus on sensations, emotions, and behaviors can help in this endeavor. In other words, it is difficult to separate the mind, body, and spirit, or the physical, behavioral, and biological selves.

The following is adapted from the book *Treatment of Chronic Pain by Integrative Approaches*, by Dr. Albert Ray, and describes some principles that have been attributed to neuroplastic development and functioning.

1. Our brain is constantly changing, based on our current experiences.

2. Cells that fire together, wire together, and, through practice, stay together.

3. "Use it or lose it" works for brain activity and numbers of neurons.

4. Our brain works best when the system is "balanced".

5. The left and right hemispheres work together within this balance, under normal conditions, as a whole and not separately.

6. Right brain makes more connections with centers below the cortex and hence has more to do with emotional things.

7. Prefrontal cortex provides our most complex cognitive, behavioral, and emotional capacities.

Author's Note

This illustrates a reason why 'name it to tame it' is important in creating downregulation as it stimulates the left, analytical brain.

Often times musculoskeletal pain is neurogenic inhibition masking as pathoanatomy. Neurogenic inflammation is a fancy way of saying peripheral nerves get irritated from the processes of inflammation. Neurogenic inflammation alters body maps and overall representation in the brain.

As Albert Ray articulately describes, "neuroplasticity can account for 'the good, the bad, and the ugly' of pain perception". A "normally" developed nervous system should use pain as a warning system, such as breaking a bone, when it says, "something is wrong", and less traumatically from overwork or being consistently overloaded or not able to go through the full lengthen to shorten spectrum. Some examples include working out too hard and having DOMS (delayed onset muscle soreness) longer than normal, running too far, positioned too long, or trying to lift something too heavy. In each case, load exceeded capacity and resulted in tissue irritation and pain or dysfunction. Ray describes the process of transduction of skin nociceptors. These nociceptors respond to mechanical, chemical, and temperature extremes, which turn responses into electrical/chemical signals that conduct information to the dorsal horn of the spinal cord.

The Process of Neuroplasticity: The Brain is Predictive

Just like roots would feed the leaves, feet, by moving, feed the brain information.

The brain is predictive because it integrates real time sensory information with its own expectations from the past, and intentions for the future, based on the context of the current situation. (Bubic, A., von Cramon, D. Y., and Schubotz, R. I. (2010).). In her book, *Dermoneuromodulating*, Canadian physiotherapist Diane Jacobs describes in great detail the concept of predictive embodiment, stating, "The brain is predictive, not reactive. This means it takes account of everything, then ignores most of it. It exhibits hierarchical functions, which means it is great at ignoring and inhibiting sensory input and feedback it regards as inconsequential." Jacobs goes on to say because the brain is predictive and not reactive, sensory input from the skin (and also from muscle contraction), can affect the somatosensory process in the respective representational area, and that novel input may help it make descending modulation changes".

In essence, this means our brain, based on previous experiences, sensations, and emotions, will predict upcoming events. This is despite the inaccuracy often associated with the prediction. Making changes to the brain requires novel and non-threatening input. I've observed a high association that most people, particularly those in pain already sympathetically driven, predict the worst. This perpetuates a negative feedback loop and illustrates the importance of parasympathetic stimulation and input change. In other words, pain is an output, so change the input. Inputs include thoughts, emotions, touch, temperature, vibration, or pressure, to name a few.

The experience of pain usually starts with activation of nociceptors, which are subtypes of chemoreceptors or mechanoreceptors in the skin. When tissue is damaged or inflamed, certain chemical substances are released from the cells, and these substances activate the chemo sensitive nociceptors and continue to reinforce the process of neurogenic inflammation. The chemical substances often result in hypoxic tissue, lowering the pH and aggravating the peripheral nerve which easily ends up sensitized. This peripheral sensitization over time turns into central sensitization and also less representation in the brain to the painful region.

Understanding the roles of specific proprioceptors provides useful strategies to increase or decrease tone, bring more awareness to a region, and also deal with pain. In other words, interventions will change based on upregulating or downregulating the region. Proprioceptors serve many purposes, as Golgi's and Ruffini's assist in downregulation while Pacini assists in bringing more representation to the somatosensory cortex. Interstitial nerve endings are the most abundant and found throughout the superficial tissue and can be influential in intervention for chronic pain sufferers.

The experience of pain usually starts with activation of nociceptors, which are subtypes of chemoreceptors or mechanoreceptors in the skin. When tissue is damaged or inflamed, certain chemical substances are released from the cells, and these substances activate the chemo sensitive nociceptors and continue to reinforce the process of neurogenic inflammation. The chemical substances often result in hypoxic tissue, lowering the pH and aggravating the peripheral nerve which easily ends up sensitized. This peripheral sensitization over time turns into central sensitization and also less representation in the brain to the painful region.

Author's Note

The importance of proprioceptors was initially highlighted for me by Gary Gray and David Tiberio of The Gray Institute in the Functional Video Digest: "Proprioceptors: The Spirit of Function" series. What stuck from those videos was that the body needs to lengthen before shortening in order to 'turn on' the proprioceptors. Initially I didn't think of the specificity of receptors, however since watching then over fifteen years ago, I've realized that working to stimulate specific receptors has tremendous value in creating change. An awareness of how stimulating specific proprioceptors affect the NS helps to create specific interventions based on the individuals. Based on pain science, some regions will be down regulated to the nervous system and some will be upregulated. Understanding how to access specific proprioceptors to influence the NS in the desired direction allows specificity in intervention.

"A great tool for any patient dealing with pain, regardless of the origin of the pain, is to teach them how to properly breathe. Typically, this is best taught while in a supine position, but should also be taught in a seated and standing position. Proper breathing mechanisms excite the parasympathetic nervous system while simultaneously delivering appropriate amounts of oxygen to the brain and tissue that is painful. Often times, five minutes of mindful diaphragmatic breathing will decrease pain, especially if that pain is derived from, or exacerbated by, neurogenic factors such as anxiety."

In his book, *Motor Control*, Vernon Brooks, PT, stated, "When the tone of opposing muscles is unequal, one muscle shortens and the other is stretched, rotating the joint to a new angle where their tensions are equal." This potentially describes why often longer muscles are inhibited while others are more connected to the nervous system. Potentially due length tensions being altered, tissue length adapts, which in turn, affects its ability to control forces. This illustrates why length tension relationships and joint centration are important. It assists to balance the nervous systems connection to tissue. The brain is responsible for coordinating and synchronizing muscle action and reaction and also reconciling the afferent input from the environment.

Insight about if a muscle is "dialed up" and easily engaged by the NS, or "dialed down" and exhibits a latency (a delay in the timing of the muscle to fire), directs the course of treatment. Generally speaking, longer muscles are less connected to the NS, which can be thought of as "dialed down" or inhibited. Shorter muscles tend to be "dialed up" or facilitated because there's a better connection in the tissue; while inhibitions often (but not always) tend to be in the longer anti-gravity extensors. This isn't always true, yet simply based on this information, it makes sense to work towards balancing the length of the muscles around a joint.

"Recognition of the cause of pain is important as a clinician. Is the pain due to tissue injury? Is the pain from hypertonic tissue? Is the pain from hypotonic tissue? Is the pain as a result of protection against re-injury? Is the pain as a result of anxiety and a heightened perception to nociception? Is the pain allodynic (pain that is in response to a non-painful stimulus)? Is the pain due to general inflammation in the system? Is the pain superficial or deep? Is the pain consistent with the presumed injury? Is the pain due to the brain being unaware of exactly where that body part is in space? Does the onset of pain match the current pain? Is the pain referred from another location? Is the pain psychogenic? All of these questions should quickly filter through the mind of the clinician immediately, with the caveat the clinician should have a therapeutic answer to any of the questions answered with a "yes" above. A thorough enough history will answer all of these questions, maybe simultaneously."

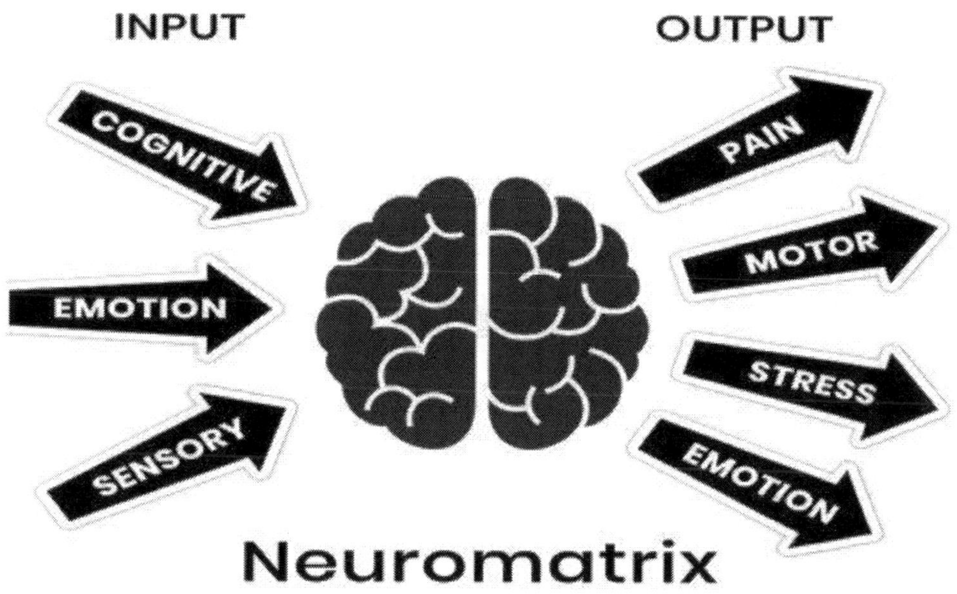

Pain is an output, and therefore to change pain, changing correct inputs is necessary. Inputs, like drivers which create a reaction, include physical, behavioral, and biological afferents.

Why an understanding of the different receptors is important.

Touch incorporates tension and compression which stimulates intrafascial mechanoreceptors. This results in a change in tone of the motor unit associated with that tissue, creating a cascade of neurochemical reactions. Evidence demonstrates that touch can change local fluid dynamics, tissue, and metabolism. Steady touch stimulates interstitial and Ruffini receptors, which create parasympathetic responses including relaxation and less emotional arousal, both of which are necessary when working with those in pain. As previously discussed, those in pain require behavior change and behavior change requires parasympathetic dominance.

Myofascial manipulation involves a stimulation of intrafascial mechanoreceptors, leading to altered proprioceptive input to the central nervous system; resulting in a changed tonus regulation of motor units associated with this tissue. Understanding the roles of the specific receptors in the body helps to create an individualized program. Within a motor control paradigm, understanding which regions are 'dialed up' and which are 'dialed down' is necessary to provide the intervention which is most appropriate. For example, if the tissue is thought to be "dialed up", interventions geared towards creating parasympathetic responses would be warranted, understand this would help to 'dial it down". Knowledge that Ruffini endings respond to deep, slow, sustained pressure is then helpful. Motor control dictates this wouldn't be the end of treatment, because there will likely be a corresponding region needing to be "dialed up". Upregulating tissue can be accomplished through many stimuli. One strategy is through touch and manual intervention that is geared towards accessing the Pacinian corpuscles, which respond to light pressure and vibration. Another useful way to upregulate tissue is through isometric muscle contractions, a topic discussed in later parts.

Clinical gem

"The use of various receptors can be hugely beneficial when trying to relieve pain. Test out the various types of receptors to see which has the best representation in the brain and/or which decreases pain in the area that is affected. For example, if a patient is experiencing left knee pain, first test if they can feel all of the stimuli similarly. Test hot, cold, light touch, deep touch, pinprick, and vibration. If one of these is not felt as well as the others, you know this is the stimulus you need to use to increase cortical representation of the painful area. If all are felt equally, then compare each stimulus to the contralateral body part that is affected, in this case, the right knee. If you find one of the stimuli is not felt as prominently or is felt differently from one side to the other, you know this is the stimulus to use. Once determining the stimulus, there are various ways each can be utilized which is where the art of practice comes into play. You will not find these differences in everyone but when you do, the changes can be phenomenal for the patient."

The following is a list of some of the receptors found in the skin and superficial tissue. It does not represent an exhaustive list, rather as an introduction. It is recommended to learn more from the resources mentioned in the body of the text as well as in the additional readings list.

Mechanical Stimulation:

- Paccinian – fast stroke + ANS = Stimulation
- Ruffini – slow, steady stroke + ANS = Relaxation
- Interstitial – slow, feather like + ANS = Pain and Wellbeing
- Golgi – contraction or fast stretch = Decrease Tone

Intrafascial receptors consist of the large Pacini corpuscles plus the slightly smaller Paciniform corpuscles, and also the smaller and more longitudinal Ruffini organs which do not adapt as quickly and therefore respond also to sustained pressure.

Sensory receptors in the skin

Cutaneous Receptors

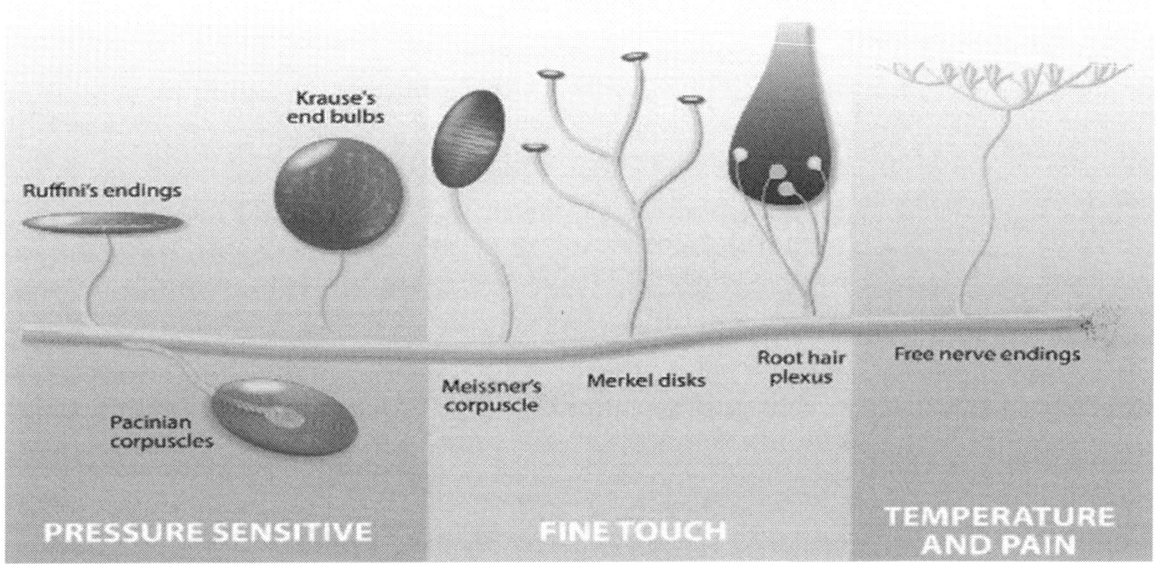

Through an understanding of the effect on the nervous system of stimulation of various types of mechanoreceptors and interoceptors, intervention specificity can be improved.

Golgi Tendon Organ. Type I & II

A Golgi I neuron has a long axon and begins in the gray matter of the nervous system. Golgi tendon organs are located in the tendons, as its dendrites are interwoven with the collagen fibrils. When a muscle contracts, the fibrils are pulled tight, activating the GTO, called a LB afferent, and provides information about muscle tension (Ray).

The analogy I've heard numerous times, is if a muscle is chronically too short, the GTO becomes inhibited. To me, this illustrates another reason why length tension is so important, as well as taking the system through a lengthening moment before shortening.

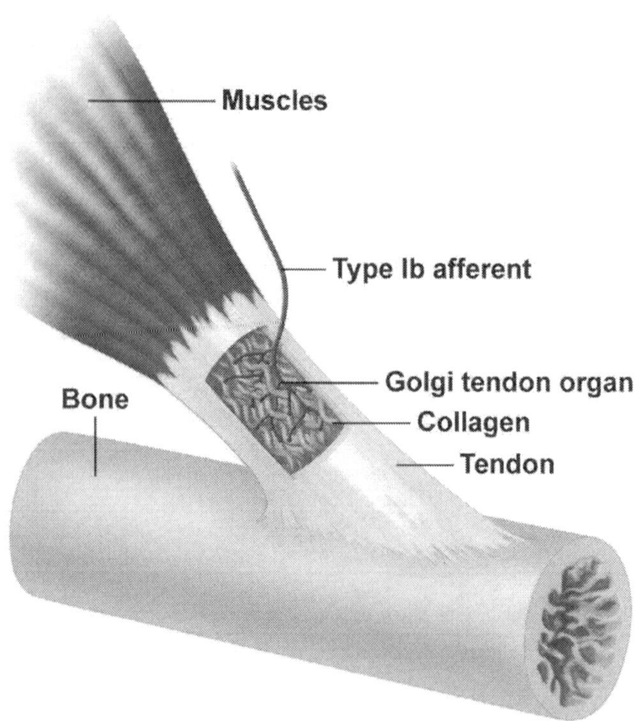

Golgi tendon organs are located in the tendons, as its dendrites are interwoven with the collagen fibrils.

Pacini & Pectiniform Receptors. Type II

Dr. Schleip describes the egg-shaped Pacini bodies respond to rapid changes in pressure and vibrations, however not constant unchanging pressure, while the smaller corpuscles have a similar function, sensitivity, and can assist in improving tactile acuity and somatosensory cortex representation. Found in myotendinous junctions, deep capsular layers, the spinal ligaments, aponeurosis and fascia, they're also known as Type II receptors. Pacini stimulation can improve the awareness of self by improving cortical representation of the area, rather than specifically activating or inhibiting motor output. Stimulation of Pacini should be considered when working with chronic pain populations because 'smudging' of the cortex and loss of perception to the affected body part occurs. Therefore, stimulation of these Type II receptors can help to create more representation in the cortex.

According to Dr. Schleip, "It seems likely that the Pacinian receptors are being stimulated only by high velocity thrust manipulations as well as in vibratory techniques. In myotendinous junctions the Pacinian corpuscles are more frequent on the tendinous site, as opposed to the Golgi tendon organs which are more frequent on the muscular site." Regardless of the exact specifics, understanding the role of specific receptors helps to create the desired ANS response.

"Clinically, it has been recognized that vibration to a joint and/or muscle rapidly reduces pain and allows more appropriate movement of that body part. It is recommended that a high frequency vibration is used rather than a low frequency vibration, to reduce the potential shearing of already damaged tissues. A great way to assess if vibration will be of use as a therapy from a central standpoint is to check two point discrimination and/or graphesthesia over the injured body part. Remember, even if there is local tissue damage, it very well could have been caused because the cortical representation of that body part was not as appropriate as it should have been. Or the injury has caused a reduction of cortical representation to that area. Either way, it is important to check graphesthesia and two point discrimination over the area. If there are errors, even if subclinical, apply high frequency vibration then re-test immediately to see if graphesthesia or two point discrimination improves. If it does, you know vibration in conjunction with typical rehabilitation should provide quicker and better results."

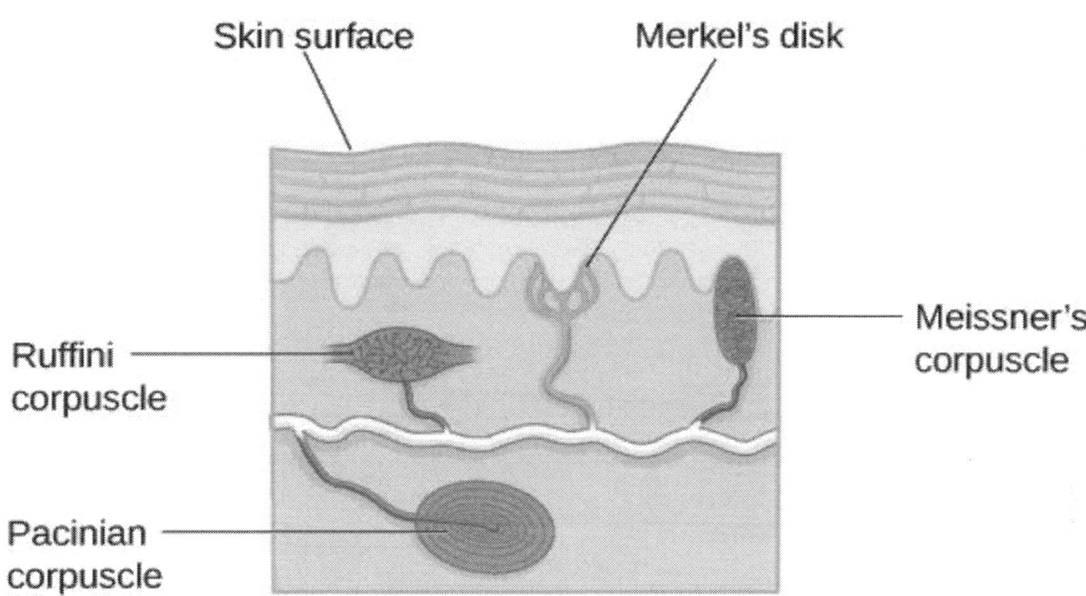

Pacini stimulation can improve the awareness of self by improving cortical representation of the area, rather than specifically activating or inhibiting motor output. Stimulation of Pacini should be considered when working with chronic pain populations because 'smudging' of the cortex and loss of perception to the affected body part occurs. "Ruffini endings are especially responsive to tangential forces and lateral stretch (Kruger 1987), and that stimulation of Ruffini corpuscles is assumed to result in a lowering of sympathetic nervous system activity (van den Berg & Capri 1999).

Ruffini Endings. Type II

Ruffini endings are typically activated by slow, deep techniques, and are found in all types of connective tissue including in muscle fascia, tendons, ligaments, aponeuroses, and joint capsules. According to Dr. Schleip, "The Ruffini endings are especially dense in tissues associated with regular stretching like the outer layer of joint capsules, the Dura mater, the ligaments of peripheral joints, and the deep dorsal fascia of the hand." He goes on to say, "Ruffini endings are especially responsive to tangential forces and lateral stretch (Kruger 1987), and that stimulation of Ruffini corpuscles is assumed to result in a lowering of sympathetic nervous system activity (van den Berg & Capri 1999). This seems to fit to the common clinical finding slow, deep tissue techniques tend to have a relaxing effect on local tissues as well as on the whole organism."

Author's Note:

Extrapolation of research information is an art. The last passage, specifically the portion of tangential forces to stimulate Ruffini endings, speaks to the fact that improving the ability of the interfaces of tissue to slide past each other (via application of tangential forces) can improve tissue mobility. When tissue can get fully long and short, the pressure differential in the tissue increases, causing more blood to flow through the tissue, ultimately helping to lower the pH. Lowering of pH means the tissue and peripheral nerves are in a less acidic environment, which is often found in cases of neurogenic inflammation. Neurogenic inflammation is often involved in pain experiences. Therefore, working tangential to the tissue can stimulate parasympathetic responses while also improving tissue glide and helping to improve body mapping which is reduced in painful situations.

Van den Berg & Capri also found that, in the knee, Ruffini endings are more frequent at anterior and posterior ligamentous and capsular structures, whereas Pacinian bodies are found more in the medial and lateral aspect of the joint, and likely reflects a similar distribution through the entire body. What's interesting is of all the sensory nerves, only 20% are Type 1 and 2 (described above), and primarily found in muscle spindles, Golgi organs, Pacini corpuscles, and Ruffini endings, while the rest are found to be Type III and IV, called interstitial nerves, number four times as many vs. Type I & II, and are found almost everywhere including inside bones (Mitchell & Schmidt 1977).

Interstitial Nerve Fibers. C-Fiber Stimulation Type III & IV

The role of Interstitial nerve fibers are numerous and are the largest group of sensory nerve fibers. They include vasomotor functions, which are important for blood flow and creating pressure differentials. According to Dr. Schleip, they seem to be involved with sensory refinement vs. motor organization, are much smaller in diameter and found abundantly in fascia. Type III interstitial receptors are covered in a very thin myelin sheath, however Type IV receptors, totaling 90%, are unmyelinated, slower than Type I & II nerves and originate in free nerve endings. Approximately 40% are unmyelinated, and afferent muscle fibers have a low mechanical threshold, and can be activated by non-painful deformation of muscle, demonstrating its nociceptive function (Hoseisel et al (2005)).

It has been demonstrated that interstitial receptors can function as both mechano and pain receptors. Their sensitivity changes during painful experiences, as mechanisms behind affective touch reinforce how important touch is for pain modulation. A role for social touch in stress alleviation has been suggested, including the contact pressure of holding hands which reduces the anxiety posed by an impending threat (Coan, et al., 2006). Touch can convey thoughts and feelings and regulate them in others (Hertenstein, et al. 2006).

Specifically, C-tactile afferent nerve fibers, which are a subtype of C-fibers, respond to gentile stroking touch. They show a preference for stimuli that move gently over the skin, such as a caress (Löken et al, 2009), and functional MRI studies show increased posterior insula activation for CT-fiber stimulation (Olausson et al. 2002, 2008). CT-mediated affective touch may have more in common anatomically with interoceptive and visceral systems than to afferent systems processing other classes of tactile and nociceptive stimuli (Björnsdotter, 2010).

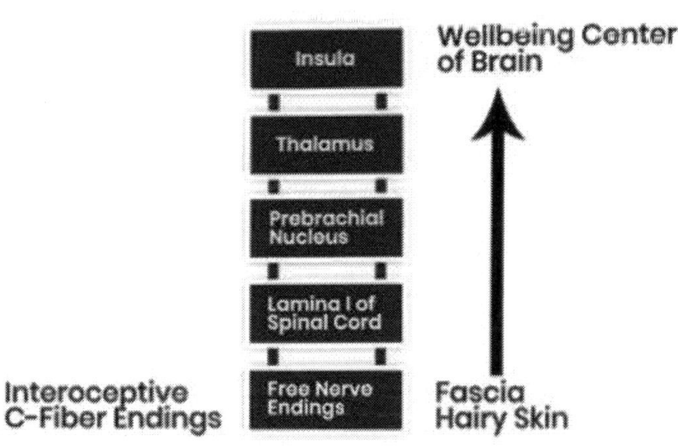

"In cases of spasticity such as with cerebral vascular accident sequela, light stroking of the skin over the antagonistic muscles to those that are spastic in the direction of shortening, often times will neurogenically relax a spasticity to some extent. Sometimes the spasticity is minimally affected with this, while other times remarkable results can be seen when traditional therapy is unresponsive."

C-tactile fibers are unmyelinated and therefore are slow conducting. They respond to gentle, slow stroking or caresses, and project to the insular cortex. C-fibers are polymodal, meaning they respond to different stimuli, including noxious and pleasant. When noxious stimulus is dominant and the corresponding neurogenic process occur, the result is often neurogenic inhibition. The discovery of the C-tactile system suggests that touch is organized in a similar way to pain; fast-conducting A-fibers contribute to sensory–discriminatory aspects, while thin C-fibers contribute to affective–motivational aspects (Löken, Wessberg, Morrison, McGlone, & Olausson, 2009).

In other words, stimulation of C-tactile afferents stimulate a sense of wellbeing that is helpful if changing a painful experience. A main part of the brain responsible for the sense of wellbeing is the Insula and Anterior Cingulate Cortex, which together are part of the Limbic System. This direct connection into the Limbic System highlight the importance of light and caressive tough of the skin as a potential modality and modulating the nervous system

THE LIMBIC SYSTEM

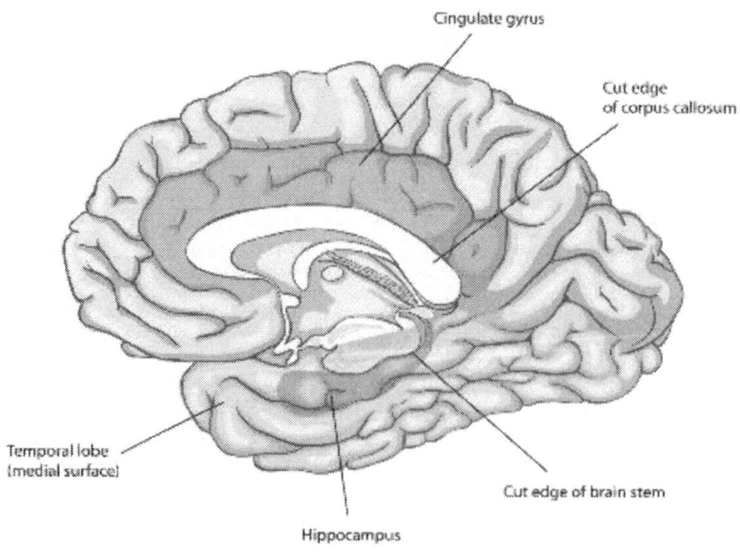

My experience is often people in pain consciously or subconsciously tighten their bodies and limit motion. This restricts blood flow and oxygen to the tissue and creates a reaction that lowers the tissue pH, sensitizing the nerves peripherally before centrally. Approximately 52% of group III & IV afferents are chemosensitive, 34% respond to mechanical stimulation, and 14% respond to thermal stimuli. Therefore, stimulation of the afferents affecting the Limbic System will assist in creating a sense of wellbeing and relaxation of the body, feeding forward into more blood flow and oxygen to tissue.

Through FNOR (Functional Neuro-Ortho Rehab), I have concluded that during manual therapy intervention, what's likely occurring, at least partially, is the liberation of the peripheral nerves' ability to slide freely through tissue. When mechanical intervention is successful there's also likely also opportunity for chemical and thermal stimulus because these receptors are polymodal. Research demonstrates that, "Under experimental conditions sensory neurons can be electrically or chemically stimulated. Under pathophysiological conditions direct mechanical activation is less important than chemical activation." (Holzer-Petsche, 2009). Reasons for chemosensitivity include a drop in pH, an increase in proton (H+) concentration, and also from ATP production.

Clinical Concept

For me, this illustrates reasons that patients/clients often need to make lifestyle changes, including diet. While not directly within my scope of practice as a PT and LMT, recognizing these potential issues, and having a medical team to refer to is important. My medical referral team includes a dietician, because sometimes changes in diet should be part of a plan to get out of pain. Personally, I have recognized the importance of an alkaline diet in managing the pain I experience from an autoimmune disease.

In addition, when mechanical liberation of peripheral nerves helps, creating alkaline responses in the tissue can be beneficial. Neuro Prologel is a dextrose based topical agent that works to alkalize the superficial nerve receptors. Group III & IV are majority chemosensitive, and so the gel is another way to assist in changing input, as the chemo receptors can be alkalized, lessening the nociceptive signal being sent up. The gel can also be used diagnostically, because if pain changes after application of the topical gel, it's fair to rule out deeper structures, including joints.

Receptor type	Preferred location	Responsive to	Known results of stimulation
Golgi Type I b	• Myotendinous junctions • Attachment of areas of aponeurosis • Ligaments of peripheral joints • Joint capsules	Golgi Tendon Organ: To Muscular Attachment Other Golgi Receptors: probably to strong stretch only	Tonus decrease in related striated motor fibers
Pacini & Paniniform Type II	• Myotendinous Junctions • Deep capsule layers • Spinal ligaments • Investing Muscular Tissues	Rapid Pressure Changes & Vibration	Used as proprioceptive feedback for movement control (sense of kinesthesia)
Ruffini Type II	• Ligaments of peripheral joints • Dura matter • Outer Capsule Layers • Other tissues associated with regular stretching	Like Pacini, yet also sustained pressure Specifically, responsive to tangential forces	
Interstitial Type III & IV	• Most Abundant Receptor Type, found almost everywhere even inside bones • Highest density in periosteum	Rapid as well as sustained pressure changes 50% are high threshold units and 50% are low threshold units	Changes in Vasodilation Plus apparently in plasma extravasation

This is a representation of a chart created by Robert Schleip's article "Fascial Plasticity-A New Neurological Explanation.

Pain & Neurogenic Inflammation

Negative changes in the transmission of pain tend to occur through a process of sensitization. The nervous system can become sensitized at peripheral sites as well as centrally at dorsal horn and/or brain. Hence, a system that once worked to protect us can transform into one that produces ongoing pain. Neurogenic inflammation is a very common pain mechanism and is tremendously underappreciated in chronic pain. It's associated with a number of pain processes, including tendon, local tissue, ligaments, and skin.

NEUROGENIC INFLAMMATION

- With pain: immediate changes in brain chemistry
- Chronic pain leads to less representation in the somatosensory cortex
  - Becomes 'harder' to find the muscle

Neurogenic Inflammation & Pain

- Very common mechanism & under appreciated in chronic pain
- Associated with tendon, muscle & ligament pain.
  - Tendon degradation involves neurogenic etiology and/or complicated by neurogenic inflammation
- Manual therapy producing pain relief is likely liberating sensitized nerves

1' goal of early rehab

David George & Stuart Fife; FNOR

What's true mechanism?

I believe manual therapies work for pain relief because they mechanically liberate the sensitized nerves, including Group III (myelenated), and Group IV (Unmyelinated), afferent fibers. This creates temperature and chemical changes that also change input. “These afferent fibers respond to numerous stimulants, including mechanical stimulation (representing 34%), thermal (less than 32%), and chemosenstitive (52%)” (Hoheisel et al (2005).

This is relevant because when the nerve is mechanically irritated, a chemical reaction occurs that bathes the nerve in acidic tissue. This process sensitizes it first peripherally, before centrally, and highlights why changing nociceptor and mechanoreceptor afferents early on is important in limiting a pain experience.

Reconceptualizing Trigger Points

The concepts of neurogenic inflammation and peripheral sensitization explain what is traditionally considered trigger points in muscle. Due to the wide use of the term “trigger point” (TrP), it will be used in this text. However, recognizing the traditional concept of trigger points put forward by Simon and Travell (and countless others), has been debunked, a more believable narrative is layers of tissue get “kinked” and lose the ability to slide past each other; this irritates the nerve, which has predictable referral patterns.

The concept surrounding sliding of layers of fascia is discussed at length in many articles, and best represented through the work of Geoffrey Bove; where he demonstrates these phenomena in rats. Please note, in this text when Trigger Points (TrP) are discussed it refers to tender regions consisting of sensory and motor combinations of sensitized nociceptors. Irritated nociceptors between layers of tissue and at the periphery can occur secondary to mechanical irritation and ischemia. This feeds up into the dorsal horn, contributing to the central sensitization and lack of somatosensory representation occurring in a pain process.

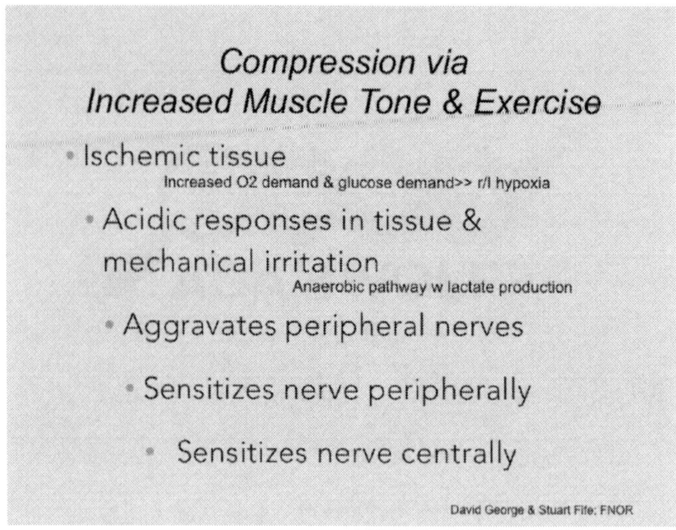

The inability of nerves to floss through tissue and tissue to slide result in irritation of the nerve and a predictable downward spiral.

Albert Ray describes how neuropathic pain reorganizes the cortical somatotopic maps in the sensory-motor areas, with increased activity in nociceptive areas. This is in conjunction with numerous brain, chemical, and hormonal changes that result in, "changes in excitatory and inhibitory transmitter systems, and significant structural changes of neurodegeneration". Chronic pain and central sensitization symptoms show a marked change in self-perception and significant neuroplastic changes, particularly with memory problems, non-restful sleep, decreased energy, decreased mental focus, anxiety, depression, anger, and more.

This means chronic pain and sensitization processes result in changes in the brain. These include anatomic cellular changes, transmitter, neuromodulator, and also physiological functional changes. It is perpetuated through anxiety, fixation, and the overall processes associated with sympathetic dominance. Sensitization results in neuroplastic changes that account for decreased pain thresholds, increased pain perception, recruitment amplification of pain signals, and the intermingling of pain and non-pain related inputs. Simply put, pain creates neuroplastic changes in the brain, illustrating the need for early interventions geared towards creating new maps and stimulating parasympathetic response.

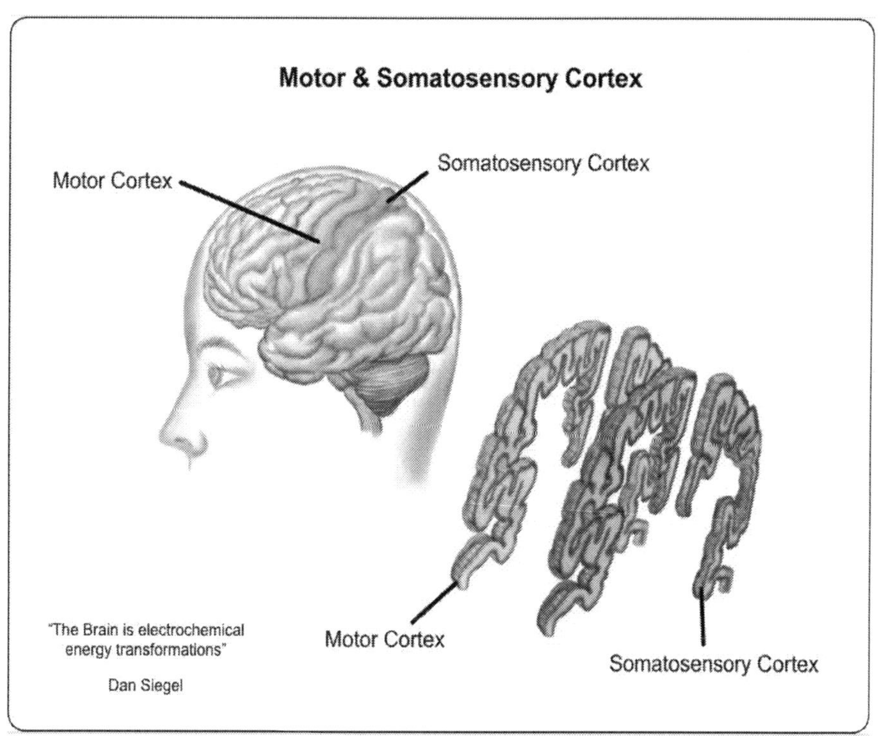

The Somatosensory Cortex can simply be thought of as where many types of 'maps' of the body are housed, along with other parts of the lower brain and cerebellum.

Behavior Change and Changing Input

In the book *The Whole Brain Child,* Dr. Dan Siegel (7), describes the strategy of naming it to tame it. As a parent, this strategy has been helpful in raising my children to be aware and conscious beings. It also helps for those dealing with pain because pain produces anxiety and fear. Like many people, anxiety is something I personally deal with, and naming it to tame it helps me.

Emotional centers are typically found in the right brain. Naming the emotion/anxiety stimulates the left brain's desire for words and reasoning, which provides an opportunity to change the narrative. Other methods include "move it or lose it", recognizing physical activity can alter emotional states, and also "SIFT", which teaches mindful attention to *sensations, images, feelings and thoughts*. Strategies that deal with the cognitive aspect of pain work to change input from an emotional and verbal perspective. The key is to create non-threatening environments in order to down regulate the system because parasympathetic dominance is the best way to retain plasticity for new activities. Pain is an output, therefore change the input.

There are many neurological processes associated with pain, including what Dr. David George, (co-founder of Functional Neuro-Orthopedic Rehab), refers to as "maladaptive cognitive and behavioral changes.'' Persistent behaviors can prime active inhibition of motor behaviors. Dysregulation of motor function may be actively maintained through negative emotions and beliefs regarding stimulus associated with chronic pain. Dr. George illustrated the point during non-invasive human brain imaging there's enhanced activity in the emotional and motivational cortical-limbic circuitry, rather than increased nociceptive representation in chronic pain sufferers (Mansour et al 2014). Changes in behavior may be more important than changes in physical markers or performance, particularly for people with chronic pain (Wessels et al 2006). In other words, a change in behavior is necessary when trying to get out of pain. The trick is to identify what contributing behaviors need to change and as a patient have the discipline to do it.

Author's Note

While this text won't get into the specifics of what's required for behavior change, recognizing it is a part of the process of 'rewiring the system' is helpful. For more information, I recommend the work of Dr. David George and FNOR, amongst other resources.

There are common sites of mechanical compromise where peripheral nerves can get aggravated. Below is a description of these sites and a general order and suggestion of strategies to improve tissue glide.

Common Sites of Mechanical Compromise

- Superficial nerves
    - More restriction points form along superficial nerve trunks than along deeper ones
    - Superficial nerve receptors generally become sensitized more readily than nerves located in deep tissue

- Depth Changes
    - Areas where deep nerves penetrate deep fascia, emerging close to the surface
    - With palpation, taut bands and ridges, very painful and irradiating pain

- Neuromuscular, -tendinous, -ligamentous attachments
    - Sites where the nerve trunks attach to the tendon

- Nerve/Soft Tissue Interfaces
    - Ligaments

- Retinacula
- Thick fascial sheets
- Joint capsules
- Collateral ligaments

Chapter Conclusion

Understanding the process of pain and how to harness the nervous system in various ways to improve representation in the somatosensory is necessary to make lasting and effective changes. Pain is complicated, individualized, and an output from the nervous system and anchoring to principles that are consistent, regardless of the person, provides the largest opportunity for improvement of their sensation. Oftentimes a multiple pronged strategy is necessary that effects change to biology, psychology, and also sociology, and not everything works with everyone. Therefore, having many ways to accomplish the task is necessary, recognizing the words chosen and stories told about the why's and what's part of the process to get out of pain.

Additional Readings List

- Butler, D, Mosely, L: *Explain Pain Supercharged*
- Kandal, E., Schwarts, J. Jessel, T.; *Principles of Neural Science*
- NeuroOrthopedic Institute; www.noigroup.com
- Jacobs, Diane; Dermoneuromodulatoin
- Lehman, G: Recovery Strategies Pain Workbook; http://www.greglehman.ca/
- Craig, B; *How Do You Feel? An Interoceptive Moment with Your Neurobiological Self (book)*
- Goldberg, S; *Clinical Neuroanatomy Made Ridiculously Simple*
- Bubic, A., von Cramon, D. Y., and Schubotz, R. I. (2010). *Prediction, cognition and the brain. Frontiers in human neuroscience*, (*4*, 25. Doi:10.3389/fnhum.2010.00025
- *Treatment of Chronic Pain by Integrative Approaches*, by Dr. Albert Ray
- *Siegel, Dan; Whole Brain Child*
- *Liebenson, Craig; Rehabilitaiton of the Spine*
- Bove GM, Harris MY, Zhao H, Barbe MF. Manual therapy as an effective treatment for fibrosis in a rat model of upper extremity overuse injury. *J Neurol Sci*. 2016;361:168-180. Doi:10.1016/j.jns.2015.12.029

- Mansour AR, Farmer MA, Baliki MN, Apkarian AV. Chronic pain: the role of learning and brain plasticity. *Restor Neurol Neurosci*. 2014;32(1):129-139. Doi:10.3233/RNN-139003
- Robert Schleip, Fascial plasticity – a new neurobiological explanation: Part 1, Journal of Bodywork and Movement Therapies,Volume 7, Issue 1,2003,Pages 11-19,ISSN 1360-8592, https://doi.org/10.1016/S1360-8592(02)00067-0.
  Wessels, Tina & Tulder, Maurits & Sigl, Tanja & Ewert, Thomas & Limm, Heribert & Stucki, Prof. Dr. med. Gerold. (2006). What predicts outcome in non-operative treatments of chronic low back pain? A systematic review. European spine journal: official publication of the European Spine Society, the European Spinal Deformity Society, and the European Section of the Cervical Spine Research Society. 15. 1633-44. 10.1007/s00586-006-0073-4.
- Tactile thresholds are preserved yet complex sensory function is impaired over the lumbar spine of chronic non-specific low back pain patients: a preliminary investigation, Wand, Benedict M. et al., Physiotherapy, Volume 96, Issue 4, 317 – 323
- Coan, J. A., Schaefer, H. S., & Davidson, R. J. (2006). Lending a Hand: Social Regulation of the Neural Response to Threat. *Psychological Science*, *17*(12), 1032–1039. https://doi.org/10.1111/j.1467-9280.2006.01832.x
- Hoheisel U, Mense S, Simons DG et al. (1993) Appearance of new receptive fields in rat dorsal horn neurons following noxious stimulation of skeletal muscle: a model for referral of muscle pain? Neurosci Lett 153:9–12
- Hertenstein, M. J., Keltner, D., App, B., Bulleit, B. A., & Jaskolka, A. R. (2006). Touch communicates distinct emotions. *Emotion, 6*(3), 528–533. https://doi.org/10.1037/1528-3542.6.3.528
- L.S. Löken, M. Evert, J. Wessberg Pleasantness of touch in human glabrous and hairy skin: order effects on affective ratings Brain Res., 1417 (2011), pp. 9-15
- Björnsdotter M, Morrison I, Olausson H; (2010) Feeling good: on the role of C fiber mediated touch in interoception. Exp Brain Res **207**:149–155.
- Loken, L. S., Wessberg J., Morrison, I., McGlone, F. & Olausson, H; (2009). Coding of pleasant touch by unmyelinated afferents in humans. *Nature Neuroscience*, 12, 547–548
- Holzer P, Holzer-Petsche U: Pharmacology of Inflammatory Pain: Local Alteration in Receptors and Mediators. Dig Dis 2009;27(suppl 1):24-30. Doi: 10.1159/000268118

PART 6: HIGHER LEVEL INTEGRATION, ADAM'S STORY

"In examining disease, we gain wisdom about anatomy and physiology and biology. In examining the person with disease, we gain wisdom about life." --- Oliver Sacks

Chapter Introduction

This chapter was, by far, the hardest for me to write and is written in a different manner compared to the rest. It Is more of a personal narrative of my experience with applying neurology to some of my issues, and the medical editor of this book, Dr. Mike Drzewiecki and I co-wrote this chapter. Unlike the other parts where Mike adds his two cents in the "neuro-boxes" that are based on my thoughts, this chapter really was filled in with relevant information by him. Due to my relative inexperience with the specificity of this information compared to the rest of the book, I felt it more authentic, and accurate, to share my story in more of a case study manner. Mike then fills in the what's and why's about his clinical interventions while I was under his care. The pictures and clinical notes are taken directly from my charts in order to provide as much specificity as possible.

It will begin with a little background about me, where my studies and attempt to better understand why I am how I am, before discussing some of my experiences that led to my anxiety and seeking a brain-based treatment. Mike will then fill in the clinical specifics of both my evaluation and our treatments, before the conclusion about general strategies about why a brain-based approach is so effective.

Why a Brain Based Approach?

Clinically, applying neurology is much like applying integrated movement because both require knowledge of the interrelatedness between specific anatomy in order to effectively utilize the information. Both can be 'modalities' where specific movements are performed in order to see if the intended outcome is observed, and for those versed enough, a lens through which to view and effect movement. The initial draft of this chapter was written in a manner comparable to the rest of the book, both in how thoughts were put together (bullet point outline), and also the process of synthesizing, then writing out the information. However, after reading it, I wasn't satisfied because my depth of knowledge about the specific anatomy and how to apply neurology, particularly compared to some friends and colleagues (Traster, Drzewiecki, Studholme to name a few), was limited. It was then that I put it down, telling myself if I was to learn more, and while this may be true, it coincided with stopping lots of daily practices including journaling, learning, practicing yoga and music, and an increase in my anxiety and depression.

Personally, journaling has always taken on different forms, including a place to summarize information, hashing out my thoughts and feelings, and synthesizing information. It has served as a place to put what I consider to be where relevant information was obtained about particular subjects. Journaling has helped me to categorize information, both personally and professionally, and is a place to safely express opinions, thoughts, desires, and emotions. It is something I've always done, and thinking back, have continually been learning about music and movement, except during periods of stagnation, since my twenties. There haven't been many times since then I wasn't consciously learning something, except when I was not in a great mental space.

'Adam being Adam' is something I always heard from my family, which perhaps meant I'm often direct, perceived as sharp, and also moody. To most, my feelings are obvious, or not obvious at all, because I'm a bit quiet and reserved when in new situations, depending on the person and situation. Yet, there is always an intensity, or what my wife calls a 'slow simmer', and there always has been. Learning about neuroanatomy and brain development has added perspective because it has brought up questions about my own brain development. Obviously, nature and nurture contribute to why I am me; learning about childhood brain development milestones (and what may or may not have been well developed) has offered a lens to develop parts of my brain that perhaps aren't as well plasticized. Specifically, I'm trying to slow down and also be more compassionate with myself, both of which have always been challenging. I'm attempting to understand more about how adult resting cortisol levels are influenced by early childhood development. Comprehending the role of the hypothalamic-pituitary-adrenocorticoid axis development between the ages of 3-5 has been particularly helpful, as for me it was a particularly challenging period. While there is an element of 'so what am I going to do about it', knowledge of development provides insight and can be useful for better understanding of myself.

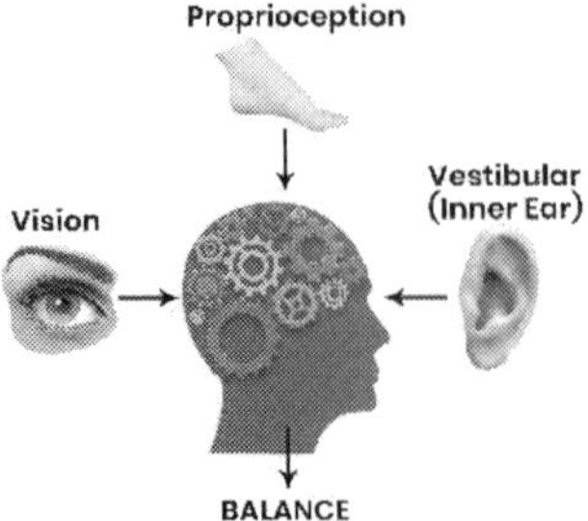

The brain receives the majority of its information from three major systems, proprioception, vision, and vestibular.

Neurodevelopment and the HPA Axis

The hypothalamic-pituitary-adrenocorticoid (HPA) axis plays an influential role in brain development and in early childhood development particularly. Research has found the HPA becomes activated with stressors, causing the release of corticotrophin releasing hormones (CRH). The HPA axis maintains an organism's capacity to respond to acute and prolonged stressors, and is a major focus on Early Life Stress (ELS) research. CRH is produced in the amygdala, a structure involved in orchestrating emotional responses, and activates behavioral stress responses, including sympathetic dominance. Research suggests that ELS may result in dysregulation of the neuroendocrine stress response system and limbic dysfunction, including regions in the hippocampus, medial prefrontal cortex, and amygdala. It's also suggested that severe ELS may have mental and physical consequences lasting into adulthood, including increased risk of depression, anxiety, and post-traumatic stress disorder.

This last piece of information has personally resonated with me, and truth be told, much of my desire to learn and apply neurology is due to a desire to feel better and be less anxious. My anxiety increasingly around social situations, and anything where I could control the situation, to the point of increased anxiety and physical symptoms with anticipation of the unknown. While I've always known many people and associated with many 'groups', since college I have primarily come and gone alone and have always felt comfortable bouncing between and bringing different groups together. I've always been good at identifying people who work well together, and also bringing various pieces of information together to create something new, that plays out to this day.

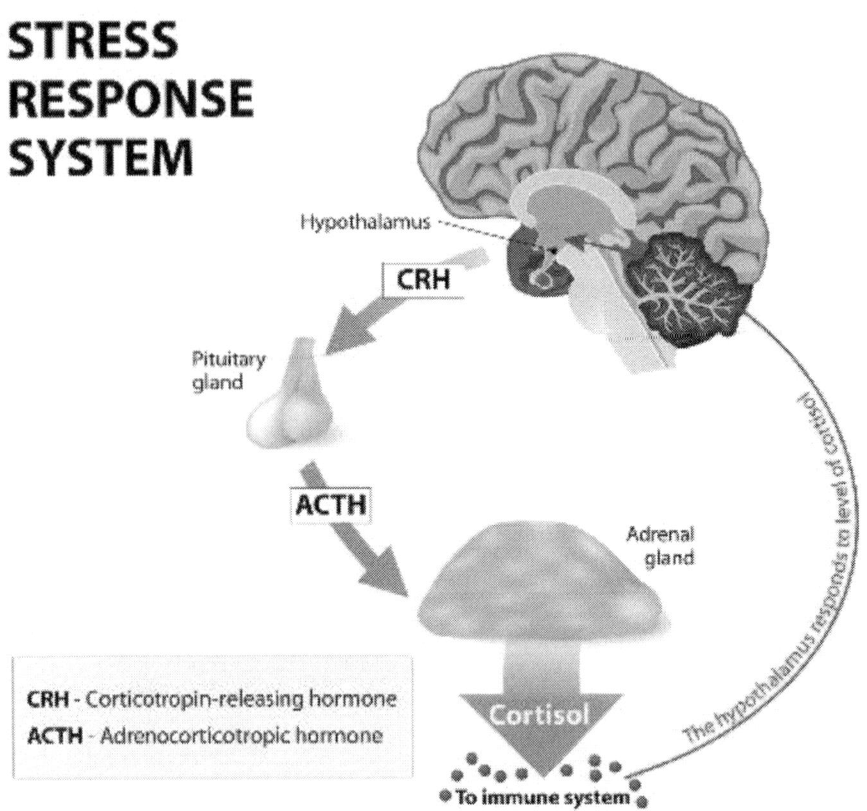

The hypothalamic-pituitary-adrenocorticoid (HPA) axis plays an influential role in brain development and in early childhood development particularly.

Entering my forties, the pressures of family, work, and life, left little desire to be social, to the point where I realized some of my patterns were inhibiting my success. The irony is, shortly after turning thirty, I made a commitment and created a goal of being the best PT I could at the expense of relationships, social opportunities, or anything that would get in the way. I found that goal written in a journal shortly after turning forty, and recall saying, "mission accomplished". However, I had become a talented therapist at the expense of losing life balance, including friends, opportunities, and important relationships.

Reflecting on those choices brings a mixture of pride for the skill set developed, and also sadness, tinged with regret, about how choices affect those I love. My decisions created a feed forward situation that reinforced control issues and contributed to depression and anxiety. They were accelerated when daily grounding practices that kept my 'head above water' ceased.

Control plays into my life in many ways, including self-employment, preferring to face the door when at a restaurant, and only going to movies where seats can be reserved ahead of time. I've learned the laid back and 'it doesn't matter' attitude I often display is a mechanism employed when I can't control a situation. Instead of stressing about the unknown, I become quiet and withdrawn.

It took a personal shit-storm, waking up at night with anxiety attacks, to realize how much anxiety had gotten in the way. As motivation waned, leaving little desire to work, write, read, or be social (not that I was ever very social), every part of my life including the relationship with my wife, family, friends, and work was affected. Waking up in the middle of the night with anxiety attacks made me realize I needed outside help to improve my situation. I felt ashamed and find it ironic I see people with anxiety all day long as a physical therapist, can easily recognize it in others, but wasn't seeing it in myself. As a PT, I have observed that anxiety is evident for those in pain, physical or otherwise. According to the New Oxford American Dictionary, anxiety is defined as a feeling of worry, nervousness, or unease, typically about an imminent event or something with an uncertain outcome. It is a feeling and should be considered in an overall approach to get out of pain.

My studies continued and led me to neuroanatomy, which simultaneously was implemented at a basic level into my clinical assessment and PT practice, and my self-movement practice. I began to think perhaps my 'wound upness' and "quick/fast thought' were simply the result of plasticity of a specific pattern, from what I could tell in the brain stem. The brainstem is where most afferent/efferent information pass through on the way to/from the higher brain levels, and where autonomic responses are regulated.

Getting Treated

I quickly realized the difficulty in assessing and treating myself and made the decision to seek someone with a better understanding of the brain and how to holistically (rather than via 'medicine') assist me in feeling better. I sought out Dr. Mike Drzewiecki (Mike D for all you Beastie Boys fans), for direction on how to deal with my symptoms, which included anxiety, slight depression, and a recent flare up of inflammatory bowel disease. Mike D had become a friend and was introduced to me by Dr. Nick Studholme. He is the co-owner of The Neurologic Wellness Institute, a functional neurology based Chiropractic practice in Chicago, where I often refer patients I feel demonstrate a central integration dysfunction that aren't progressing with me. Their depth of knowledge about brain anatomy and how the specific "circuits" work together is unparalleled, influenced heavily through a functional neurology thought process taught by the Carrick Institute.

Watching a functional neurology practitioner work reminds me of when AFS is used as a thought process to tease out dysfunction. It's often a simple intervention utilized to elicit a desired reaction. While

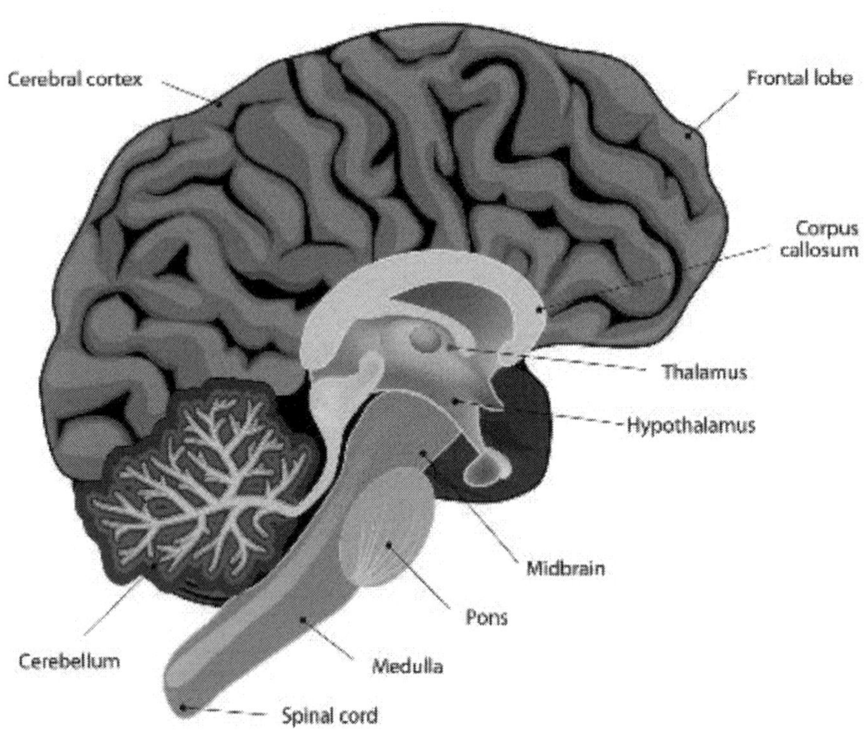

functional neurology utilizes movement to create a desired reaction, it can be more difficult to observe secondary to the subtlety of the input. From my observation, looking for changes in bedside neuro exam findings including in the eyes and vestibular system as an indicator for and direction to treat. What's most impressive to me is what is often the simplicity of an intervention. Like AFS, watching a skilled practitioner work and understanding what is happening requires a specific thought process based on applying an understanding of neuroanatomy, which is often less observable, compared to a knee joint. While I have observed a number of their three hour intake evaluations, being on the receiving end was an enlightening (and tiring) experience. It included a traditional neurological bedside exam, cognitive assessments, along with a tool, measuring eye reactions, called a videonystagmography (VNG) or video oculography (VOG) test. A VNG test is a technology for testing inner ear and central motor function. Testing these parts of the vestibular system involves the use of infrared goggles to trace eye movements during visual stimulation and positional changes and will be referenced specifically later in this part. As a movement geek and someone who has been learning this information, experiencing it on the patient end was an eye opening experience, pun intended.

Neuro Editors Notes: Based on Clinical Intervention on Adam

"The process with Adam was the same as for all patients, including a detailed history to learn what the patient is currently experiencing in order to identify potential components of the past that can provide clues to why they landed in my office. Sometimes these clues are obvious such as physical trauma (like a concussion), other times they are subtle and cumulative over a lifetime. Examples include emotional abuse, poor self-talk, emotional traumas, and overall loss of control, leaving the body and mind in a state of fear and panic, with a patient being stuck in a state of sympathetic dominance, always on edge and ready for the next insult. This state often leads to poor breathing patterns, poor blood flow to the brain and the gut, all of which create signs of chronic illness such as anxiety, panic attacks, and inflammatory bowel disease, which Adam was dealing with here.

Following the history, a detailed physical examination was performed to look at all of the systems of Adam's body, though through the lens of neurology. Because it isn't possible to test only one system such as the proprioceptive, vestibular, or visual systems without testing the others, deficits must be summated through multiple tests. Much of how Adam assesses his PT patients is similar to the way I assess in that he watches them move, finds errors in movement, and gives feedback and exercises to correct those poor movement patterns. Although these movements involve neurology and orthopedics, which is similar to my practice, we tend to use very specific drivers to stimulate regions of the brain based on an understanding of the specific brain pathways.

For example, with abnormal gait patterns, I think more of the central brain mechanisms first rather than the biomechanics of the gait pattern. With that being said, this is where a detailed history is very important, particularly if the patient has an abnormal associated arm swing during gait. It could be musculoskeletal, however without specific trauma to the tissue, it's just as likely it could be because they have poor integration between the contralateral frontal lobe, spinal cord central pattern generators, and the muscles or joints. Or it could be because they have had several injuries and surgeries to that shoulder. Through thoughtful, investigative, and 'test, re-test' assessments, the deep-seated problems that cause many ailments, especially in the chronic patients can be uncovered.

Another example is when a saccadic intrusion to smooth pursuit happens when the brain knows the task of following a target from point A to point B must be performed but somewhere along the pursuit pathway is an error resulting in inability to smoothly track the object. In this situation, the frontal lobe takes over this task and supplants a fast eye movement to continue following the object, although not in a smooth fashion. From the clinician's standpoint, it is hugely important to be able to observe this error before attempting to correct the error and restore smooth pursuit. It is easy to say, "well the frontal lobe did the job and technically the subject still completed the task," yet there are many other conditions potentially arising from the 'lesioned area' in the pursuit pathway that may be causing deficit in function. For example, pursuit pathways begin in the ipsilateral parietal lobe, and if the saccadic intrusion error is due to a lesion in the parietal lobe (such as a stroke), the patient may also be suffering from sensory loss in the periphery. Rehabbing this smooth pursuit finding affects the parietal lobe and can help decrease the amount of sensory loss to the area affected. Some clinicians may never work with a stroke patient, and only with performance athletes, but the same holds true for an athlete who may have the same saccadic intrusion to smooth pursuit, due to a functional deficit in the ipsilateral parietal lobe. While the deficit may be as small as not fully understanding where their foot is in space and suffering repeated ankle sprains, only through a thorough understanding of the specific pathways, and by summating the results of all the tests, can the exact deficit be best recognized. When this occurs, the most effective and efficient intervention possible can then be provided to help rehab the ankle sprain. Also, using a brain-based treatment to provide better understanding of where the foot is in space by creating faster and more appropriate spinocerebellar input and vestibulospinal output, the system should be better protected against future sprain injuries. Understanding the various inputs and outputs of the system opens a huge toolbox for rehab purposes. The interactions of the neuroaxis; the cerebral cortex, basal ganglia, limbic system, brainstem, cerebellum, spinal cord, peripheral nerves, and end organs/muscles/receptors, and all of the connections between them, allows for great laterality in treatment protocols if it is understood how to access each of these systems. It's interesting to note there is no one way to access any specific pathway because it is so interrelated, although areas of deficit and areas of proper function can be tested, recognized, and re-tested after intervention to identify what will work best for the individual patient.

Adam demonstrated classic symptoms of someone 'wound up' and living in a state of sympathetic dominance, essentially living in a consistent state of 'fight or flight', contributing to the heightened anxiety, depression, inflammatory bowel disease, and nighttime panic attacks he was experiencing.

His positive finds included:

- Hyperkinetic optokinetic reflex, particularly to the right and downward.
- Bilateral convergence spasm left > right.
- Hypoactive myotatic stretch reflexes, or MSRs (formerly named deep tendon reflexes, DTRs).
- A pathological ocular tilt reaction; OTR (left head tilt with a right hypertropic eye).
- Hypersensitivity to pinwheel in the right hand and left side of the neck.

Definitions:

Optokinetic reflex (OPK) –

- a vestibular and ocular reflex that is elicited by two scenarios.
    - 1) When someone is turning their head or rotating without fixating on an object.
    - 2) When a visual scene, for example a train, is moving in front of the eyes even if there is no head rotation. The eyes will track smoothly and slowly in the direction of the visual scene then quickly jump in the opposite direction to catch the next portion of the visual scene. In the scenario of spinning, the eyes will fixate on the next portion of the visual scene to allow continued rotation without losing balance. In the example of the train, the eyes will follow one train car then quickly jump to the next car.

Convergence spasm

- Convergence and divergence of the eyes happens when an object is moved closer or farther from the eyes, respectively. This can be either if the object is moving or if the head is moving towards or away from the object. Convergence and divergence allow proper depth perception and the ability to look at both near and far objects.

- When one or both of the eyes become 'stuck' in a converged position (closer together or crossed), it is referred to as a convergence spasm. This must not be confused with a primary muscle weakness causing the eye to turn in, which should be differentiated and is beyond the scope of this text.

- Often, a convergence spasm will be only present with certain eye movements, stimuli, or after a convergent scenario where the eyes become stuck in a medial position, relative to each other. In cases of primary lateral rectus weakness, the eye will remain in a medial position regardless of stimulus and is rarely transient. Often times in cases of head injury the vergence mechanisms become disrupted and is a common finding of patients following head injuries.

- In Adam's case, the convergence spasm could have been a result of long term increased output from his mesencephalon, the top part of his brainstem, where the sympathetic nervous system originates. The convergence spasm may also have contributed to the wind-up due to constant feedback from the muscles and nerves associated with that eye position, creating a feedback loop.

    - To illustrate a convergence spasm, place your thumb in front of your nose, then move it to about 12 inches and hold it there for an extended period of time. After a few moments you will understand how having a convergence spasm will lead to increased anxiety, headaches, brain fog, and general uneasiness.

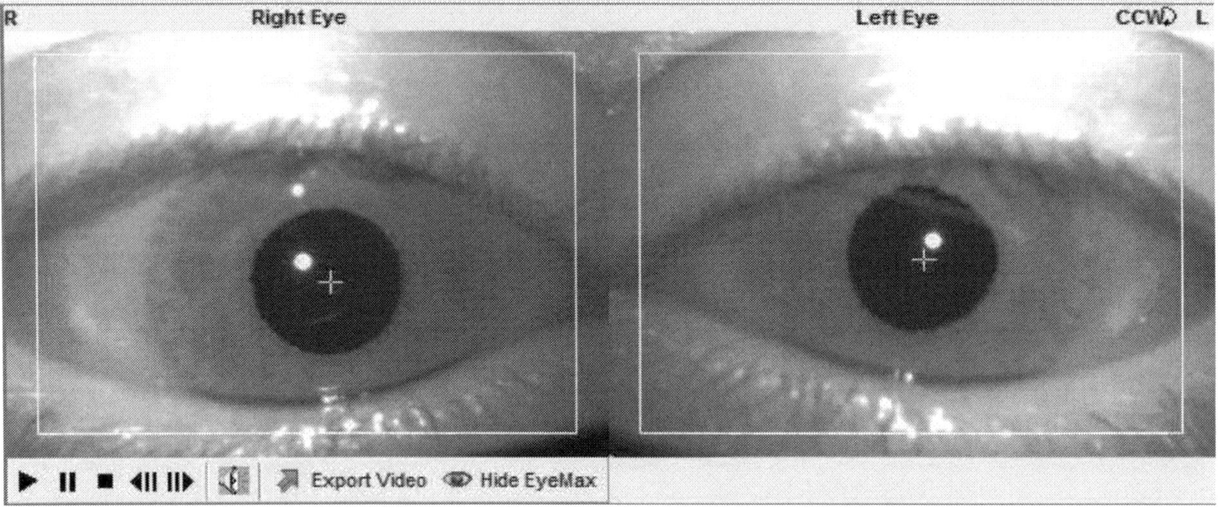

Above Image: Upward Optokinetic test at 30 degrees/second for 15 seconds. Appropriate OPK response throughout with minor horizontal deviations as seen in the top portion of the graph. The horizontal deviations are most likely a result of the ongoing convergence spasm (sustained esodeviation of the eyes) throughout the test.

Below image: Still close-up image of the video that was taken during the upward OPK test. During the test, the eyes should be in a neutral position in the X-axis. If in a neutral position, the white light would be in the midline of the pupil. The light is eccentric in the pupil which gives away the convergence spasm, also described as an esodeviation of both eyes.

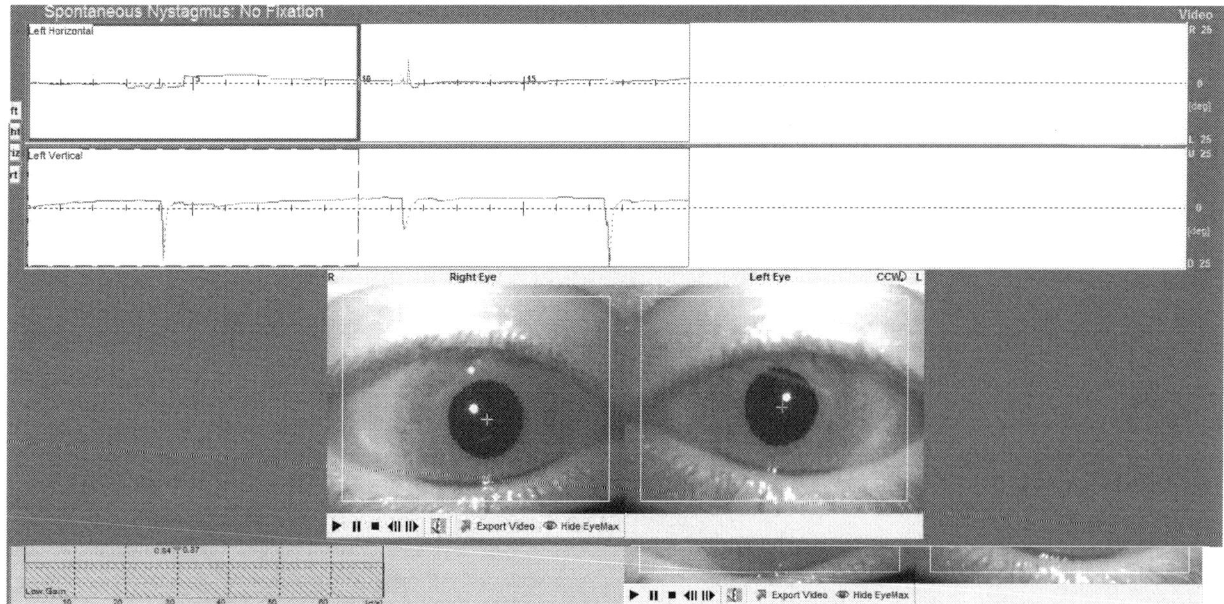

Above image: Normal OPK reflex during a rightward stimulus with appropriate consistency and amplitude. The green lines depict the slow phase and the red lines depict the fast phase of nystagmus. The lower portion of this graph is the vertical movement of the eyes showing slight vertical deviation, although within normal limits.

Below image: Leftward OPK stimulus with inconsistent and hyperkinetic result. The amplitude from peak to peak is inconsistent with many small amplitude peaks. The optokinetic system is present throughout, but not as fluid as the rightward OPK for Adam. This is consistent with his other findings of left brain instability. By many accounts this would be considered a normal OPK graph but in comparison to his right OPK result and in combination with his other findings, nuances in subclinical findings were important for assessing and treating his complaints.

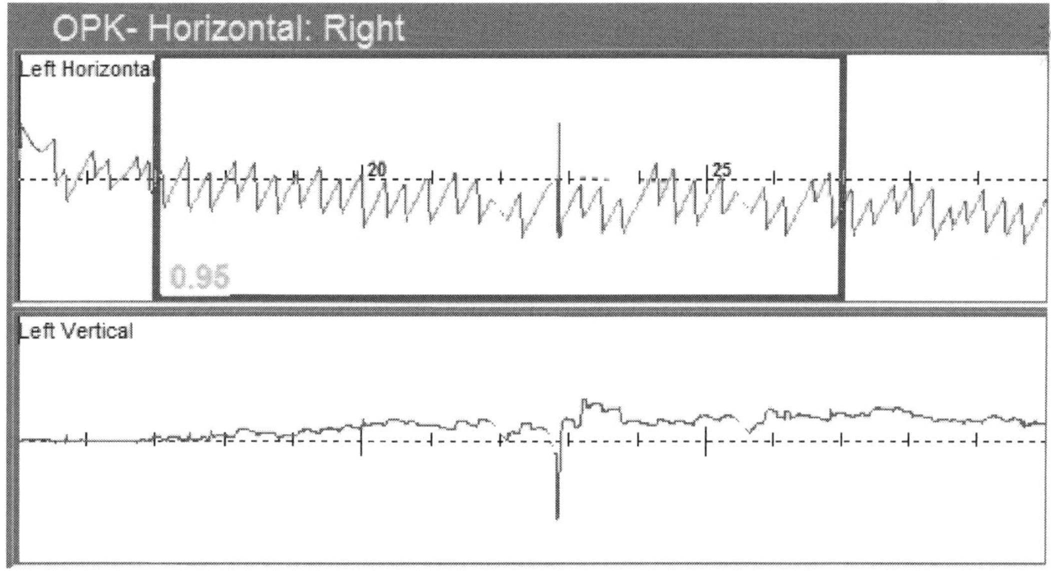

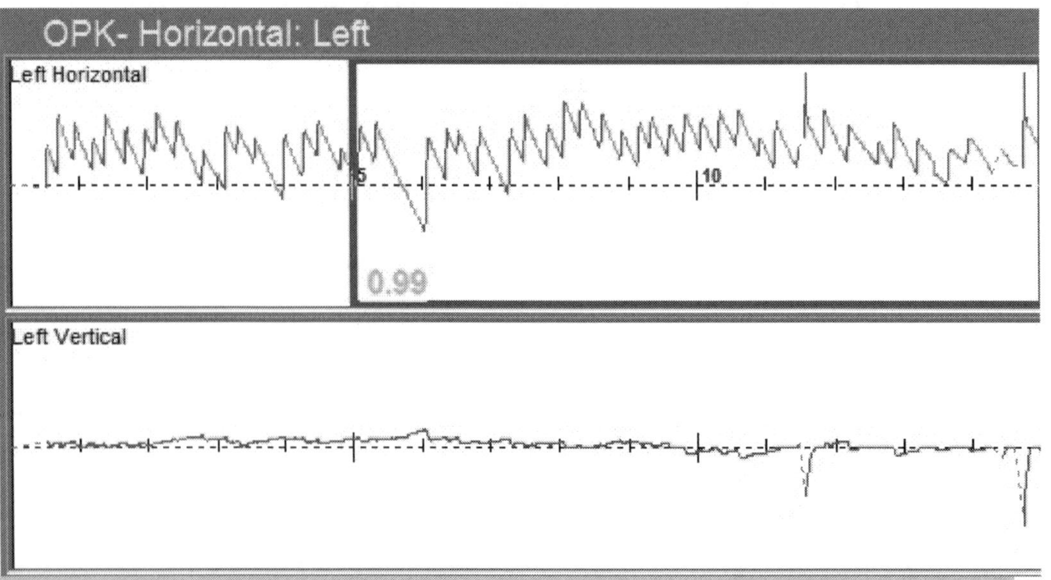

Above image: Spontaneous nystagmus test performed with a cover over the eyes to provide total darkness. No nystagmus is noted but a static convergence spasm can be seen in the still image of the video with esodeviation of the eyes and eccentric location of the infrared lights in the x-axis of the pupil.

Below Image: Horizontal smooth pursuit at 0.1 Hz for 3 cycles. The pursuit is appropriate and accurate. In the still picture of the video, the convergence spasm is again highlighted. The size of the pupils are equal but the light is at different locations. The tone of the medial rectus muscle is too high causing less lateral excursion of the eye. This was true throughout the video for both eyes, highlighting that the relative distance between the eyes is in a converged position. Although this is abnormal, his brain has adapted over time with a result of an appropriate smooth pursuit mechanism.

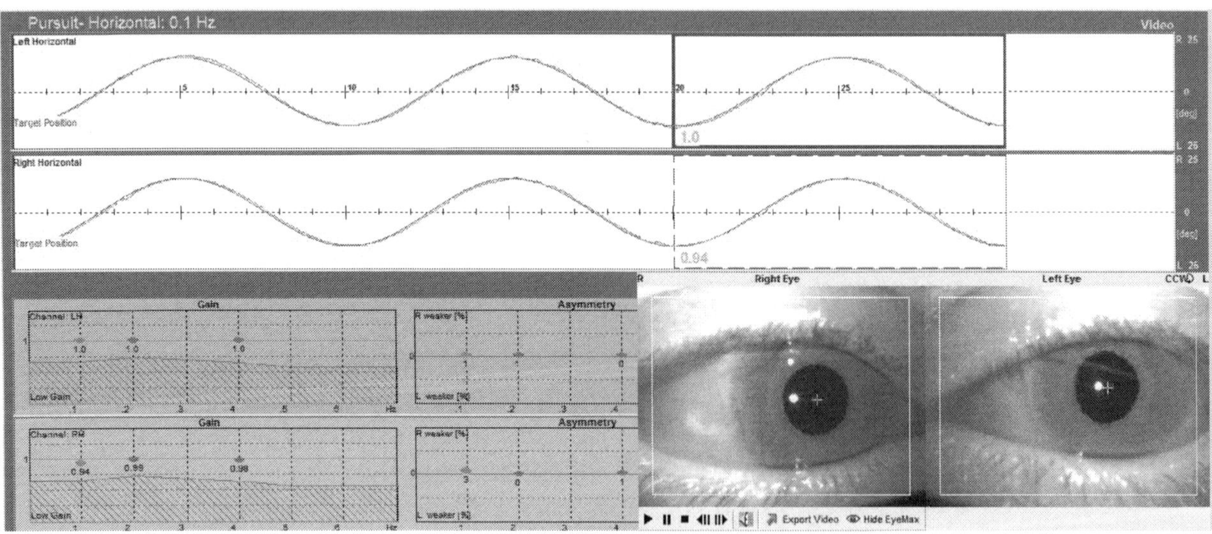

Myotatic Stretch Reflexes (MSRs)

- Previously called Deep Tendon Reflexes, MSR's are tested by using a reflex hammer, with the most common MSR being the patellar reflex. MRSs checked include patellar tendon, Achilles, biceps, brachioradialis, triceps, and clavicular reflexes. They provide insight about which muscles are at a higher tone and may give clues into postural reflexes.

- In Adam's case, all of his MSRs were dampened at a 1+ in all of the aforementioned areas. This alone did not tell me anything other than his reflexes were all decreased or that the functional tone of his spinal cord is slightly decreased. Essentially this was just an abnormal box checked. It wasn't until interventions were performed and the reflexes returned to a normal brisk 2+ that it was assumed that they were abnormally hypofunctioning during the exam.

Pathological Ocular Tilt Reaction (OTR)

- Normal ocular tilt reactions occur when the head is tilted in the roll axis to keep the eyes level with the horizon and give the brain a true sense of being upright relative to gravity.

- As the head is tilted to the right, a normal ocular tilt reaction is for the right eye to move superiorly in the orbit and for the left eye to move inferiorly. Simultaneously the eyes should roll to the left. In a pathological ocular tilt reaction, the eyes do not react this way. Conversely, the right and left eyes maintain their neutral position or move opposite to what is described in the normal ocular tilt reaction. This is often seen as a static hypertropia (unlevel eyes with one eye higher than the other in their obits when the head is neutral) that worsens with a head tilt away from the high eye.

- This information illustrated that Adam didn't have enough vestibular information being delivered to his brain from his left vestibular apparatus compared to the right. In other words, there was hypo-function of the left inner ear or hyper-function of the right inner ear.

- It's significant to note that this is a greatly simplified definition of the pathological ocular tilt reaction. For an in-depth explanation of this vestibular reflex, read the article Skew Deviation Revisited by Brodsky et al.

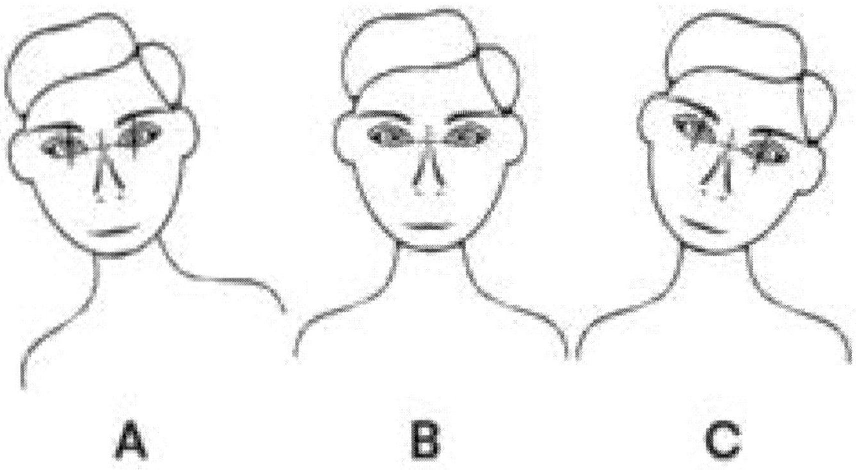

Utricular ocular tilt reaction in humans. When the eyes are frontally placed, a torsional component becomes necessary to neutralize a tilt in the roll plane. A, Physiologic ocular tilt reaction. A rightward body tilt activates right utricular and inhibits left utricular pathways subserving graviceptive tone in the roll plane, resulting in vertical divergence with conjugate torsion of the eyes and head tilt toward the lowermost eye. B, Normal eye position with head upright. C, Pathologic ocular tilt reaction. A leftward ocular tilt reaction can be caused by an inhibitory lesion of the left utricular pathways or an excitatory lesion of the right utricular pathways.

Pinwheel hypersensitivity

- There are many reasons why skin sensitivity is assessed, especially in cases where someone is suffering from pain either physically or emotionally. Pinwheel/pinprick is often assessed to determine if there's a lack of sensitivity, which was not the case for Adam and is often not the case for many of my patients who are experiencing a wind-up condition as he was.

- Adam experienced a reproducible hypersensitivity to painful stimuli, which led to the idea that the brain was not effectively blocking pain. Patients with sympathetic nervous system dominant syndromes often demonstrate heightened pain, leading to both physical and emotional suffering.

Adam's convergence spasm, increased frequency of the optokinetic reflex, along with a pathological OTR response meant that his inner ear and central brain components of the inner ear signals were not calibrated appropriately. His brain was perceiving more motion than was in reality, leading to an increased OPK reflex gain and a bilateral convergence spasm. What complicated this more was the pathologic OTR response which means that the inner ear mechanisms were measuring gravity and visual vertical differently left to right. All of these errors created a state of instability in his central nervous system which led to the increased sympathetic, 'fight or flight' response.

A loop was created where the convergence spasm was the result of inaccurate signals from the inner ear that led to a wound up mesencephalon. The mesencephalon is the upper brainstem area and controls convergence and sympathetic output. This made the convergence spasm stronger, elevating fight or flight responses to everyday activities. In other words, Adam had trouble turning the figurative 'sympathetic faucet' down to let the 'parasympathetic faucet' dominate, potentially explaining the heightened anxiety. Interestingly, many people with anxiety that are 'high performers' demonstrate convergence spasms and increased OPK gain which may be due to the environmental overload of stress due to being high performers or may contribute to being a high performer as their brain is working overtime, all the time.

The other finding of increased optokinetic reflexes, particularly to the right and downward, also are indicative of increased activity in the central vestibular system, also contributing to increased mesencephalic wind-up. Optokinetic reflexes are most easily thought of when sitting at a train crossing and a long train is passing, as the specifics of each car is attempted to be seen. In this situation, eyes will bounce rapidly, until eventually they fatigue out and slow down. There is a known rate/velocity that should occur which should be a 1:1 ratio of stimulus to response, however Adam's reflexes were too fast. His eyes were moving at a rate faster than the stimulus provided which creates a situation where his perception of reality and actual reality did not match.

Based on these findings I performed a modified Epley maneuver that was similar to a standard BBQ roll to the left, as well as Brock bead string exercises and zero-times viewing exercises horizontally and vertically. The goal of these oculomotor/brain exercises was to break the convergence spasm and reduce the gain of the hyperkinetic OPK system. In other words, the recalibration of the central vestibular mechanisms through the exercises allowed his brain to recognize that visual and vestibular motion were paired at the same sensory frequency. Thus, his perception of reality and actual reality matched. This creates less confusion in his brain and less need for sympathetic output due to the confusion of sensory inputs. Following the modified Epley maneuver, the pathological OTR response lessened, the hypersensitivity to pinwheel findings normalized, and the MSR responses became more brisk. All of this happened immediately. The combination of thorough examination and strong hypothesis of where the dysfunction was coming from, as well as a depth of knowledge of how all of the affected neurological systems interplay with each other created a situation that created positive change right away. Although it is great when this happens so quickly, it is not always this way. Many times, with patients, there is a peeling back of layers of dysfunction that takes time and patience by the practitioner and the patient. The work was not done there, as with anything involving the brain, for neuroplastic effects to take place and maintain the activity must be performed repetitively over time. Adam was given other exercises for at home self-guided therapy to continue the positive effect of the initial treatment.

Clinical Note

Professionally, I've referred many patients to Mike and his partners because what I was seeing was beyond my limits of intervention. On more than one occasion, it was validating for me to know that I was seeing something, such as observing what I thought was a lack of convergence of one eye, which turned out to be a bilateral convergence spasm where one eye wasn't converging because it was already converged. Similar to 'motion vs. position' and 'real and relative' motion, the converged eyes meant they weren't able to go through full convergence, which is easily observed with sophisticated (expensive) equipment. I wasn't incorrect in my observation of one eye not moving into convergence, however because I don't use a VNG or record eyes to that specificity, which is the primary way to identify this information, it was missed.

On a second clinical note, it has been challenging to grasp this information and often quickly reach my limits of intervention. In all therapeutic instances, particularly when working with a non-clinical central integration dysfunction, I try and abide by the rule "if it's not better in four, you're out the door". Said differently, if there hasn't been any change in four sessions I'm going to refer out because something is being missed. In these cases, an understanding of the specifics of the eyes and vestibular system with a VNG is warranted, which for me entails referring out.

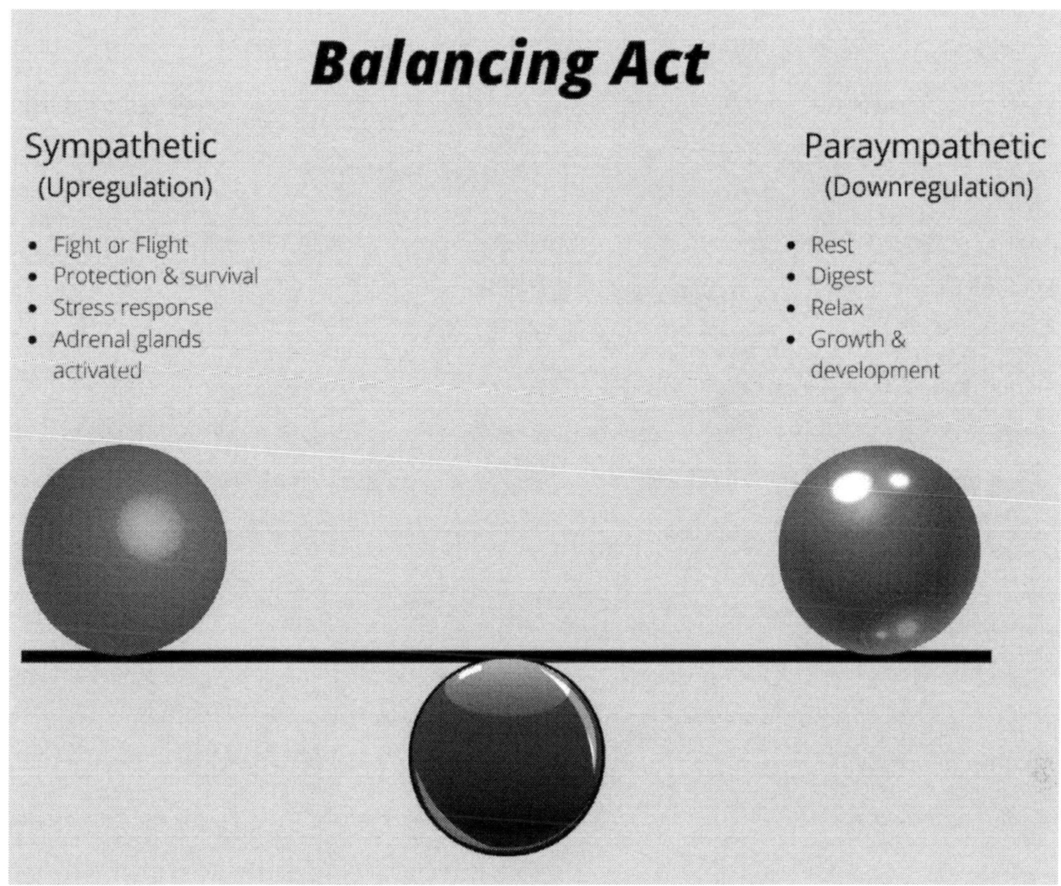

Balance in the nervous system is important for overall health, and those in pain often demonstrate sympathetic dominance of the overall nervous system.

Personal Description of Being Treated

The first exercise Mike D taught was an inphase pursuit in order to decrease my optokinetic reflex, which was too fast. This occurs via exercises to help create better pathways of my eyes into the mesencephalon. My layman's terms (Mike D will fill in the specifics), the optokinetic reflex is the combination of slow and fast eye movements in order to follow an object that is moving in a field of vision, which can sometimes be misleading. According to "*Principles of Neural Science* (p 828), "The contribution of the visual system to spatial orientation can be misleading when the whole visual scene moves steadily relative to a stationary subject, as in the familiar impression of backward movement caused by the forward motion of an adjacent train pulling out of the station. This form of optokinetic stimulation can have a dramatic destabilizing effect on posture in the newly walking infant or an adult performing a difficult balancing task". The exercise he prescribed included cervical spine rotation as the thumb stays in line with the nose while looking left and right, otherwise known as zero times viewing, creating movement at the same rate as the world moving. As a movement geek and clinician, I also purchased an (expensive) app allowing inphase pursuits with the optokinetic strip moving in the same direction at the same speed as what is being pursued (basically a dot moving along the screen with lines moving in the same direction at the same speed as the dot).

Exercises to dampen sympathetic dominance also included eye divergence exercises, requiring a 'thumbs up' placed in front of something, so that when I look at my thumb it covers the target behind it. Once this is accomplished, the goal is to change my focus to the far object, while trying to see 'two' thumbs and focusing on the details of the entire thumb. It's important to note when focusing on the far object to first work on making out the details of two entire thumbs (it's really one thumb that is being seen separately by the eyes). In addition, the thumbs should be on the same horizontal plane, and when they're not it's good biofeedback about a tilted head position.

Generally speaking, these interventions and my experience being a patient, have helped recognize the downward spiral I was stuck in, while assisting to create an upward spiral. It was accomplished by working to plasticize the regions of my brainstem that work to downregulate. These exercises are only part of what I do on a daily (and almost hourly) basis in order to help down regulate myself. Others include contemplative sitting, which is the term I prefer vs. "meditation", which for me has substantial pressure associated with it. Practicing yoga and making sure to get a daily bout of movement in, even if it's low intensity and for a brief period of the day is also imperative.

Chapter Conclusion

Understanding anatomy, concepts of test and retest, and recognizing an individual's opportunities for neurological and musculoskeletal improvement, creates simple and logical interventions and progressions. This chapter was by far the most difficult of the book, mainly because I don't like talking about myself. Also, because neuroanatomy is something I continue to intently study and learn. Yet, it feels good to be able to share directly how my experience helped me to become a better clinician, father, husband, and friend.

Additional Readings list

- Beck, R.; *Functional Neurology for Practitioners of Manual Therapy*
- Kandal, E., Schwarts, J. Jessel, T.; *Principles of Neural Science*
- Korb, Alex; *The Upward Spiral: Using Neuroscience to Reverse the Course of Depression, One Small Change at a Time*
- Tottenham NH, Hare TA, Quinn BT, McCarry TW, Nurse M, Galvan A, Davidson MC, Thomas KM, McEwen B, Gunnar M, Aronson J, Casey BJ. Amygdala volume and sensitivity to emotional information following orphanage rearing. Journal of Child Psychology & Psychiatry. In press.
- Bremner JD, Vythilingam N, Vermeetn E, Adil J, Khan S, Nazeer A, Afzal N, McGlashan T, Elzinga B, Anderson GM, Heniger G, Southwick SM, Charney DS.. Cortisol response to a cognitive stress challenge in posttraumatic stress disorder (PTSD) related to childhood abuse. *Psychoneuroendocrinology* 2003;28(6):733–750.
- Heim C, Newport JD, Mletzko T, Miller AH, Nemeroff CB. The link between childhood trauma and depression: Insights from HPA axis studies in humans. *Psychoneuroendocrinology* 2008;33(6):693-710.
- Yehuda R, Halligan SL, Grossman R. Childhood trauma and risk for PTSD: relationship to intergenerational effects of trauma, parental PTSD, and cortisol excretion. *Developmental Psychopathology*. 2001;13(3):733-753.
- Gunnar MR. Quality of early care and buffering of neuroendocrine stress reactions: Potential effects on the developing human brain. *Preventive Medicine: An International Journal Devoted to Practice and Theory*. 1998;27(2):208-211.
- Gunnar MR, Donzella B. Social regulation of the cortisol levels in early human development. *Psychoneuroendocrinology* 2002;27(1-2):199-220.
- Gunnar MR, Larson M, Hertsgaard L, Harris M, Brodersen L. The stressfulness of separation among 9-month-old infants: effects of social context variables and infant temperament. *Child Development* 1992;63(2):290-303.
- Ahnert L, Gunnar MR, Lamb M, Barthel M. Transition to childcare: associations with infant-mother attachment, infant negative emotion and cortisol elevations. *Child Development* 2004;75(3):639-650.
- Hertsgaard L, Gunnar MR, Erickson M, Nachmias M. Adrenocortical responses to the strange situation in infants with disorganized/disoriented attachment relationships. *Child Development* 1995;66(4):1100-1106.
- Skew Deviation Revisited, Brodsky, Michael C. et al. Survey of Ophthalmology, Volume 51, Issue 2, 105 – 128

PART 7: MOBILITY – AN ASPECT OF MOTOR CONTROL

"Nothing is more revealing than movement." -Martha Graham

Introduction

This chapter will introduce different concepts of mobility, and how they are different and related to flexibility. First, we will define the differences and similarities, and relate how mobility is an integral part of integrated movement. After defining mobility, the chapter will discuss various types of mobility restrictions as well as strategies to work to improve mobility.

Mobility is different than flexibility

Integrated movement is enhanced through an understanding of motor control and its relationship to mobility. Mobility and flexibility are different. Flexibility is the quality of bending easily without breaking, and flexible means an ability to passively achieve full range of motion. Conversely, mobility requires active control with the utilization of flexibility, particularly at the end range. The largest difference is that a person can be flexible and not mobile because flexibility is passive and often unloaded. In contrast, mobility is the ability to actively achieve end range of motion with motor control because it is loaded.

"This point of motor control is especially important. Mobility is only achievable under optimal circumstances in the brain, and from a cortical, sub-cortical, and cerebellar standpoint; all systems must be working in unison for optimal mobility. Specifically, the association cortices, primary motor and sensory areas, basal ganglia, and cerebellum must fully coordinate to achieve proper mobility. In addition, motor association and primary motor pathways need to develop the correct motor output with appropriate motivation. The sensory association areas and primary sensory area of the cortex must have appropriate sensory awareness of the body part that is trying to achieve mobility. The basal ganglia must be able to appropriately activate and inhibit specific muscle groups appropriately, while the cerebellum must relay appropriate sensory information providing immediate feedback and feedforward programs for the desired movement. And the limbic system must be able to handle the emotional load of moving a body part to its end range with or without perceived pain. For these reasons, mobility is a very intricate outcome that is often simplified to "can you move easily?"

THE HUMAN BRAIN

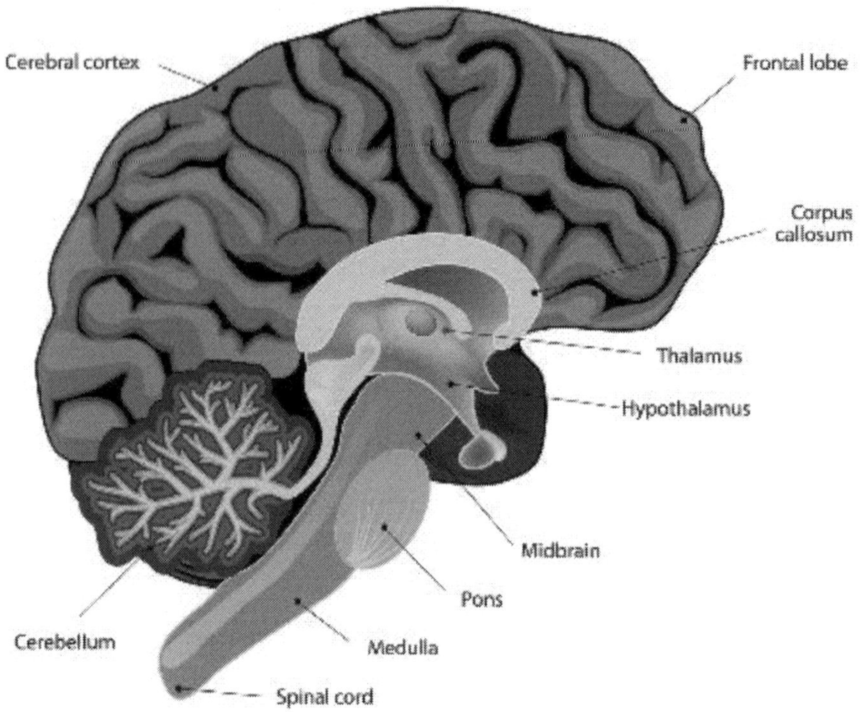

Motor control encapsulates all aspects of the brain and requires integration for full optimization.

Active is a key differentiator. Mobility requires tensioning the system and can be accomplished via isometric contractions that can be performed multiple ways at various intensities. Additionally, the mechanical force produced by an isometric contraction mediates a chemical response in the neuromusculoskeletal system. In turn, this influences tissue direction and quality while also reinforcing the connection from the nervous system to the tissue.

Lines of tissue working together is application of tensegrity

Lengthening chains of tissue together can be a good strategy to enhance overall movement because it mimics real life. As such, chains of tissue can be mobilized together by lengthening under load through various points of stability. For example, holding on to a door with hands positioned, to lengthen a specific tissue line and pulling with one hand and pushing with the other, which tensions the line. The 'push and pull' creates system-wide tension where specific motion and tension in specific tissue can be accomplished. This is an example of tensegrity (discussed in previous parts) and how tension and compression can be created through combinations of tissue.

The lateral line 'stretch' is one example where stretching the line can be applied in an integrated fashion that is also specific. An entire chain of tissue including the peroneals, lateral glutes, quadratus lumborum, latissimus, and more are lengthened and tensioned together through the 'pulling' hand, while specificity in the movement is applied with compression through the 'pushing' hand.

- Standing next to door or pole, with left shoulder closest
- Cross inside (left) leg over outside leg (right)
- Take outside hand (right) up overhead and grab the pole
- Left hand goes to door at about waist height, or where desired for specificity in stretch with the lateral line
- Pull with top (right) hand and, push with bottom hand (left)

This integrated lateral line stretch encapsulates concepts of tensegrity via the push and pull, while lengthening under load, both of which are required for integration.

This movement can be progressed and regressed based on the thresholds of the individual. Regressions can include different placement of the hands or performed side lie. Progressions include isometric stabilizing by pulling or pushing more, or adding a pelvic or hand drive and moving towards an opposite side, side lunge with an overhead frontal plane hand drive to create a dynamic length to the tissue. Other variations may include lateral lunging and reaching, before utilizing external loads such as bands or dumbbells to create variability.

"When looking at mobility of a joint or a specific kinetic chain, the understanding of reflexive ocular and vestibular mechanisms can help aid in mobility and stability. In order to have proper mobility, stability must be present first. The following is to give an example of how a practitioner can think when approaching mobility with a patient. If the patient has limited range of motion in right cervical rotation, have the patient hold his/her eyes to the left at the same time as rotating the head to the right. Looking to the left is associated with a vestibulo ocular reflex (VOR) to the right. Have the patient hold their head to the right at end range in an isometric hold while simultaneously holding their eyes to the left. By introducing a gaze shift opposite of the desired head turn, along with an isometric hold, the neuronal pools associated with the VOR become more excitable and should improve the range of motion of the cervical spine. This is one example, but it should highlight how coupling isometric holds with ocular and/or vestibular afferentation should allow the patient to achieve better stability and therefore mobility. The physician will immediately have more tools to drive mobility by having a full understanding of postural reflexes as mediated by vestibular and ocular mechanisms. The above mentioned principle can be applied to any joint in any range of motion once postural reflexes are understood."

Not All Joint Sensations Mean the Same Thing

Creating tissue change takes focus, consistency, and intensity. Dr. Andreo Spina, developer of Functional Range Conditioning (FRC), defines mobility as the combination of flexibility and strength. Strategies to mobilize a joint are going to be different compared to soft tissue and understanding which is limited directs treatment (they both may be limited). Recall, a joint is simply space between bones, and during motion, sensation should be on the 'opening', or progressive side of the joint rather than on the 'closing', or regressive side. Generally speaking, closing angle sensations and/or limitation are typically indicative of joint or capsule, while opening side tends to be soft tissue restrictions.

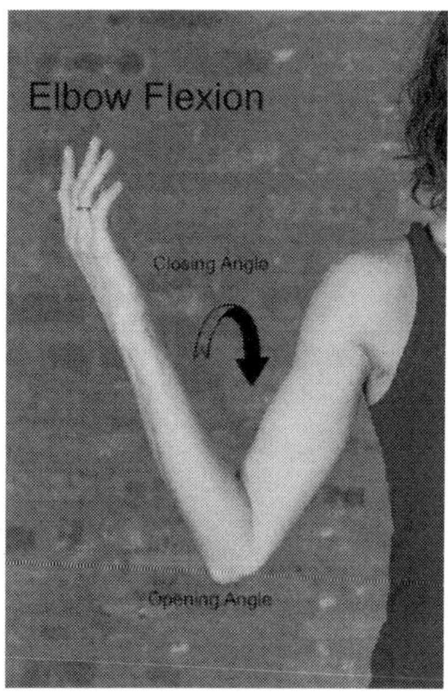

Simply put, when one joint is limited compared to the other side, knowing if the limitation is driven from soft tissue or joint helps direct the course of treatment. There shouldn't be dramatic differences in the way a joint passively 'feels' or plays when comparing one side to the other. When there's restricted movement or joint play, further assessment may be warranted, particularly when there is pain surrounding the joint. Sensation should typically be felt on the opening side of a joint at the end range of motion.

In the book, *Movement*, Gray Cook describes an effective general thought process for reasons to mobilize prior to stabilizing:

> "Mobility and stability problems coexist. Intense focus in one region causes unintentional neglect in another. A central mistake in both rehabilitation and exercise is the attempt to create stabilization with inappropriate mobility. Revisit and attempt to maximize mobility whenever possible. True functional stabilization cannot occur in the presence of inappropriate mobility, because the instant a mobility restriction comes into play reflex stabilization is inhibited or compromised and becomes a less valuable factor in function. Once we've maximized mobility, stability is the next function to target. Greater amounts of mobility will require greater stability. Many people think it takes too long to gain appropriate mobility and since stabilization is of utmost importance, they go for stabilization exercises and programs, neglecting the requisite mobility necessary for spontaneous stability."

A Personal Perspective of Mobility Before Stability

The thought process described above works much of the time. In their view, motion is harder to achieve after strength work. If we are to coordinate thought processes, a "stiff and gunky" joint with closing angle restrictions should be mobilized. In other words, stiff joints are mobilized, and 'flexible' joints call for stabilization; and while often true, it's not always the case, to the point where specific criteria must first be met.

Brain-based approaches emphasizing motor control principles that influence the neuro-musculoskeletal system provide insight about if a limited joint actually requires more motion. It is entirely possible the limited joint requires more stability and increased representation in the brain in order to improve the motion of the joint. I find the most straightforward way to find out this information is to provide an intense bout of stability via isometric holds to the intrinsic muscles surrounding the joint. Isometrics are not inflammatory and can be applied with varying intensities, which instills a sense of safety, while concurrently creating more representation in the brain for that region. Often providing an intense bout of isometrics will create more joint motion, indicating stability prior to mobility is warranted. When an intense initial bout of isometrics to the intrinsics of the joint is performed and it doesn't improve motion, mobility is focused on first.

In other words, when ROM improves with stabilization in a limited joint, stabilization is warranted first despite the closing angle restriction. Despite demonstrating 'mobility' restrictions, in this case, stability before mobility is warranted because the joint is stiff to provide stability for an otherwise unstable system. In these cases, mobilizing can create more instability that feeds the negative loop they are already in.

Personally, I've played with this scenario for my torn right hip labrum injured about five years ago while practicing yoga. The injury may have been put into a position I wasn't ready for (marichyasana D). Despite mildly dysplastic hips and having hypermobility, I demonstrated significant closing restrictions in passive range of motion (particularly flexion and adduction), but full and above average active mobility. It could be easily aggravated with too much of the wrong activity and was best observed with supine PROM. My passive ROM when aggravated was less than 100' of hip flexion before a pinch, and when flexed 90'; I'm unable to adduct 10' before restriction, pinch and pain. However, in these situations, when my hip is pinchy and sore, an intense bout of isometrics focusing on gluteus engagement will improve my hip ROM and also create less pain for my hip. I have also experienced this with numerous patients in practice.

Clinical Concept

If ROM can be improved with a quick bout of stability, then stability is warranted despite the lack of initial ROM and closing restriction.

Dissociation Can Be Seen and Felt; Developing Palpation Skills.

The idea of synchronous dissociations between adjacent tissue and joints is also inferred with mobility. Those with mobility deficits will often demonstrate less dissociation and synchrony between segments, and instead will observe the segments moving at the same speed or with the wrong one moving faster. Put another way, when joints don't dissociate due to hypomobility, regions above and/or below may become hypermobile. Segmental dissociation creates the most neurological input and relative tissue mobility and despite difficulty in reliability of palpatory skills I believe palpation skills should continue to be developed.

Palpation skills take time to develop, which is a reason to obtain numerous data points that are anchored in objectivity not related to manual therapy skills. While subtle and not necessary to be a successful clinician, soft tissue and joint restrictions can be felt by an experienced practitioner. The sensations typically experienced with a joint restriction include abrupt end feels with a binding on the closing side. When viewed from the lens of AFS and real/relative motion, this is possible due to one bone moving faster or slower than it should relative to the corresponding bone. A question becomes which bone should move faster and being able to identify if it is or not and intervene is important. Sensations associated with soft tissue restrictions include an abrupt and quick tension in the tissue on the opening side of the joint. It tends to be in a specific spot rather than uniform, and the tissue often feels thicker. When manipulated, restricted tissue typically provides a more intense sensation to the client compared to non-restricted tissue.

Educating on self-care, including what to do and why to do it, is important. This includes self-tissue work, as well as likely a stability movement and a mobility movement. In addition, vestibulo-ocular or cerebellar layers may be added, depending on who, what, and why. Providing a narrative, the patient/client can understand what makes sense is most important. Often this means putting things in simple terms, or at the very least, at their level of understanding. Regarding soft tissue therapy (self or otherwise), the narrative should include improving the ability tissue interfaces to slide past each other and also changing the viscosity of the extracellular matrix (ECM). At both a structural and neurological level, the ECM plays many roles which will be discussed later in the text. Currently, we now know manual work doesn't release adhesions or break down scar tissue, and telling this story is irresponsible because it's been debunked numerous times and doesn't empower the patient.

At the minimum, manual therapy creates pressure changes in tissue, and physics dictates that pressure moves from high to low concentration. Pressure changes occur in various ways, but mostly through movement secondary to tissues getting long and short resulting in increased delivery of blood, oxygen, and nutrients to the tissue. Healthy tissue will slide past itself, however sometimes (sections of) tissue does not slide past itself, reducing the relative intratissue pressure. This is palpable and often more tender to the patient due to deoxygenated nature of this tissue. An inability to fully lengthen<>shorten reduces the pressure difference and consequently the amount of blood and oxygen that flows through the tissue. Less oxygen in tissue lowers the pH due to numerous processes (including lack of oxygen), creating a cascade of events that perpetuate the cycle of limited tissue slide/glide and irritation of peripheral nerves.

Author's Note

I recognize research around palpation skills isn't great, yet still feel it is an important skill to develop. The ability to identify limited tissue will only come through touching a lot of people. This palpation skill must be in conjunction with reproducible evidence and never used as a stand-alone measurement.

Clinical Applications: What should be mobilized first?

While mindful of red flags, I assume most pain is neurogenic inflammation where peripheral nerves that are aggravated mimic pathoanatomy until proven otherwise. Therefore, when mobilizing, I start with superficial tissue mobilization before moving to joint mobility, assuming that if peripheral mobilization makes positive changes, it's likely not anything deeper. This is followed by working with one, then two, joint muscles. In other words, I now mobilize superficial tissue first because irritated and sensitized peripheral nerves can and do present as joint pain. If the pain doesn't change after peripheral nerve mobilization, I assume pain isn't driven from neurogenic inflammation or the palpation site is incorrect.

Clinical Correlation

Often superficial tissue over a painful (or once painful) region will be restricted in motion and mobility compared to the other side. It will exhibit limited glide either up or down, and also in or out, in addition the combination of the two. For example, if limited up compared to down, and in compared to out, it's safe to say the most limited direction would be up and in, compared to down and out. In addition, the tissue will be difficult to 'pill roll' or lift and will be exquisitely tender to do so.

Regarding the direction to mobilize, most prefer into the direction of ease, however some feel better with mobilization into the restriction. It should therefore be checked on an individual basis.

The order I tend to mobilize (and stabilize) tissue in is:

- Superficial tissue
- Joints
- Single Joint Muscles
- Multiple Joint Muscles

The following sections will go further in depth about the specifics of working with joint restrictions, as well as further qualities of soft tissue that should be accounted for when working with joints and soft tissue.

Improving Mobility in Joint and Capsule Restrictions

Closing angle joint restrictions are bad and often indicative of limited capsule mobility or joint restrictions. Hierarchically, joint restrictions should be worked on prior to one joint then two joint muscles. Once neurogenic inflammation and peripheral nerve irritation have been ruled out (or not resolved the symptoms fully). Education on self-manual and movement strategies that enhance joint and tissue mobility is imperative, as is having numerous ways to accomplish the same task. This is also a reason to keep learning, and developing teaching techniques, as not everyone learns the same way or have the desired outcomes with the same strategies.

When a joint continues to demonstrate limited mobility after an initial bout of isometric stability input, joint distraction techniques have proven useful. In clinic, a Mulligan Strap is often used to increase space between bones and improve capsule mobility. This technique can easily be combined with other modalities such as 'contract-relax' or 'contract-contract' techniques in order to drive input into the CNS. For those experiencing relief with these strategies, their homework will often be mimicking the distraction with a superband with isometric contractions at the end range upon the conclusion of the stretch. I like that these types of mobilizations can be reproduced easily and progressed to include 'contract-contract' or 'contract-relax' techniques when appropriate.

Contract-relax is a form of proprioceptive neuromuscular facilitation (PNF) that can be useful to improve both joint and soft tissue mobility. I tend to use contract relax techniques in acute populations to reintroduce stabilization during early stages of rehab. There are many useful resources that discuss in depth the concepts of PNF (some listed at end of chapter), which are beyond the scope of this text, however, readers are encouraged to learn more about the thought process. PNF gently introduces muscle recruitment via minimal isometric contractions upon the conclusion of a passive stretch in order to teach the nervous system how to stabilize the increased motion from the hold. Progressions for 'contract-relax' are varied and can include 'contract-contract', or what functional range conditioning refers to as progressive and regressive angular isometric loads, or PAILS & RAILS.

PAILS are similar to a post-isometric relaxation (PIR) technique, which allows a temporary reduction in the stretch reflex threshold. Leon Chaitow describes the thought process associated with PIR, "any muscle, or group of muscles, which is isometrically contracted is obliged to relax afterwards. So, if a muscle is tense or tight and it is then isometrically contracted, it will, to some extent, release and relax afterwards, allowing it to be more easily stretched afterward." This means immediately following increased ROM, contraction of the opening angle muscle helps to develop strength in the new range. The stretch reflex is the body's automatic response to keep the system safe and can be thought of as the built-in 'governor' that automatically determines safe range of motion at any given moment.

When tissue is lengthened past a point deemed safe, the stretch reflex is triggered. This signals the central nervous system to increase tension that tightens tissue to prevent further lengthening from occurring. An example can be seen with a straight leg raise. As the hip is flexed with knee extension, tension in the hamstring triggers the stretch reflex which registers a lengthening of the muscle past normal range. This causes a contraction of the hamstring group to prevent further lengthening to prevent injury to the muscle and other soft tissue structures. However, the CNS has built in safeguard systems to allow more length without injury, so the potential for further safe movement exists. This is why upon long axis distraction of the lower extremity by the clinician, the client will demonstrate improved range of motion with a passive straight leg raise. This is because when the golgi tendon organ is stimulated through distraction, it sends an inhibition moment to the tissue allowing the nervous system to allow more length.

Therefore, the CNS can be trained to allow more movement without these reflexes being stimulated. People with chronically shortened tissue often demonstrate increased stretch reflex sensitivity. They also will not be strong enough to recover from or control a specific range of motion, or the body simply won't allow the motion. For example, when attempting to do the splits, when the CNS believes it no longer able to maintain a stable position, the stretch reflex is triggered causing your muscles to tighten and preventing further movement. Isometrically engaging the progressive angle muscle inhibits the stretch reflex and allows more motion to the system.

In Functional Range Conditioning vernacular, RAILS stands for regressive angular isometric loading and are isometric muscle contractions in the closing angle, or short muscles of the joint. For example, if the hip was flexed, the regressive tissues would be the hip flexors and quads. I use RAILS (or contract-contract as I describe it to patients) as progressions to contract relax. The simplified explanation to patients is after lengthening through stretch the CNS needs to actively use the length. This can be accomplished in many ways including an isometric contraction of the lengthened tissue, which tells the body to let the tissue work in the lengthened position. However, for a long tissue to work long, a short tissue must work short, and so after contracting the lengthened tissue, a regressive (or short side) contraction is performed, telling the CNS to "let the short tissue work short". For more specific information about the FRC system, I highly recommend attending a course and checking out the website and blog. More resources can be found at the end of this chapter.

Contract-contract is an effective way to improve both capsule and soft tissue mobility. When the holding position is assumed and the sensation is on the closing side, rather than hold a passive stretch, it's recommended to immediately perform a PAIL, which should relieve the closing angle sensation and be followed by a RAIL to 'move' (or at least stabilize) the joint into new range of motion. When sensation is on the opening side of the joint is a stretch, it can be held as a stretch for upwards of 2-5 minutes. Holding the position is supported by literature that suggests this time frame is required for myofibroblastic changes to occur. Following the hold, isometrics (of varying degrees and intensities) are performed on the opening then closing side of the joint.

Isometrics at end range are effective for a number of reasons. They teach the body that end range motion can be safe while stabilizing that range through contraction each side of the joint. Over time, this helps to improve end range tissue tolerance and access to the motion. Isometrics don't cause inflammatory response and also build brain representation. For more information about strategies surrounding isometrics please read more about the integrated through isolated spectrum in Part 9.

Starting on the left, picture 1 & 2 above illustrate the position of 90/90, emphasizing the front hip. Picture 3 demonstrates 90/90 for the back hip, while picture 4 illustrates a PAIL/RAIL for the front leg hamstring.

Soft Tissue Restrictions and Extracellular Matrix

Soft tissue continually renews, and can be remodeled and influenced, and from the smallest to largest piece is interconnected three dimensionally through a network of tensegrity. Tensegrity describes the property of structures maintaining their integrity as a result of continuous tensile integrity, rather than continuous compressive integrity (Pienta & Coffey, 1991). In soft tissue, tensegrity is seen as a series of continuous tension resistant components and as a discontinuous series of compression resistant elements, such as bones, and describe structures that stabilize themselves mechanically by balancing local compression with continuous tension. Tensegrity structures are pre-stressed and require continuous transmission of internal tensions to maintain stability, analogous to the resting tone the central nervous system (CNS) keeps in muscle. In other words, the body is set up as a three dimensional structure where compression and tension are interrelated, and one can be enhanced through the application of the other. Therefore, too much of one can easily lead to an imbalance in the system.

Clinically, I use the principles of tensegrity both through manual therapy and also in the "push-pull" scenario in the lateral fascial line stretch described above. While there are many potential explanations about what is happening, fascia responds to mechanical interventions. Mechanical stress mediates chemical responses in tissue, as force is the language of the cell. Mechanical intervention can change volume and consistency of ground substance and also decrease cross linked fibers that develop as a result of the inflammatory process and lack of intratissue glide. In other words, manual therapy can change the viscosity of the ECM in order to improve the glide of layers of tissue, which can allow peripheral nerves to pass through tissue including aponeurotic rings with less friction.

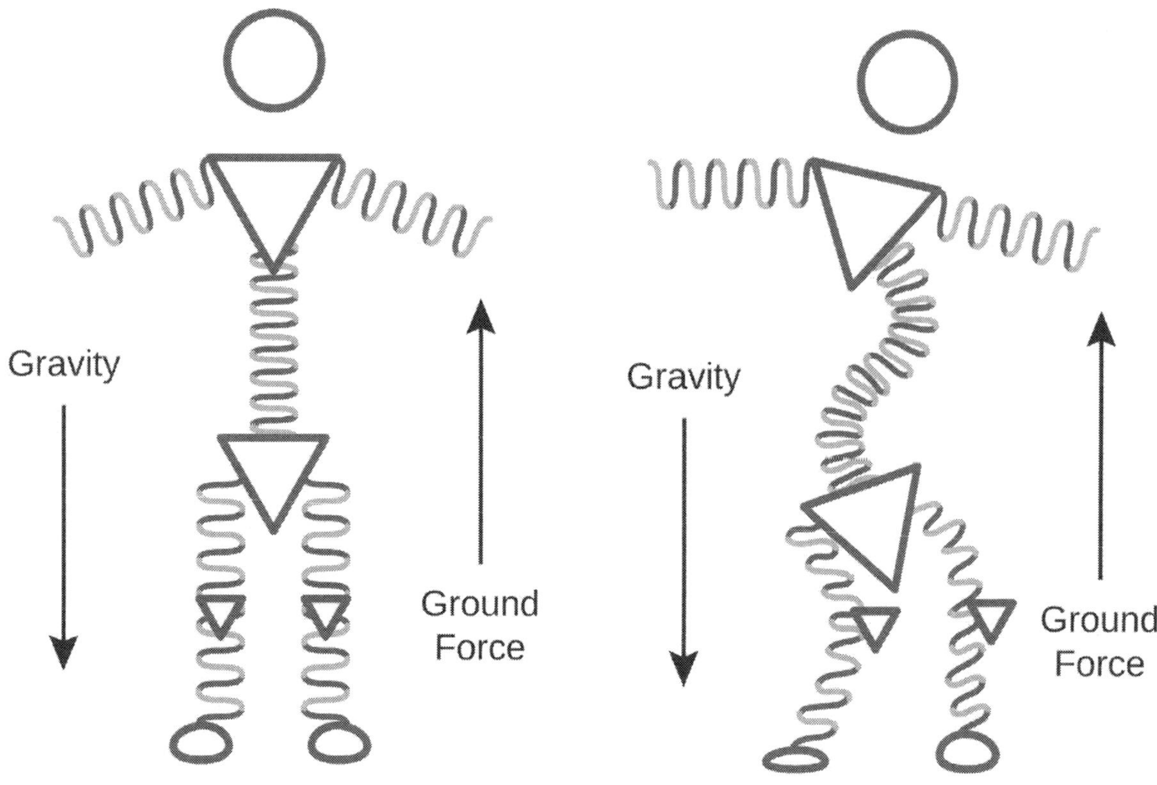

When tissue is unable to slide it often compresses and densifies, resulting in a cascade of events that perpetuates itself. Soft tissue restriction can often be felt in the tissue as a localized abrupt end feel and includes the loss of bulk water found between the tissues. Inherent asymmetry in the body results in asymmetrical distribution of forces through the system. This pulls the helical body into further asymmetry because rotational dysfunctions occur around a vertical axis.

The extracellular matrix is very changeable and has far reaching effects on the nervous system and movement output. Simply put, the act of placing hands upon tissue changes the pressure of what's underneath versus what's around it, and, under the right circumstances, can influence the ECM. "The extracellular matrix (ECM) is the non-cellular component present within all tissues and organs and provides not only essential physical scaffolding for the cellular constituents, but also initiates crucial biochemical and biomechanical cues required for tissue morphogenesis, differentiation, and homeostasis. The ECM is composed of water, proteins, and polysaccharides, each tissue has an ECM with a unique composition that is generated during tissue development through a dynamic and reciprocal, biochemical and biophysical, dialogue among the various cellular components (e.g. epithelial, fibroblast, adipocyte, endothelial elements) and the evolving cellular and protein microenvironment." (Frantz, Christian et al 2010).

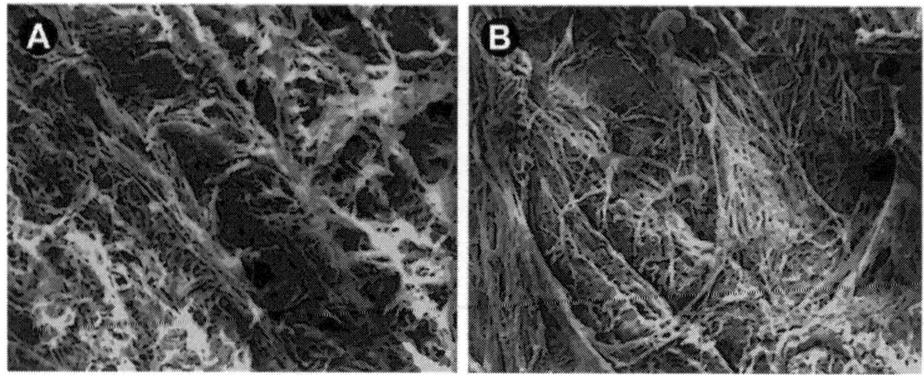

With injury, collagen crosslinking contributes to tissue stiffening so an aged tissue is mechanically weaker and less elastic, but also more rigid, than a young tissue. Picture A illustrates healthy tissue, while picture B illustrates cross-linked tissue.

"...the ECM is a highly dynamic structure that is constantly being remodeled, either enzymatically or non-enzymatically, and its molecular components are subjected to a myriad of post-translational modifications. Through these physical and biochemical characteristics, the ECM generates the biochemical and mechanical properties of each organ, such as its tensile and compressive strength and elasticity, and also mediates protection by a buffering action that maintains extracellular homeostasis and water retention" (Frantz, Christian et al 2010). In other words, the ECM can be modified through tensile and compressive forces. "The relaxed network of collagen and elastin fibers allow the healthy ECM to resist a wide range of tensile stresses. A functionally competent normal tissue can also easily resist compressive stresses because of the binding of the hydrated glycosaminoglycan (GAG) network to the fibrous ECM molecules (Scott, 2003). Thus, the tissue ECM is a highly dynamic entity that continuously undergoes regulated remodeling, whose precise orchestration is crucial to the maintenance of normal function (Egeblad et al., 2010).

With injury, collagen crosslinking contributes to tissue stiffening so an aged tissue is mechanically weaker and less elastic, but also more rigid, than a young tissue. This aberrant mechanical state can severely compromise ECM organization, and modify epithelial function. The ECM is continually remodeling according to the stress and strain applied, and therefore can be influenced by mechanical forces applied specifically. This means that after tissue injury there's an opportunity to influence the direction of tissue reformation. Injury deforms fibroblasts and is destructive, and an irony is, at times, manual therapy can also influence and deform fibroblasts, yet is curative because it's based on the thresholds of the individual and progressed through a continuum of movement.

An important aspect of bodywork, self or otherwise, is the reintroduction of movement that delivers blood, nutrients, and oxygen, to the tissue. Manual work creates pressure change, and at the very least, pushes fluid around the body, in addition to other potential reactions (such as up or down regulation, depending on the specificity of the application). Once tissue mobility has been improved, reinforcing it through specific movement that loads tissue authentically should be assigned via concepts of loaded movement training.

Applying principles of tensegrity to tissue work by 'winding up' the tissue through both compression and tension creates the specific application of force necessary to 'shear' apart layers that would otherwise be 'velcroed' together. Tissue limitation is something that can be felt by the practitioner as an abrupt tensioning of `tissue in a specific area', and when compared to the other side. It is also described by the client as an increase in sensation (more painful?) compared to the contralateral side. When tissue doesn't slide past what is around it, a stagnancy is perpetuated that creates a lowering of the pH. This eventually 'binds' or crosslinks the layers together, sensitizing the peripheral nerves that perpetuates a cycle.

Once the inflammation cycle begins due to injury, the process eventually includes fibrosing to the injured area in order to repair the tissue. It is lower in tensile strength and stiffer than normal tissue due to randomized collagen fiber direction limiting the ability of collagen bundles to slide easily over one another. Due to the cross linking fibers and lack of hydration, the substituted collagen types aren't as strong as the original. Yet tissue direction can be influenced by the application of force that tensions the tissue in a specific direction. Mechanical forces mediate chemical responses, illustrating another reason that isometric contraction and also grips that wind up the tissue will create the most opportunity to preserve intertissue slide. It's also worth mentioning the CNS also influences tissue extensibility and tissue tone, both of which can be regulated through manual therapy and isometric contraction.

Recognizing working with soft tissue is most likely a combination of a musculoskeletal and neurological process, depending on the situation, is important. Soft tissue work can trigger sympathetic or parasympathetic processes and also improve the ability of tissue to glide. Assuming it's nonpathological and the client is compliant with the homework assigned (and it's the right work), regions that continually require repeated work are indicative of a subclinical sensory integration dysfunction which has been discussed in a different part of this text, and at the very least isn't creating the desired changes.

Chapter Conclusion

Mobility encompasses both joint and soft tissue, and the consistency lies in being able to control end range and control and tolerate lengthening under load. Ensuring that both tissue and joints have synchrony in the way they dissociate creates the necessary pressure changes in the tissue to ensure proper fluid dynamics and overall tissue health. Limitations in mobility lead to dysfunction in a number of ways and is a reason to address and maintain the ability to be mobil*e*. This chapter discussed primarily what's required to improve end range capacities without diving into the specifics of controlling end range via isometrics and triplane movement. Part 9 will have more information on movement specifics and end range isometrics.

Additional Readings

- *The extracellular matrix at a glance*, Christian Frantz, Kathleen M. Stewart, Valerie M. Weaver; J Cell Sci 2010 123: 4195-4200; doi: 10.1242/jcs.023820

- https://functionalanatomyseminars.com/

- *Biotensegrity: The Structural Basis of Life;* Scarr, Graham

- *Movement;* Cook Gray

- https://kinstretch.com/pails-rails-good/

- *Peter Wright, Ian Drysdale, A comparison of post-isometric relaxation (PIR) and reciprocal inhibition (RI) muscle energy techniques applied to piriformis, International Journal of Osteopathic Medicine, Volume 11, Issue 4, 2008, Pages 158-159.*

- Lewit K, Simons DG. Myofascial pain: relief by post-isometric relaxation. Archives of Physical Medicine and Rehabilitation. 1984 Aug;65(8):452-456

- K.J. Pienta, D.S. Coffey, Cellular harmonic information transfer through a tissue tensegrity-matrix system, Medical Hypotheses, Volume 34, Issue 1,1991, Pages 88-95.

- *Chaitow, Leon; Maintaining Body, Balance, Flexibility &* Stability: A Practical Guide to the Prevention and Treatment of Musculoskeletal Pain and Dysfunction.

- Egeblad M, Rasch MG, Weaver VM. Dynamic interplay between the collagen scaffold and tumor evolution. *Curr Opin Cell Biol.* 2010;22(5):697-706. Doi:10.1016/j.ceb.2010.08.015

- Institute of Motion & Michol Dalcourt; https://instituteofmotion.com/

- Scott J. E. (2003). Elasticity in extracellular matrix 'shape modules' of tendon, cartilage, etc. A sliding proteoglycan-filament model. *J. Physiol.* 553, 335-343

PART 8: MUSCLE TESTING: APPLYING MOTOR CONTROL

Introduction:

The purpose of this chapter is to further understand aspects of motor control and how to apply these principles in practice. The first sections will lay out more information about motor control, followed by a section defining some key terms that are helpful. This will be followed by a discussion about how muscle testing as insight into the nervous system is a useful but limited tool. Specifically, how isolated tests can provide insights into the nervous system and how to apply these principles via strategies that help to specifically increase somatosensory representation, which is often the goal of rehabilitation.

As a young clinician, I envied the ability of experienced practitioners to test and retest. It wasn't something taught in school, and only through experience and clinical acumen has more specificity in assessments created more specific interventions. It was a natural process in getting there aided through the concept of trying to prove myself wrong rather than right, because self-bias is easy. Gary Gray teaches "if it is still there after trying to prove it's not, then it likely is". It's a concept continually returned to in an effort to recognize inherent self-bias. Gary also taught me to ask, "why am I doing *this* right now?", and if I'm honest, it's sometimes hard to satisfactorily answer (although I can more than I used to). However, trying to remain neutral and remove bias creates more effective interventions.

While this text doesn't get into specific assessments, the very nature of understanding anatomy, musculoskeletal or neuro, means the response can be checked, via the appropriate input and expectation of what should happen. When it an expected outcome doesn't occur, further investigation is likely warranted.

Why apply Motor Control:

It is well established that the primary and secondary somatosensory cortical regions possess a map like organization. Neuroscience demonstrates how important the brain is in maintaining an accurate and up to date inner map of the location of our muscles and joints in 3D and space, and how a faulty inner map can be detrimental for an individual, Dr. David Traster, DC, teaches every point on the body, along with each internal organ, and every point of space to the end of the fingertips, is mapped inside the brain. The ability to sense, move, and act, in the physical world arises from a rich network of flexible body maps distributed throughout the brain, which can grow, shrink, and morph, based on needs and repetitive actions.

It Is understood that immediately upon a pain experience the brain chemistry changes, and over time, results in less representation to the somatosensory cortex, or, what Lorimer Mosely and David Butler of the Neuro-Orthopedic-Institute (NOI) Group refer to as "smudging". This can also be thought of as diminished representation of "maps" of specific body regions.

The motor cortex receives instructions from the association cortex, cerebellum, and the basal ganglia, issues commands to the spinal cord, and are connected through various feedback loops for messages going up and down. The motor cortex operates at a lower part of the brain than the cerebral cortex and assists in how to carry out movements for a given strategy. Often times dysfunction arises when there is an aberrant afferent signal into the MCC, creating compensatory firing patterns, potentially causing facilitation and inhibition relationships. Current pain research illustrates that pain produces a cascade of events in the brain, including neurogenic inhibition. Neurogenic inhibition can be defined as the process in which activity in one nerve cell suppresses activity in another.

Clinically, I've often observed that those in long standing pain verbalize can't "find" or "connect" with the muscle and this potentially makes sense when understanding that pain decreases representation to the region. This also illustrates the necessity of creating somatosensory cortex representation in numerous ways, particularly to the inhibited region that demonstrates latencies.

Motor Control & Muscle Testing Terms & Definitions

Defining key concepts and terms will be helpful in ensuring a proper foundation in which to work. This is necessary because I have concluded movement professionals don't necessarily possess or learn from the same base of movement knowledge. Therefore, ensuring everyone is 'singing from the same hymnal' leads to preventable misunderstandings and furthering divisions about how to work with the body. Within a motor control paradigm, stretching and strengthening have different effects on the NS, just as slow, sustained pressure versus rapid vibration provide different input stimulus. Therefore, insight if a region is up or down regulated is important because it directs the course of treatment.

DEFINITIONS

Reciprocal inhibition – In the book *REAL Movement: Perspective on Integrated Motion & Motor Control*, reciprocal inhibition (Chapter 4), is described as: "a neuromuscular reflex, where an increased neural drive of a muscle or group of muscles reduces the neural activity of functional antagonists. It is not a simple function of "on or off", as postural dysfunction resulting in adaptive shortening and hypertonicity inhibits functional antagonists, such as an upregulated or facilitated piriformis that could potentially inhibit the psoas. The piriformis does not decrease the neural drive to the psoas completely, as it's possible to move and function, just less than optimally."

According to Physical Therapist, Vernon Brooks, in the article, "Motor Control How Posture and Movement are Governed": "strong reciprocal inhibition allows the limb to swing loose, that is, to be compliant. Joints are made more compliant before the onset of a planned movement. Weak reciprocal inhibition, in contrast, permits co-contraction of opposing muscles, which makes the joint stiff. The golfer holds his arms fairly stiffly during the hold before the swing, but they are compliant during the swing and then stiffen again before the impact. Therapists can increase or decrease unwanted actions through appropriate touch, pressure, or imposed postures. Repetition of these movements and understanding of what is wanted by the patient can help involve larger task systems and can thus build new, voluntary capabilities on the initial changes produced by the therapist".

A simplified example of reciprocal inhibition is the nervous system sending a message to a muscle to contract, creating tension in the opposing muscle on the other side of the joint, and inhibiting (decreasing the impulse from the motor neurons) in order for the joint to move. Sometimes, there are aberrant, afferent inputs, which results in altered efferent motor output.

Inhibited/Inhibition – According to the dictionary, relative to anatomy and biology, an inhibition can be defined as, "The act of inhibiting or the state of being inhibited. 2. Something that restrains, blocks, or suppresses. 3. Psychology, Conscious or unconscious restraint of a behavioral process, desire, or impulse."

From a neuromusculoskeletal standpoint, it means the timing and ability of the nervous system to engage the tissue is decreased, resulting in a delayed and often weakened muscle contraction. Please note that the term 'inhibited' does not mean that a muscle is not "working", or not connected to the system. Rather, the muscle demonstrates a latency, or decrease in the ability of the NS to 'find the muscle'. A normal functioning muscle should demonstrate a two to three second steady state ramp up, a steady state contraction at the top, and a steady ramp down. However, an inhibited muscle demonstrates a short quick ramp up, a short contraction ability, and the muscle will show no ramp down. Rather, it will 'fall off'. This can be felt during a muscle test as not having a 'neural grab'.

In his book *Applied Kinesiology*, Robert Frost defines inhibition as, "The blocking or holding back of one physiological process by another. In muscle function, when a muscle is active, it lowers the tone of (inhibits) its antagonist." It's also of use to note the Applied Kinesiology world refers to an inhibited muscle as a "weak" muscle, defined as, "one that cannot resist the pressure applied in muscle testing,'' despite that an inhibited muscle can be physiologically strong.

AUTHOR'S NOTE

I feel it important to mention the term "weak" as described in this type of muscle testing doesn't necessarily mean that the muscle is weak, as defined by most textbooks. I've found often that initially upon muscle testing, an inhibited (what's called weak) muscle can be strong, however, it demonstrates a latency, or difficulty in engaging the muscle in a timely and efficient manner. I do try my best to call it a delay in the timing rather than weak, but I do find myself on occasion referring to it as "weak", recognizing the importance of words and the ones we choose to use around our patients/clients.

"Inhibition of a neuron moves the membrane potential of the neuron away from its threshold potential and decreases the probability the neuron will produce a calcium ion potential. These same concepts can apply to neuron systems, recognizing that a neurological system involves input stimulus, a series of integration steps, and an output". Some examples of inhibitory strategies used by the nervous system include direct inhibition, feedforward inhibition, feedback inhibition, and disinhibition, to name a few.

Facilitated/Facilitation – Robert Frost in the book *Applied Kinesiology: A Training Manual and Reference Book of Basic Principles and Practices*, defines facilitation as "literally "aiding". When a muscle contracts, its synergists and stabilizers are automatically contracted (facilitated) at the same time. Relative to neurology, Merriam-Webster defines facilitation as "a) the lowering of the threshold for reflex conduction along a particular neural pathway especially from repeated use of that pathway; b) the increasing of the ease or intensity of a response by repeated stimulation" (*Merriam Webster Dictionary).* In other words, facilitated tissue tends to demonstrate an increased connection to the nervous system.

Often the terms 'upregulated', 'strong', and 'dialed up', are used to describe facilitation, and so a clear understanding about the intent and communication of the term to patients and colleagues is necessary in order to provide the correct narrative. Clinically, I've found the upregulated, or 'facilitated', region has the ability to dial down numerous regions, however, there tends to be a stronger connection with a specific muscle, therefore the trick becomes how to find it, however… it's beyond the scope of this text.

In general, most times (not all the time), short and tight tissue tends to be upregulated, while longer tissue under a constant tension will often be downregulated and is another reason to work on improving length tension relationships between joints and tissue. Recall that stretching and rubbing (especially parallel) provides a down regulatory moment, while engagement provides an upregulation moment. In order to create the most individualized program possible, it is necessary to have insight into tissue mobility, extensibility, and if a muscle can engage in a timely and efficient manner. In the book *Touch for Health: A Practical Guide to Natural Health with Acupressure Touch* by Drs. John and Matthew Thie, they describe, "For fluid, well-coordinated movement to occur, there must be a balanced coordinated, gradual relaxation of antagonists and agonists. The stimulation of agonists is called Facilitation, the relaxing of antagonists is called Inhibition. If we take this concept to whole body movements of fluidity, coordination and precision, it becomes obvious a great deal of communication through our proprioceptive networks and energy circuits is necessary" (p 293).

KEY POINT

From this view it is clear how the engagement threshold of a muscle is reduced when the region it is connected to demonstrates an increased firing threshold. Reduced thresholds feel like a delay or latency in muscle engagement. Remember, upregulated tissue must first be downregulated before providing stimulus to the inhibited region.

Therapy Localize – Dr. Robert Frost, author of *Applied Kinesiology: A Training Manual and Reference Book of Basic Principles and Practices,* defines therapy localization (TL) as, "The effect… upon a body area whose effect may be measured with muscle testing", which can be active or passive in nature. Active therapy localizations include active muscle stretching or engagement, while passive TL simply implies touch, or rubbing on a muscle. In *Applied Kinesiology* (AK), from a musculoskeletal perspective, TLs are used as an insight about if muscle 'A' might be 'connected' (for lack of a better term) to muscle 'B'. Said differently, the engagement ability of muscle A shouldn't change based on therapy localizing muscle B (and vice versa) and when it does, often means a relationship exists.

In Applied Kinesiology, a *passive therapy localization* (TL) is most often the testee's palm or finger placed upon the suspected dysfunctional area, muscle B, to see if muscle A changes, or 'flips', which means there is a potential relationship. An *Active Therapy Localization* is similar to a passive TL, except muscle B is actively engaged via a contraction or stretch rather than a simple hand placement. Regardless of active or passive, it's providing information about how firing one muscle affects the engagement ability of another muscle, and at this stage no direction of dysfunction has been specified. Therefore, when a strong goes weak or a weak goes strong, it only means they're potentially related. The question then becomes best guessing the up to downregulated relationship.

Why Muscle Testing is Useful.

Muscle testing can be understood when appreciating neurological pathways are often predictable and observed through muscle inhibition, or a diminished response to resist a modest pressure. This inhibited response could be a result of many different factors including internal chemistry, dehydration, or emotional issues, to name a few. There is innate subjectivity to this discipline, and trying to eliminate bias is necessary, recognizing that I can't/won't with everyone. Only combined with other, verifiable information should muscle testing be used, despite some utilizers of the discipline doing otherwise. The rules that are described here are not to be held as absolute truth, rather are guidelines that have worked for me, recognizing it isn't for all patients/clients. It is also important to note that professionally I do not muscle test everyone, because mindset and belief system come into play. This also highlights the importance of concurrently gaining objective information.

Recognizing muscles and glands are a direct representation of the nervous system (NS), muscle testing has provided insight/best guess about what's upregulated and/or downregulated in the NS. For most people, one would expect a specific group of muscle fibers to produce and maintain a consistent contraction when a perpendicular line of force is applied to the line of pull, described as a 'neural grab'. When a muscle test is performed appropriately, the neural grab should be virtually immediate, without needing to 'search' for the engagement. Therefore, when working in this mindset, testing both sides and multiple muscles above and below is important in order to gauge the overall ability of the person to sustain contractions. At this stage, at least in my head, the answer is yes or no, meaning there is or is not the described neural grab.

"The above mentioned 'neural grab' is the proper coordination of anticipatory postural adjustments (APAs), as set up in the corticoreticulospinal tract and act as postural control prior to any volitional movement. If these APAs are not appropriate, there will be a lag in the 'neural grab' and the muscle tests will feel 'spongy' compared to the contralateral side. It must be noted that these muscle tests are functional in nature, meaning the muscle may not exhibit gross weakness as seen in, for example, peripheral nerve injury, rather has the inability to 'lock-out' when being tested as other joints in the chain or contralaterally are able to."

AUTHOR'S NOTE

> *Regarding muscle testing, I recommend for anyone with the funds or opportunity to practice with a hand-held dynamometer (MicroFET) to know what 5, 10, and 15 pounds of pressure is, and how to ramp it up over two to three seconds. This will provide more consistency, and if also linked to objective information, can provide tremendous value.*

Inherently, this isn't a problem until it is a problem, as everyone has muscles that test 'weak in the clear' or even demonstrate a delayed timing to a region, yet it doesn't mean anything, except when it does. Simply demonstrating inhibitions doesn't mean anything, becoming relevant if there is pain or dysfunction. Correlating this to pain science, a painful region has reduced somatosensory cortex representation, in addition to aberrant firing patterns.

Nothing is absolute. It is all 'best guess' and therefore correlating results of a group of diagnostic tests helps shape the narrative and approach to intervention. There are many ways to try and make changes, and while there are numerous 'protocols' for muscle testing, it all flows from the same source, Applied Kinesiology. While muscle testing can become very in depth, it doesn't have to be, and as long as it is tied to the basics, there can be tremendous value to a muscle test. The key is to *anchor to consistencies*, which will be discussed in future parts, as muscle testing can test what efferent changes occur based on the afferent stimulus provided. In other words, observing how input changes (or up/down regulates), it can potentially change output and directs intervention. This information can help identify up and down regulated regions, as they typically go together, which leads to specificity in intervention. In addition, experience proves an upregulated tissue can down regulate numerous tissues, and there's likely to be one main connection. Pairing those muscles is possible and beyond the scope of this text, however, understanding motor control theories and the interaction with the nervous system helps to create the most individualized program possible. In my experience, most times a 'specific protocol' isn't necessary because simply finding a region to downregulate, understanding it is changing the afferent leads to an opportunity to drive intense input of whichever region/system needs more representation.

In other words, typically, there is a relationship between dialed up muscles/regions and numerous dialed down muscles, while most often there are numerous relationships between up/down regulated muscles. Most times, I simply try and find the (a) muscle that's dialed up and try and dial it down and then blast the region that has the most compromise in capacity with input, typically via isometric contractions with or without layering of other systems. Wherever the biggest observed deficit lies is where I try and drive input, recognizing pain is an output.

For example, someone with hip or low back pain, after assessing and filming gait (and possibly other movements), I first try and see where the biggest deficit is right to left and top to bottom. Things to assess include knee angle at heel strike, the amount of knee flexion from heel strike to foot flat, in addition to hip angles at specific phases of gait. This process is followed by assessing the system first globally, then locally, before again globally. In addition, as emphasized through AFS, it also holds true with neurological testing including beside neurological exams and muscle testing. After establishing up and down regulated regions, the idea is to try and balance the system by repeatedly and specifically blasting the system with safe, intense stimulus in order to help change the output. This also builds 'representation' to specific brain regions. In other words, after down regulating the upregulated region, the goal becomes to drive as much non-threatening somatosensory representation for the inhibited muscles. This is often initially done via isometric contractions performed at the threshold of the individual, which is a concept that will be discussed further in later parts.

In normally functioning muscles, when applying a perpendicular force to the angle muscle pull, that specific tissue should engage first and sustain a contraction for two to three seconds. However, often another muscle surrounding the region not perpendicular to the tissue engages first, indicating a potentially altered relationship, because the specific muscle tested (the one perpendicular to the line of force) would be expected to engage first. When a muscle not perpendicular to the muscle engages first, the relationships with that region should be further investigated.

Author's Note

One would expect a "neural grab", or the ability to sustain a contraction when a perpendicular line of force is applied to the line of pull of the muscle if performed correctly.

Under these circumstances, when a dialed up, or facilitated/upregulated muscle fires, it dials down the region it is related to for that pattern. Conversely, when an inhibited muscle fires, it improves the contraction ability of the muscle it is connected to, further lessening the inhibited muscle's ability to sustain a contraction and also perpetuating a cycle. These relationships will remain until the input is changed because I believe these dysfunctions are the result of aberrant afferent input. Therefore, from a neuromusculoskeletal view, if input can be altered, possibly by soft tissue mobilization, stretching, engaging, distracting, or compressing a muscle, then a window of opportunity to change the output is potentially created. In addition, recognizing one region can be dialed up for one pattern and dialed down for another, should be considered.

What are the limitations of muscle testing?

Despite the inherent bias and subjectivity of the discipline, muscle testing can provide a place to start, and provide insight (best guess) about if a region is, for lack of a better term, up or down regulated. It can also provide insight about if the work being done is working, and if treatment is heading in the right direction. Muscle testing is subjective because isolation can't reflect the true interconnected nature of the body, and to research anything requires isolation. I've also never seen anyone *exactly* fit a study, and so utilizing non-validated thought processes is acceptable so long as it is anchored to objectivity. However, this illustrates the importance of extrapolating information based on unifying principles that everyone can anchor to. Less research doesn't make it less valuable, it simply needs to be linked to unifying principles that are well established.

Obviously, muscle testing is an imprecise discipline, yet this doesn't mean it shouldn't be used. It simply means it should be used alone, highlighting the importance of anchoring to objectivity. Discussing specific protocols about how to find and tie a facilitated-inhibited relationship, is beyond the scope of this text, but there are numerous thought processes to do so. Instead, we will discuss what I feel is the least amount of information required to make the most and quickest impact, without getting too specific about any of it.

Muscle testing can provide insight to where to start, direction of treatment, and also what should be focused on during treatment. Dr. George Goodheart, founder of Applied Kinesiology emphasized the importance of "always measure independent objective measurements", because it is easy to test a test. Recognizing that muscle tests aren't very sensitive or specific, however if paired to an objective measurement, believe it provides insight to know where, when, and what to treat. Also, muscle and glands are direct representation of the NS and unlike the heart, stomach, or organs, which can survive outside the body and keep 'functioning' albeit a bit differently, muscles have no intrinsic nervous system. Therefore, muscles are a direct representation of the nervous system and so insight about if a region needs to be up or down regulated directs treatment.

Muscle testing can provide a starting point and direction of treatment, and simultaneously be a huge rabbit hole because it is subjective. In addition, it is easy to test the test, so is a lot of what's done in the movement profession, illustrating the importance of anchoring to objective information.

According to the Urban Dictionary (1), a rabbit hole can be defined as: a bizarre, confusing, or nonsensical situation or environment, typically one from which it is difficult to extricate oneself. Relative to muscle testing, it means that it is easy to find connections that may or may not matter to the whole and chasing these connections feeds into tester bias. There are numerous ways to affect the nervous system, therefore, ensuring interventions have the desired result is imperative, and muscle testing assists in this endeavor.

For those newer to the thought process, it becomes easy to select the first deficit identified, regardless if it is the primary driver of dysfunction. However, experience demonstrates this isn't always the best strategy because it can often be a large rabbit hole, and so being extremely sure it's correct is necessary (see above for proving yourself wrong). Another way to say that is, don't lose the indicator, or area being keyed in on until it is absolutely necessary, because once treated, things change. Rabbit holes are easy to get lost in, and therefore ensuring it is the best one is important, which necessitates a thorough assessment in order to make a best guess about the primary driver of dysfunction.

Other examples of rabbit holes include working only the site of pain or pairing an up/down regulation movement when not called for, which perpetuates their cycle. My general rule is if the patient/clients isn't improving in four sessions they're out the door and referred on to someone on my 'professional referral team'. Note, they don't need to BE better in four sessions, there simply needs to be change, and if not, something is being missed. It's also worthy to note that not everyone gets muscle tested, and it's not always a part of every session.

Author's Note

Be careful of using online 'groups' to talk specifics of any patient. This is another huge rabbit hole I observe, particularly around muscle testing and those that offer certifications. It contributes to dogma and discredits the individuality of the person and larger thought process of how muscle testing can be utilized. Only through applying principles everyone can anchor to can learning occur, rather than just throwing out possible suggestions that often are what I call 'unicorns'. These unicorns tend to be found on social media platforms in 'private groups' only for those that have taken "the" course.

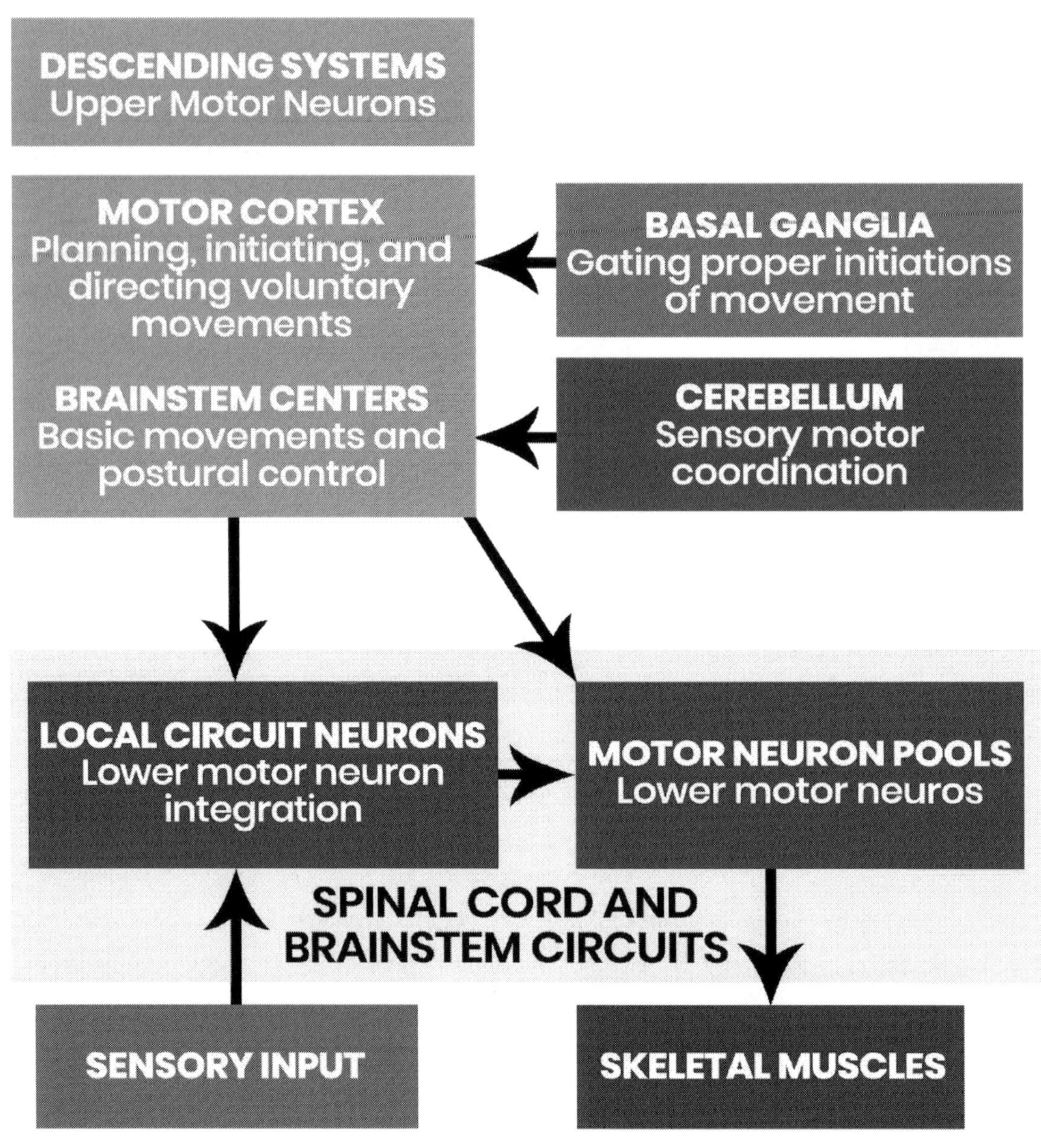

Muscles reflect the nervous system and understanding the process and pathways of sensory information up and motor information out is helpful for specificity of intervention. This picture demonstrates how sensory input affects muscle output. While a reduced output often may be present, this graph also illustrates that the reason for the diminished output can vary.

How Isolated tests can provide insight into the Nervous System.

The point of a muscle test is insight in order to find better direction and course of treatment and shouldn't be used in isolation. Early in my career, I never knew if the work was working or not, but muscle testing has provided better insight based on these principles. Muscle 'A' should demonstrate a 'neural grab' in fairly consistent and repeatable ways, and also not demonstrate a 'neural grab' in other tests, regardless of muscle 'B'. Sometimes muscle 'A' improves after stretch/rub/engage muscle 'B', and other times it's reduced. Both provide insight towards specific treatment.

At this point it is useful to see what changes when one muscle is fired 'against' another muscle, or what happens to one muscle's ability to engage immediately (within one to two seconds) after another is fired. I wouldn't expect the first to change based on another muscle firing immediately prior, and when there is, it's fair to say there's potentially a relationship between the two.

Key Point

Please note, while muscle testing can also provide insight into if a region is up/down regulated, that is not its purpose at this stage, and instead is being used to answer if there is or is not the described 'neural grab' of the tested muscle.

Research demonstrates that pain produces neurogenic inhibition. Therefore, if pain is an output, attempting to understand the possible relationships of how input can change output is helpful. Changing input is potentially an effective strategy to assist in getting out of pain and can be accomplished in numerous ways. In my opinion, if pain produces inhibition, there's value in trying to understand what is potentially creating an inhibition, because if something is inhibited something is inhibiting it. While answers are best guess, there's value in looking to see what changes when one muscle is tested against another. For example, if muscle 'A' fires (which has already been deemed less connected) followed by an immediate activation of muscle 'B', and then muscle A is again engaged, did muscle 'A' engage more or less efficiently? It is not expected to, and in these situations (which occur often), there's value in further exploration to find up<>down regulated relationships. This information is useful to allow more specificity in creating an individualized experience, because it guides the course of treatment and also what comes next.

When a perpendicular line of force is applied to a muscle, an immediate 'neural grab' would be expected, depending on the position of the tissue. For example, while standing, the right latissimus dorsi would be expected to demonstrate a neural grab when the left (opposite) foot is forward, and not demonstrate it when the right (same) foot is forward. This makes sense when gait is considered, where the right arm and left leg go through similar motions during gait, meaning when the left leg is swinging forward while walking, so the right arm tissue is loaded more. Based on positioning, the latissimus should be engaged more when opposite leg is forward and less engaged when the same side leg is forward. This is consistent with gait, and why, when in this position, a neural grab would be expected with a contralateral forward leg and not with an ipsilateral forward leg.

From an Applied Functional Science, motor control, and also capacities perspective, understanding what's not doing enough and what's doing too much is helpful. Applied Functional Science (AFS) teaches the site of the pain is not the cause of the pain, and if something isn't doing enough, something above or below is likely doing too much.
Therefore, when looking at 'joint' relationships, looking at the joints above and below before moving to two joints above and below can be a powerful strategy. Most times, the relationship between what's doing too much and what isn't doing enough lies one joint above or below, often even two joints above and below. Local relationships should attempt to be identified before global relationships.

The same is true from a motor control perspective, relative to what's dialed up and what's dialed down, and therefore asking the questions, "What combinations of tissue work together to control the painful motion?" From an up/down regulated perspective, starting within eighteen inches of the painful region, looking first at the same side of the joint before looking at the opposite side, a thought process of "testing muscles against each other" is applied, meaning what happens to one muscle "A" immediately after muscle B is up or down regulated?

A logical thought process allows for improved efficiency of treatment and having more tools in which to 'best guess' can be very helpful. The following thought process has helped me to assess and "best guess" a direction of intervention.

Muscle testing in relation to lines of tissue. After assessing WIC tissue:

What combinations of tissue work together to control the motion?

Step 1.

- **Attempting to find a relationship within 18" on same side of joint, then opposite if relationships can't be found.**

Step 2.

- **Assess a joint above and below on same side, followed by opposite side**

Step 3.

- **If unable to find connection, look toes to nose, same then opposite side**

Concepts of Upregulated and Downregulated: Neural Grabs, Neurogenic Inhibition, and What Changes?

As a general rule when muscle testing, if the answer is 'no', or the test is a 'fail' the first time, it can't yet be assumed that the tissue is inhibited. Because repeated engagement will either improve or reduce the 'neural grab'. Therefore, in step two (described above), I'm looking to see what is still a 'no' upon repeated testing, understanding there will likely be numerous dialed down muscles. Step two is utilized to see if repeated muscle testing improves or reduces the "neural grab" when repeatedly fired. That's it.

As a general rule, to 'dial up' one that is 'down', first the dialed up muscle needs to be dialed down in order to 'steal its juice' before 'redirecting the juice' towards another region/muscle, otherwise the relationship will likely remain. Said differently, dialing down a 'facilitated' muscle is necessary prior to dialing up an inhibited region. This opens a proverbial 'neurological window' or opportunity to dial up or upregulate an inhibited tissue.

Author's Note

The most effective strategy I have found to date to deal with an inhibited region is to drive intense isometric contractions at the individual threshold, with the trick being where to drive it. There are many times when I'm unable to find a connection or choose not to, and in these cases, look for where the biggest opportunity for improvement of control is and drive input there. I also look to see what fires first when muscle testing because this is often a clue about what the compensatory relationship includes.

Changing output requires input change, and the trick becomes to provide the input that has a desired effect on the output. Therefore, understanding what tissue is up or downregulated is helpful, but in itself is not enough to make a lasting output changes for many, especially when it is a chronic situation where more neuroplastic changes may be required. It is also relevant to have insight into what is creating the up or down regulation, recognizing that one upregulated tissue can downregulate numerous surrounding tissues. In addition, there are many relationships that likely exist and not all of them will be relevant.

Put another way, for 'neural grab' to improve, lowering the contraction threshold of the upregulated region needs to occur before increasing the contraction threshold of another. Downregulating can be accomplished by rubbing or stretching and should happen prior to 'turning the volume up' of the inhibited region via recruitment or engagement. When there's a relationship, experience dictates that dialing down has to occur before dialing up. If muscle ‘A’ changes after muscle ‘B’ fires, it means there’s a relationship to muscle ‘B’, because this isn’t expected. The question then becomes what is the direction of dysfunction, meaning what is potentially causing the inhibition.

This text won’t discuss specific protocols to ‘pair’ muscles and directions of dysfunctions, but please recognize there are many ways, all of which have numerous certifications of various lengths. The goal of this text is to provide enough basic information to quickly be successful integrating basic principles of motor control. A primary driver (behavioral) for me to write this book is because I didn’t have a centralized resource when introduced to the material. It isn’t designed to be a stand- alone resource, especially considering the difficulty in objectifying information. Rather, it should be seen as a guide with insight about blending motor control and integrated movement. I recognize the lack of research and the inherent subjectivity will disqualify its use for many, and I’m okay with that. However, testing a test is different than testing an objective independent measurement verifiable across disciplines, and is why A-B-A can provide a useful starting point about where to start. Another way to say it is, A-B-A is consistent with trying to prove yourself wrong. It makes sense to me to have insight about the function of muscles around a painful region (and beyond), and if something is not ideally connected or too connected. It also allows for an effective test and retest strategy to have the best insight towards specific treatment.

Strategies to Gain Insight about the Nervous System.

Up to this point, we’ve discussed why I believe muscle testing can be a valuable strategy to gain insight into the nervous system. I have mentioned it is easy to test a test instead of linking a test to an objective measurement, which is what I feel most protocols I’ve come across tend to do. Dr. Traster illustrates the importance of utilizing muscle testing as a place to start, and with this in mind, feel that providing a thought process as to HOW to do this is beneficial.

When muscle testing, there are three general rules on which to focus.

1. Know your anatomy.

   When I began learning this information, I had trouble reconciling when I’d test a muscle when I didn’t believe in isolation to begin with. I have since reconciled that, realizing I’m really testing the nervous system and specific parts of the brain’s ability to connect with specific tissue. Therefore, knowledge of specificity of tissue ‘anatomy’ is important.

2. Apply a perpendicular line of force to the angle of pull of the muscle.

This is necessary to identify the specificity of particular regions of the brain to engage efficiently and will assist in the quest to understand the capabilities of the tissue.

3. Don't attach to the outcome of the test. It's just a test.

Recognize you're simply trying to assess what changes when another region fire first. It is very easy to influence and bias the outcome of the test, which is the reason to remove attachments from it and attempt to be as consistent as possible.

A-B-A Muscle Testing: Testing Muscles Against Each Other

A-B-A Muscle Testing Procedure

I learned the concepts of A-B-A muscle testing from Jocelyn Oliver, a massage therapist and developer of Neuromuscular Reprogramming (NMR). It's a simple way to identify potential relationships between muscles and is used to identify which muscle is dialed up and which is dialed down, recognizing there are many relationships that exist. The idea is to test two muscles a total of three times, looking to see if 'A' changes on the second test, before testing B-A-B, to see if muscle 'B' changes the second time. This information can help in figuring out the dialed up and dialed down muscles, directing the course of treatment, and in assigning a homeworkable program.

In essence, A-B-A helps narrow and differentiate the dialed up and dialed down muscles, as the expectation is the muscles shouldn't flip based on the activity of another muscle. Most times before utilizing an A-B-A strategy, understanding the combination of tissue/muscle/joints that work together to control the painful motion is helpful before muscle testing those muscles, taking note of the WIC muscles. A weak-in-the-clear muscle can be either dialed up or dialed down. An A-B-A thought process helps identify what muscles have desired (or not desired) relationships.

To test A-B-A

1. Find weak-in-clear muscles and make an educated guess regarding the "'weakest'* (it's not really weak), identified as muscle 'A'
2. Using muscle 'A':

   Muscle test 'A' to 'engage'

   Engage muscle 'B' (the one potentially related to muscle 'A')

   Retest muscle 'A'

   Did muscle 'A' neural grab improve or reduce?

Reverse Step 2, or B-A-B the muscle test

Engage muscle 'B'

Engage muscle 'A'

Retest muscle 'B'

Did muscle B neural grab improve or reduce?

Generally speaking, if muscle A demonstrates an improved neural grab the second time, it's upregulated, and if the neural grab stays or reduces the second time, it is inhibited, and vice versa. The term I heard from colleague, Thomas Wells, is whatever gets strong or stays strong is upregulated and whatever gets weak or stays weak is downregulated, recognizing it's not a true weakness or strength, rather the ability to engage efficiently and timely.

It is common to see people with a longstanding painful posterior hip that at some point has been intervened upon by another practitioner with no real difference. Often the intervention involves a 'piriformis' stretch (or fill in the stretch and body part), which may provide some temporarily relief, but ultimately never changes the sensation. What's typically not considered is if the tissue even needs to be stretched, the potential down regulative effects of many stretches, or if the tissue being stretched is upregulated or downregulated. In other words, identifying if tissue requires increased or decreased connection should guide intervention, otherwise it's not the best guess about intervention. Understanding the connection to the nervous system of specific tissue directs treatment and eliminates as much guesswork as possible.

As a general example regarding someone with posterior hip pain; upon muscle testing, the following muscles demonstrate a 'weak-in-the-clear (WIC)' test upon the first round of testing:

- Gluteus maximus
- Gluteus minimus
- Hamstring
- Piriformis
- Opposite side QL
- Same side QL

Recall just because a muscle is WIC, doesn't mean it's necessarily dialed down (inhibited) because a muscle that's 'too' connected will test WIC until it's engaged repeatedly, at which point the 'grab' will improve. The most efficient way to gauge if a muscle is up or downregulated is to simply engage the muscle repeatedly, as it will either improve or lose the ability to sustain a contraction. Most times, an upregulated region will improve its ability, while a downregulated region will lose its ability to sustain a contraction. This fits into the paradigm of 'what gets strong, stays strong is facilitated, and what gets weak, stays weak is inhibited'.

Author's Note

Performing the same exercise/movement for more than two to three weeks means something is missing and it's not integrating. In these instances, referencing the fundamentals of intervention to ensure pain and higher level integration (cerebellar and vestibular) is recommended. Assuming higher level integration is cleared, and it is deemed a neuromusculoskeletal issue, A-B-A can be of benefit to find the best course of treatment, and if still not improving to the desired degree (which for me is four sessions), referring to another medical professional is recommended.

Based on the five muscles listed above, a situation where a dysfunctional relationship exists is possible because they all synergistically work to control the first gait phase.

Referencing the example above about the person with high hamstring pain who has been told to stretch her/his hamstrings:

Pick two WIC muscles and practice the A-B-A concept, with the idea of first figuring out what is the most 'dialed up' and linking it to potentially what is the most 'dialed down'.

For example, of the five listed:

Hamstring & deep external rotators (ER)
Hamstring & gluteus medius
Hamstring & gluteus maximus
Hamstring & opposite quadradus lumborum (QL)

Choose:

Hamstring (A) & deep ER (B)

- Both WIC
- Hamstring (W) >> deep ER (W) >>hamstring (S)
- ER (W), hamstring (S), ER (W)

This example demonstrates that the hamstring is dialed up (facilitated) and the deep ER is dialed down (inhibited)

  - With this relationship, every time the deep ER fires the hamstring fires up, and when the hamstring fires it dials deep ER muscles down.
  - One potential correction could be to first dial down the upregulated tissue before dialing up the down regulated tissue.
    - This could be accomplished by stretching or rubbing the high hamstring followed by engaging the deep ER glute complex, initially via an isometric contraction.

The important thing is to drive input to the somatosensory cortex to the inhibited region, which likely has less representation in the brain because it's painful and the changes associated with it that result in 'cortical smudging'.

Hamstring (A)& opposite QL (B)

Both WIC

Hamstring (W) >>opposite QL (W)>> hamstring (W)

Opposite QL(W) >> Hamstring (W) >> Opposite QL (W)

No relationship because nothing 'flipped'.

Clinical Note

When someone has deep ER pain, I ask myself, "why is the gluteus complex not controlling the transverse plane?" With hamstring pain, "why the gluteus complex isn't controlling the frontal plane?" Either way, it's often gluteus complex dysfunction and something to address, recognizing that creating somatosensory representation to this region is important, especially for chronic pain. I would also ask the question, "what is the foot and hip doing during the painful motion?" before checking both regions.

Conclusion

Simply put, understanding the general concepts of motor control, muscle testing can provide direction of treatment/intervention. It also can help to explain why two people who present with the exact same pain and dysfunction can respond exactly opposite to treatment, which has undoubtedly happened to all of us. The very terms motor control and muscle testing provide a huge amount of information from which to draw. This chapter has been my best practices working with people to improve their movement and function. It is designed as a jumping off point, recognizing that these are general rules, all of which can be 'broken' under specific circumstances. However, when used appropriately, patients/clients can quickly feel a difference that can help create buy-in.

Additional Readings List

- Thie, John F., Thie Matthew; Touch for Health: A Practical Guide to Natural Health with Acupressure Touch
- Frost, Robert; Applied Kinesiology: A Training Manual and Reference Book of Basic Principles and Practices
- Beck, Randy; Functional Neurology for Practitioners of Manual Therapy
- Chronic Pain: Lost Inhibition; Luke A. Henderson, Chris C. Peck, Esben T. Petersen, Caroline D. Rae, Andrew M. Youssef, Jenna M. Reeves, Sophie L. Wilcox, Rahena Akhter, Greg M. Murray, Sylvia M. Gustin, Journal of Neuroscience 24 April 2013, 33 (17) 7574-7582; DOI: 0.1523/JNEUROSCI.0174-13.2013
- https://neuromuscular-reprogramming.com/
- https://dna-assessment.com/

Part 9: Movement and Functional Integration

Introduction:

This purpose of this part is to further highlight some logical progressions to improve overall capacities. It is arranged bottom up, starting with the feet, before progressing to the costo-pelvic complex, shoulder complex, cervical spine, and higher level 'brain-based' applications. Each section describes various movements with suggestions of progressions that follow the along the isolated<>integrated spectrum and by no means is intended as a complete list. Rather, this is a starting point in order to progress and regress through logical thought processes.

A logical thought process includes identifying decreased capacities along with strategies to improve the ability to maintain a position through motion. This spectrum works at individual thresholds, which always fluctuate and loosely have four progressions in order to provide regression and progression methods. At one end is isolation, and at the other is integration, with two steps in the middle that create various ways to isometrically and/or dynamically create efficient and effective movement. Many of the movements utilize an isometric hold in some way, which is a safe and quick way to create neuroplastic changes. Isometric holds can take on various forms as seen in the suggestions above.

1. Isolated-Isolation
    - Defined as one muscle and joint, working in one dimension, with or without an isometric hold of the rest of the body. This can best be thought of as most often what tradition teaches as 'muscle action' in isolation.

2. Isolated-Integration
    - Defined as one or more muscles and joints working together in one plane of motion while the other two planes stabilize and perform a concentric/shortening action first. Isolated integration is what tradition teaches as an isolated muscle action while moving or standing, such as a lateral banded walk.

3. Isolated-Integration
    - Defined as muscles and joints surrounding a region to be positioned in 3D isometrics holds, with a drive from above or below.

4. Integrated-Integration
    - Defined as all tissue and joints of the TZ working together in 3D to control a specific motion.

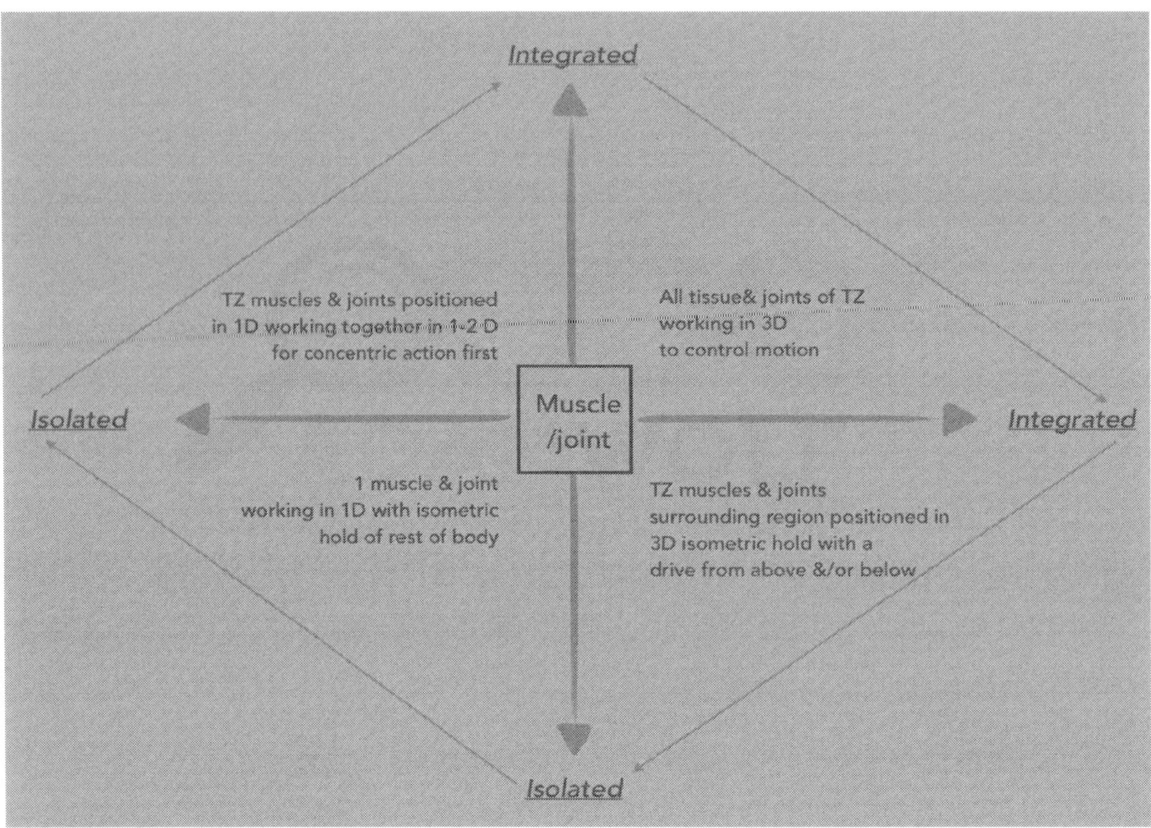

The Integration<>isolation spectrum demonstrates where, on the movement spectrum, one should start to move/intervene. It is based on being at a threshold and is based on logical progressions. Moving from isolated-isolation on the bottom left, the top left reflects qualities of isolated-integration. The bottom right of the graph demonstrates integrated-isolation, while the top right of the graph shows integrated-integration. The recommendation is to ensure one section can be mastered prior to progressing.

The Foot & Leg

When working with someone who has foot pain, it is important to consider the strength of the intrinsic muscles in the foot. Often times people with foot pain have weak intrinsics, as pointed out in the book *Human Locomotion*, where Tom Michaud states, "The role of the flexor digitorum brevis in force transmission is clinically evidenced by the fact that calcaneal heel spurs form at the origin of this muscle not the origin of the plantar fascia. By increasing tone in response to stress, the flexor digitorum brevis may behave as a variable length spring that functions as a secondary restraint to vertical lowering of the arch" (Chapter 3, Page 108). He also refers to a strength increase of intrinsic muscles coinciding with an improved ability to produce more pressure beneath the tips of the toes when ambulating. More importantly, "Reduced pressure beneath the toes produced a corresponding increase in pressure beneath the metatarsal heads, resulting in large bending strains being placed on the metatarsal shafts. A primary role of the digital flexors is to create a compressive force along the plantar metatarsal shafts that counteracts the bending moments associated with propulsion. ...Fatigue of these muscles would result in elevated metatarsal shaft bending moments, predisposing to stress reactions" (Chapter 3, P. 112). This is relevant particularly when working with a foot pain population because it is commonly seen.

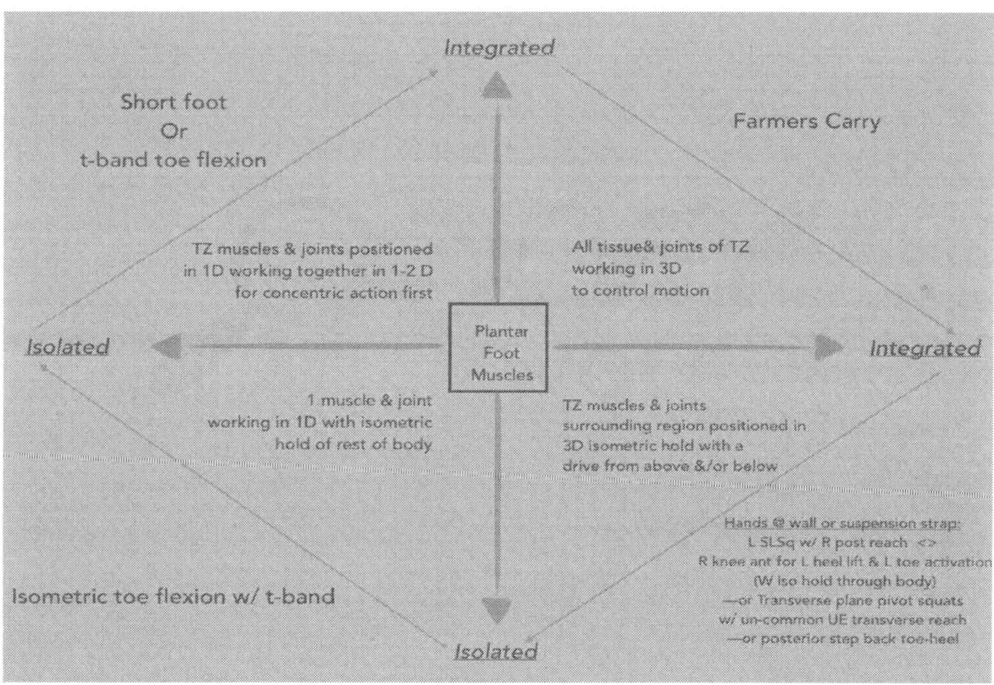

Integrated<>Isolated spectrum for the plantar foot

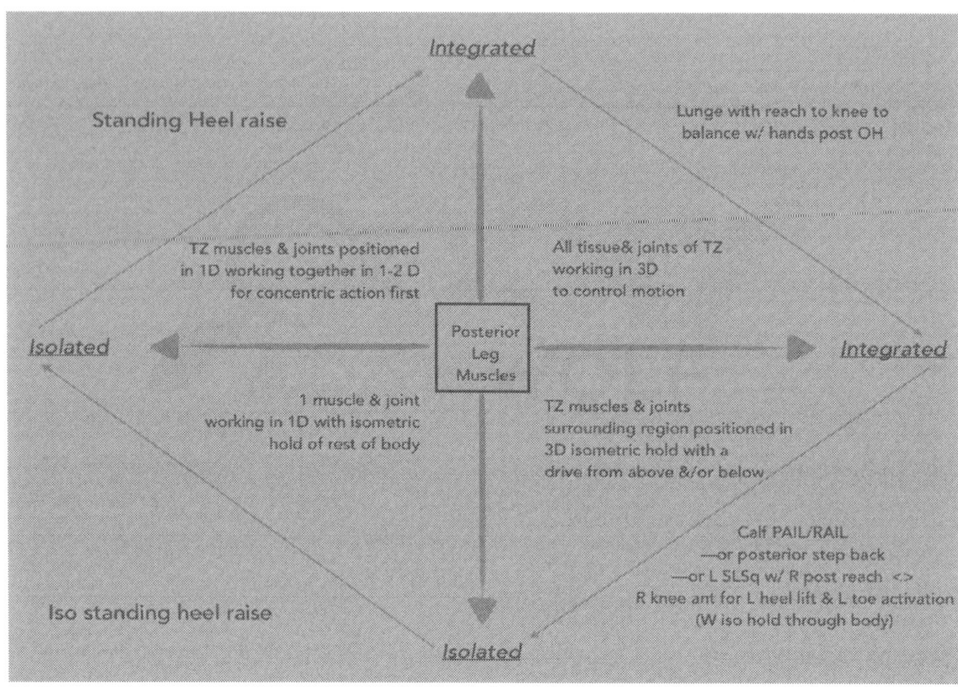

Integrated<>Isolated spectrum for Posterior Leg

Michaud does a fantastic job of describing the role and importance of foot intrinsics in great detail, including the tibialis posterior, which "functions during early stance phase as the body's most important decelerator of subtalar pronation. ...the long digital flexors play important roles during terminal midstance, as they assist with heel lift by decelerating the forward momentum of the proximal tibia. The digital flexors continue contracting throughout most of the propulsive period, forcefully maintaining the digits against the ground and assisting with supinating the foot about its oblique midtarsal joint axis (Chap 3, P. 122)."

Interestingly, the flexor digitorum brevis functions with flexor digitorum longus to compress the metatarsophalangeal joints of the second through fifth rays and allows the lesser digits to maintain effective ground contact during propulsive period. "Because it lessens the velocity in which the toes dorsiflex during the propulsive period, flexor digitorum brevis protects the plantar fascia from high tensile strains by activating as a muscular synergist to the plantar fascia. (Chap 3, P 123). In other words, the strength of these muscles plays a crucial role in offloading the metatarsal heads and redistributing forces through the shafts of the bones and also soft tissue. More importantly, decreased strength often results in foot pain, secondary to overuse, overwork to compensation.

The posterior leg tissue, including the gastrocnemius and soleus work throughout stance phase primarily as a decelerator and stabilizer, although both muscles demonstrate peak activity during terminal midstance, when they function to produce heel lift. Michaud states, "During contact period, soleus decelerates internal rotation of the tibia while gastrocnemius decelerates internal rotation of the femur. ...Soleus continues to contract throughout midstance and into propulsion, when it assists with subtalar joint supination and external femoral rotation."

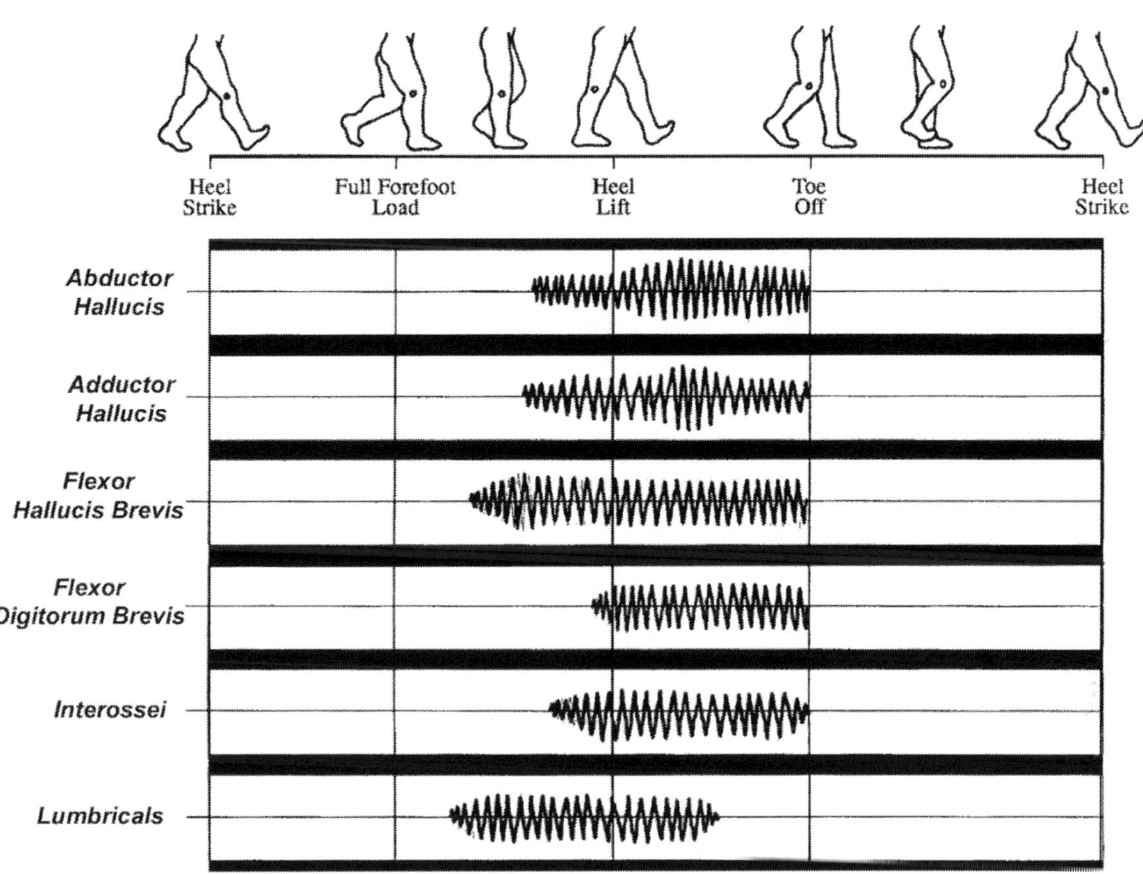

The long digital flexors play important roles during terminal midstance, as they assist with heel lift by decelerating the forward momentum of the proximal tibia. These graphs are courtesy of Tom Michaud and found in Human Locomotion, 3.53 A and 3.53 C.

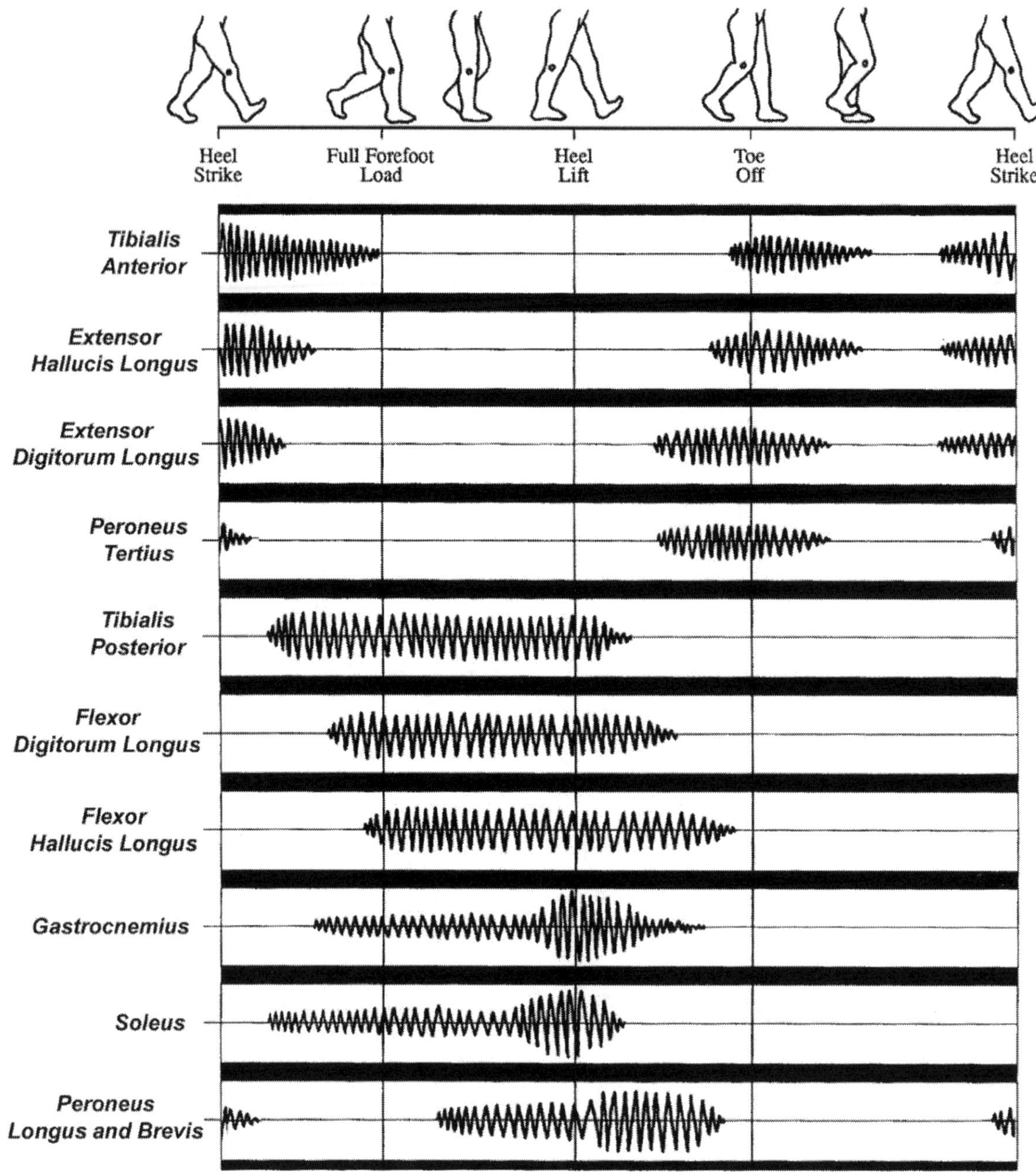

These muscles also assist in hip extension and allowing the body above the stance limb to translate further and faster than what's below, allowing the sequential dissociation necessary for the relative motion. In addition, weakness in the intrinsic muscles of the foot often lead to overuse in the posterior tissue including Achilles tendonitis.

Author's Note

Tom Michaud has some fantastic products both to help improve and stabilize motion and also to objectify the information gathered. I use his products, specifically the toe pro and dynamometer, on a daily basis. Be sure to check out his website: humanlocomotion.org and enter the discount code WOLF20 for 20% discount on his products.

The following represents suggestions of ways to begin to strengthen the intrinsic foot and leg muscles, recognizing they are starting points rather than destinations. They should be regressed, progressed, and tweaked appropriately, based on the threshold of the individual.

1 Isolated-Isolation can best be defined as one muscle and joint, working in one dimension, with or without an isometric hold of the rest of the body. This can best be thought of as most often what tradition teaches as 'muscle action' in isolation.

- Often the first strengthening exercise prescribed is isometric toe flexion exercises, with or without a band. Typically, these are performed beginning with the foot in neutral, although different positions are acceptable. Adding a band offers progressive resistance, and the emphasis of these movements should be flexion of the distal and proximal interphalangeal joints instead of extension at the distal interphalangeal joint.
    - The holds vary anywhere from five seconds x 10 reps to 60 seconds x one rep, depending on the thresholds of the individual.
    - The following are descriptions for individual toe exercises via an external load, however in clinic, I would also ensure patients move the toes independently without a band.
        - Toe intrinsic strength w/ t band

- Place theraband under foot, wrapping either the first toe, or toes two through five
- Tension band with toe(s) passively taken into extension
- Pull toes down towards floor, using proximal interphalangeal joint(s)
    - A common compensation is to extend the distal interphalangeal joints with flexion of the proximal interphalangeal joints
- One to three sets, 10-20 reps, emphasizing form rather than numbers
    - Regressions include
    - extending all toes at once, and placing toes 2-5 down (either together or 5,4,3,2),

- keeping the first toe extended
- Progressions include standing and loading the toes with t band & also winding up for to authentic positioning for toe off or foot flat.
- One to three sets, 10-20 reps, emphasizing form rather than numbers

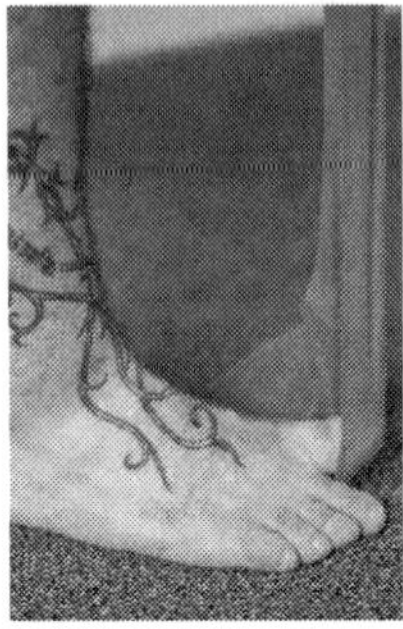 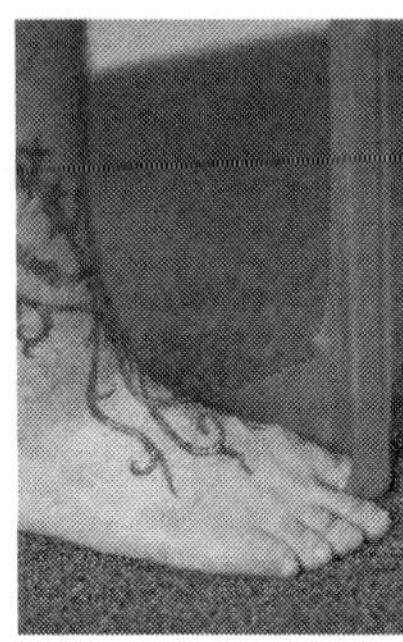 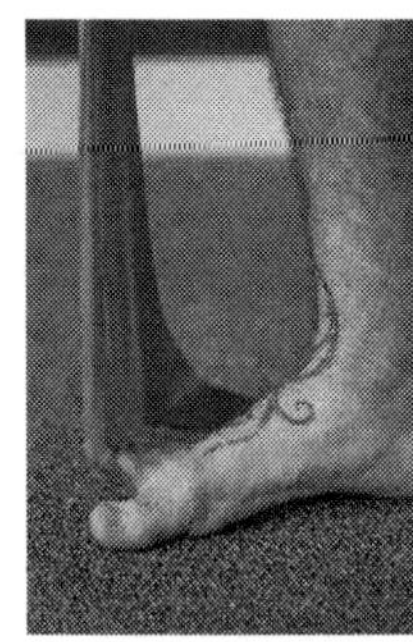 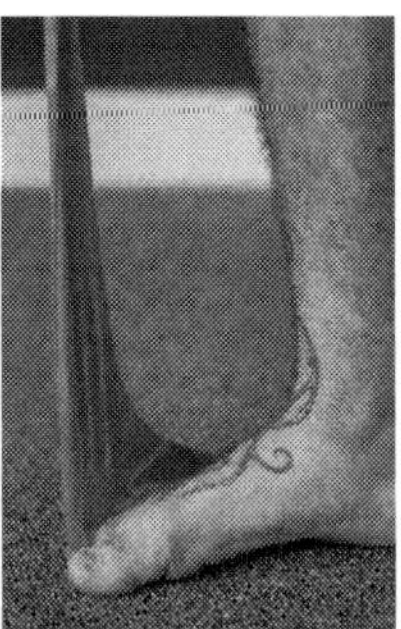

- Educating the person with foot pain, and particularly metatarsal pain, to dig the tips of the toes into the ground when standing and walking can help to lessen the stress in the metatarsal heads and distribute the forces throughout the foot in a more symmetrical fashion.

2. Isolated-Integration can be defined as one or more muscles and joints working together in one plane of motion while working together in one or two planes and performing a concentric/shortening action first.

The short foot exercise, popularized by Dynamic Neuromuscular Stabilization (DNS), is a great movement to incorporate into a routine designed to improve foot function, intrinsic strength and awareness of the foot. It's a good movement for people who also need to improve their positional awareness, or said differently, one place to start to improve posture. The movement can be taken from static through a dynamic spectrum and tailored to the individual relative to variations within the movement.

- The following are basic steps for performing a short foot exercise:
  - **Step 1:** Sit in a chair with both feet placed flat on the floor
  - **Step 2:** Raise the foot arch by sliding the big toe toward the heel without curling the toes heel lifting.
  - **Step 3:** Hold the position for six seconds then relax and repeat for the recommended number of set and repetitions. Variations can be performed by moving the feet farther away, turning the foot inward or outward to challenge the muscles in different positions.

- **Step 4:** Once you feel comfortable, progress to performing while standing, and eventually from a single-leg standing position.

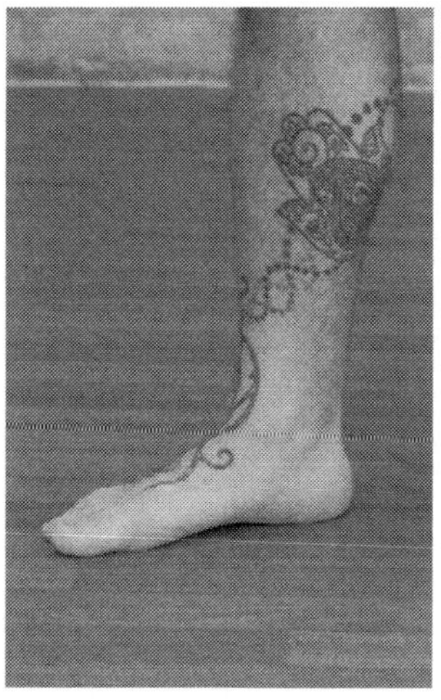 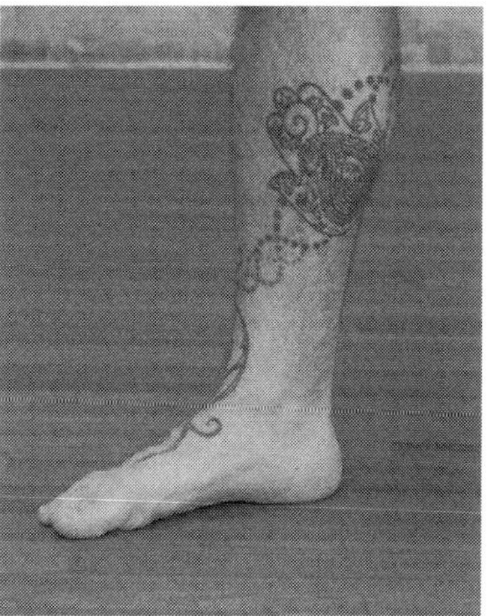

The short foot exercise can help to bring awareness to the bottom of the foot and assist in strengthening intrinsic foot muscles in a neutral position. The left picture is relaxed and the right foot has intrinsic engagement.

3. Isolated-Integration can best be defined as muscles and joints surrounding a region to be positioned in 3D isometrics holds, with a drive from above or below.
    - Integrated-isolated spectrum movements for the bottom of the foot are numerous, and the following are simply examples of different strategies, understanding everyone responds to different movement cues differently. These movements include variations on heel raises, squats, and lunges performed from different starting positions in order to mimic various foot positions.
        - Heel raised holds in different positions with various levels of stability are a great way to work the intrinsic muscles in an authentic position. It's important to think about the phase of gait that's trying to be improved because the specificity of the movement will change. The following will describe two examples of heel raised holds, one to mimic the front phase foot in gait and one to mimic back phase foot in gait.

1. Front foot. Aka the 'Elvis Presley Hold"

    a) Single Leg Stance with toe touch support (tts) with majority of weight over front foot or Single Leg Stance w/ Bilateral UE against wall

    - Knee flexed 20-30'
    - Hip flexed 20-30'
    - Long, aligned position

Emphasize front foot big toe pushing into ground

Raise heel
Hold for 30-60 seconds

Progress to 5-10 second holds with emphasis on smooth eccentric, descending with internal or external count

Internal counting emphasizes basal ganglia
External counting emphasizes cerebellum

Progress to one to two second repetitions for a total of 20.

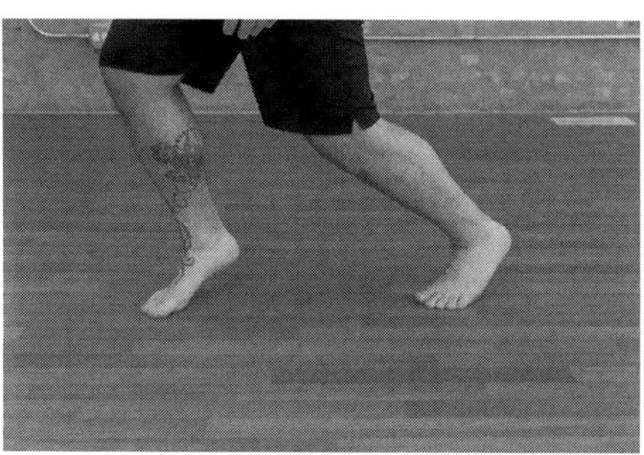

A heel raise, while mimicking the front foot in gait is one strategy to strengthen the muscles of the leg. Keep as much weight on the front foot as possible, and make sure the motion only comes from the talocrural joint, ensuring NO knee motion during the movement.

2. Back foot in gait

a) Hip & knee into extension emphasizing the back phase of gait

Hands against wall in long position, maintaining cervico-costo-pelvic relationship
Progressions include performing w/suspension straps & standing on blue airex
Plantarflex ankle, driving pelvis past shoulders

1. Hold for 30-60 seconds, progress as tolerated
2. Progress to five to ten second holds with emphasis on eccentric control
   a) Internal count emphasizes basal ganglia
   b) External emphasizes cerebellum

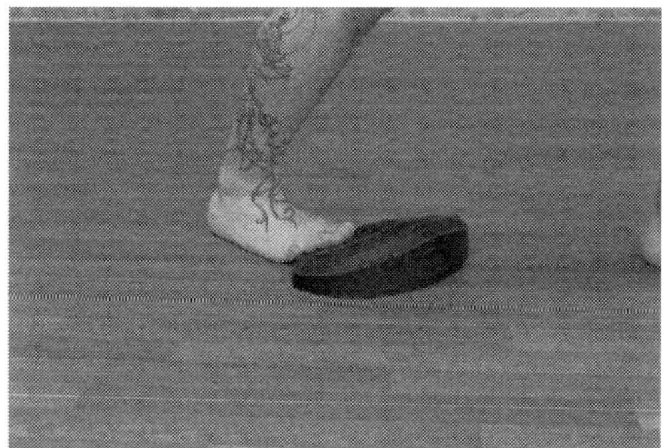

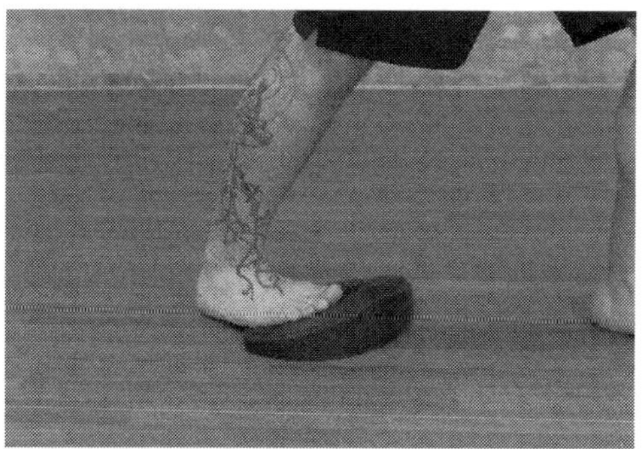

Toe intrinsic strength at the back phase of gait is necessary for proper mechanics and propulsion during the gait cycle. In the picture above, the Toe Pro is used to fully engage the flexor digitorum brevis (middle picture) and flexor digitorum longus (right picture)

Author's Note

This phase is often used as part of an active recovery phase, often coupled with cognitive and reactive drills.

Transverse Plane Pivot-Squat

The transverse plane pivot squat is a common lunge that is performed and taken straight into an uncommon lunge. When the left foot is the stance leg, it is considered a left pivot-squat.

a) The emphasis of the motion is to keep both heels on the ground

b) It can be performed with or without UE reaches and/or weighs

c) Verbal cues include drive your big toes into the ground

Left foot left rotational lunge with right hand reach towards left knee. This movement creates top down motion into the right foot/midfoot.

Left foot right rotational lunge with left hand reach in front of left knee. This movement creates top down motion into the right foot & hip that mimic the full 'wind up' of the tissue below the knee at the second phase of gait.

4. Integrated-integration.
    - Defined as all tissue and joints of the activity working together in 3D to control a specific motion. For the plantar surface of the foot, most often the activities to accomplish this include extra load to a movement in addition to dynamic balance activities.

Farmers Carry

1. This movement is great to load many regions of the body simultaneously. The simple act of lifting moderately heavy weight with the ability to maintain consistent relationships of the pelvis, scapular complex, and head results forces engagement of the intrinsic muscles in the feet.
2. A good movement to improve endurance, awareness of position in space.

A farmer's carry dynamically engages the entire musculoskeletal system and is a great way to incorporate leg and foot strength through the gait cycle. The weight should be heavy but able to be controlled.

Costo-Pelvic Relationship

The ability to maintain the relationship between the pelvis and the rib cage during movement is important, and those with difficulty maintaining this relationship through movement are at higher risk of pain vs. those who can maintain this relationship. This has been observed both in research and clinically in patients. Often people 'chunk' movements, meaning upon motion, interdependent motion occurs in separate regions. In other words, during movement, often times motion is coupled when it shouldn't have to be, such as spinal flexion with hip flexion, or thoraco-lumbar extension with shoulder flexion. In each case, the distal region should be able to move independently of the spine. Literature demonstrates those with back pain have significantly greater SI joint motion, and with greater individual difference than in healthy volunteers (Nagamoto et al 2015, Goode et al 2008). This means the SI joint moves too much because regions above and/or below aren't moving enough (hip or thoracic spine?).

In gait, the pelvis constantly rotates, reorienting itself against the changing demands of sustaining and controlling posture against changing gravitational and biomechanical context. The ability to control the pelvis, particularly in the frontal plane, is part of midline stability. Therefore, early interventions geared towards maintaining proper pelvic position through movement, with emphasis on awareness of controlled ranges in early interventions is warranted. People move around pain, not through it, and abnormal compensatory posture and movement have been strongly correlated in people with low back pain.

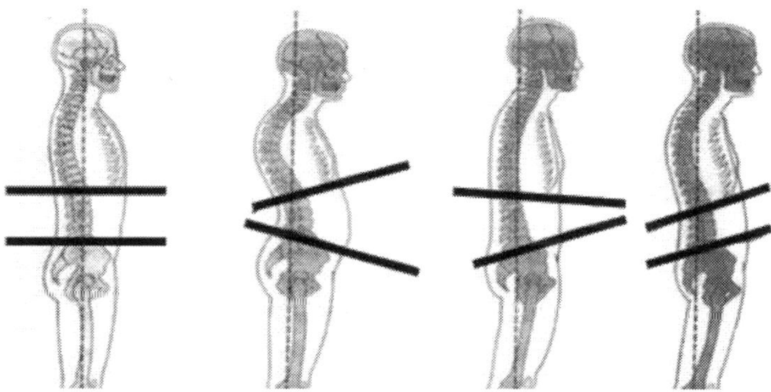

Proper costo-pelvic alignment through movement reduces shearing forces at joints above and below. The picture on the left reflects proper costo-pelvic alignment, while the other three demonstrate decreased alignment.

Lateral Gluteus Complex

The lateral gluteus complex is a key region of the body, requiring both strength and flexibility of the tissue surrounding the joint. "The Gluteus medius is the primary frontal plane stabilizer of the pelvis. It begins contracting during late swing and continues throughout midstance and into propulsion. Peak activity occurs during early midstance when this muscle vigorously contracts to prevent excessive lowering of the contralateral pelvis, which is entering its swing phase." (Michaud Ch 3 P120).

.The lateral hip muscles work in different capacities throughout the gait cycle, including when the foot hits the ground into midstance, controlling the pelvis primarily in the frontal plane. Inability to control the frontal plane results in greater shearing forces at the knee, hip joint, and low back joints. Proper lateral hip function is dependent upon correct foot function. If the foot doesn't do what it should when it should, neither will the hip.

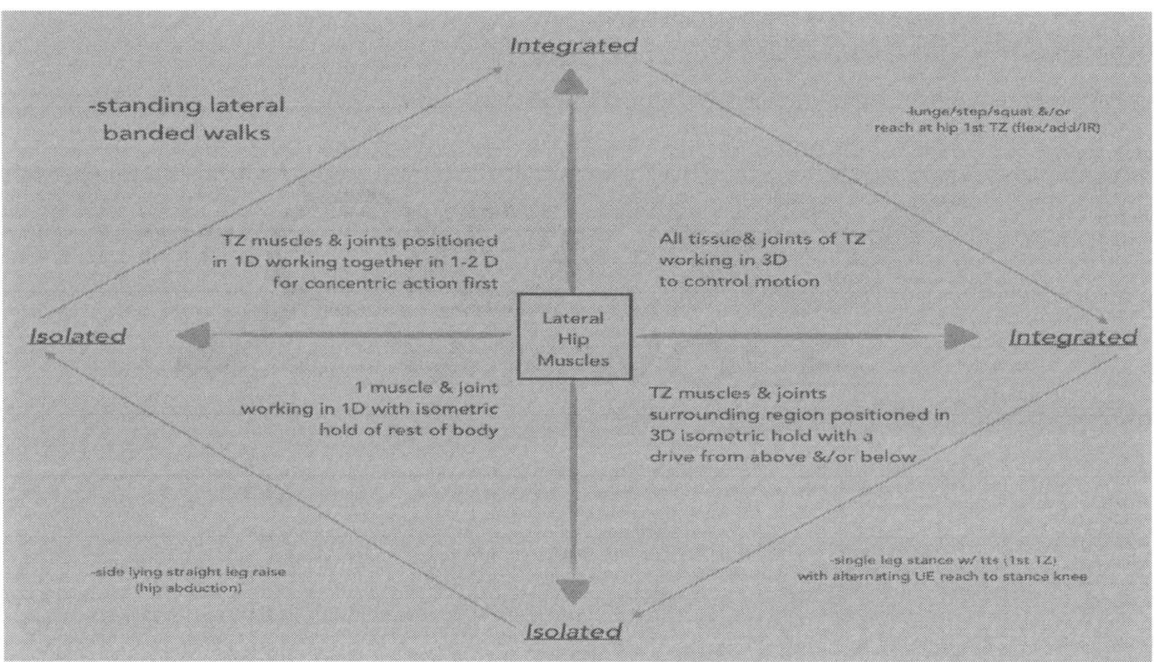

"The Gluteus medius is the primary frontal plane stabilizer of the pelvis. It begins contracting during late swing and continues throughout midstance and into propulsion. Peak activity occurs during early midstance when this muscle vigorously contracts to prevent excessive lowering of the contralateral pelvis, which is entering its swing phase." The picture and previous quote both come from Tom Michaud in Human Locomotion, Figure 3.53.

In the book *Human Locomotion*, Tom Michaud states, "Gluteus medius also plays a role in distributing pressure throughout the femoroacetabular joint during stance phase, functioning in a manner similar to the rotator cuff musculature of the glenohumeral joint," illustrating the importance of joint centration for optimal function. If the gluteus medius, along with other stabilizers of the pelvis and femur aren't able to control the motion, often the resting position of the femur isn't centrated, potentially contributing to impingement situations.

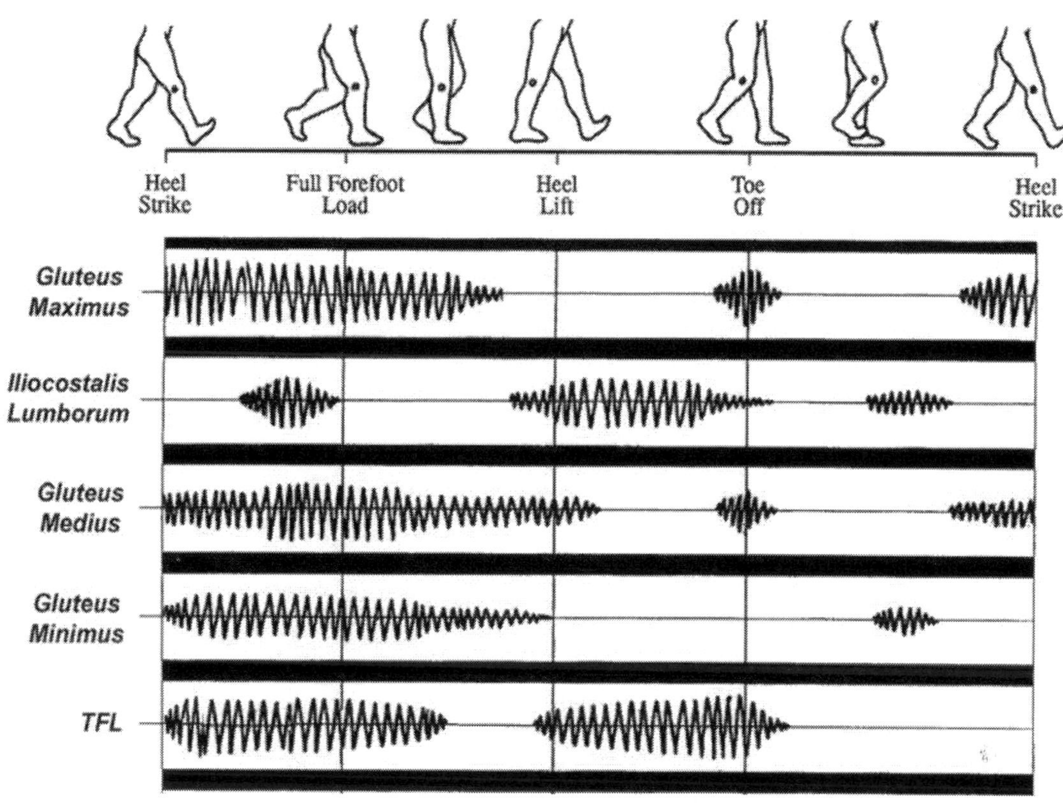

The following are suggestions that focus on the lateral hip:

1. Isolated Isolation
   - Defined as one muscle and joint, working in one dimension, with or without an isometric hold of the rest of the body. This can best be thought of as most often what tradition teaches as 'muscle action' in isolation.
     - Relative to the Gluteus Medius (GlMed), in isolation the GlMed is primarily considered a frontal plane 'hip abductor', while contributing to isolated hip external rotation. Two strategies to engage the GlMed in isolated isolation are a side lying 'clam' or side lying 'straight leg raise' (hip abduction). The ability to isometrically engage the other muscles around the hip joint allows more specificity and isolation to the particular tissue/joint being moved.
   - Sherrington's law of irradiation is applicable in these instances. It states that "a muscle working hard recruits the neighboring muscles, and if they are already part of the action, it amplifies their strength. The neural impulses emitted by the contracting muscle reach other muscles and 'turn them on' as an electric current starts a motor". It is a great way to, for lack of a better term, 'ramp up the nervous system', which simultaneously builds space in the brain to that specific region.

Isometrics are a safe way to drive input for the region into the somatosensory cortex. The lateral gluteus muscles are important to help stabilize the costo-pelvis in the frontal plane during gait.

2. Isolated Integration

   - Defined as one or more muscles & joints working together in one plane of motion while working together in one or two planes & performing a concentric/shortening action first. Relative to the hip, this can be a lateral banded walk.
   - For an understanding of the isolated integrated action, comprehension of fascial lines and continuities is beneficial. In the case of the GlMed, while associated with numerous fascial lines, is a primary component of the frontal line of fascia and joints. Some of the tissue includes the TFL, ITBand, peroneals, and Gluteus Maximus, quadratus lumborum (both or one, depending on the frontal plane movement0, the latissimus dorsi, deltoid muscles, and even scalenes. Joints working with the hip in the frontal plane include those in the foot, pelvis, lumbar, thoracic, cervical, and scapulothoracic regions.
   - Relative to the GlMed, isolated-Integrated strategies to tension and strengthen the line include frontal plane GlMed control, specifically the concentric phase, while simultaneously engaging the tissue above and below to stabilize the movement. In this instance, all of the joints above and below the hip/GM work in synergy to produce a concentric, or hip abduction moment, prior to the lengthening, with integration coming through the lateral line muscles that work together to produce an isometric hold to stabilize.

In isolated integration, the entire line of tissue, in this case the lateral line, work together in the shortening, or concentric action first. In the above pictures, start with feet wider and move wider while lateral walking 3-4 in one direction then the other.

3. Isolated Integration

- Defined as muscles and joints surrounding a region positioned in a 3D hold while driving motion into the region from above or below. Relative to the lateral hip, examples include a single leg stance with a reach, or an upper extremity warding pattern with a step or reach with the opposite leg. Note than in both examples the body is positioned at the TZ, or transformational zone, before motion is driven into the system from above and/or below.
- This strategy also incorporates static positioning, however different than integrated isolation. In this example, all the tissue/joints that control the first TZ, or loading phase of gait, would be placed into a static hold position. For the GlMed, a single leg stance with soft position of standing leg (knee bent up to 45', depending on threshold) with a toe touch of the opposite leg will accomplish this position. Contralateral toe touching can provide stability, because feeling stable and safe is a necessary component in early interventions to assist in changing output. Once placed into this position, options to drive motion into the GlMed/lateral hip are numerous, utilizing an arm or opposite leg driver.
- "It is also well described in fMRI studies that isometric contractions create the greatest amount of activity in the brain, followed by eccentric then concentric movements. Isometric holds through various positions of a joint range of motion can be greatly beneficial for joint by creating a better brain representation of each angle of position of that joint."

In integrated isolation, the lateral and posterior hip will be loaded in 3D and motion will be driven into the region via arm or opposite leg drivers. In the pictures above, the movement is started with right leg single leg stance with toe touch support (as needed) and bilateral hand reach in front of the right knee is performed in order to drive top-down motion.

4. Integrated Integration

- Defined as all tissue and joints of the TZ working together in 3D to control a specific motion. The GlMed experiences the triplane motion of flexion/adduction/internal rotation when the foot hits the ground with walking, running, jumping, lunging, up/down stairs, squatting, which is also known as the 1st Transformational Zone.
- Movements that create the GlMed working to control flexion/adduction/internal rotation include lunges, squats, and step ups, with or without an upper extremity reach. The key is to achieve as an authentic movement as possible, relative to the intended task, which requires top down and bottom up drives. Relative to gait, a simple strategy would be to choose a lunge, with upper extremity reach, that will create the motion, while also getting as many joints as possible above/below the hip concurrently feel what it should feel at the TZ.
    - For the left GlMed, a left leg anterior or lateral lunge (creating right pelvic rotation) with a left hand frontal plane reach opposite overhead (to side bend the torso away) and a left hand transverse plane reach left at shoulder height (which will create left torso rotation out of sync to the pelvis). These movement combinations mimic what happens in gait when the foot hits the ground (the 1st TZ) at the foot, hip & thoracic spine.

A same side lateral lunge with type 1 thoracic motion fully lengthens the lateral gluteus muscles in three planes of motion. Driving the thoracic spine into side bending left and rotating right (type 1 motion = side bend/rotate opposite) via arm reaches creates a top down drive into the lateral hip to fully 'wind it up'. Notice the two different ways to create type 1 thoracic motion, as the picture in the left has the right arm in the frontal plane and the left arm in the transverse plane, while the picture on the right has the right arm in the transverse plane and the left in the frontal.

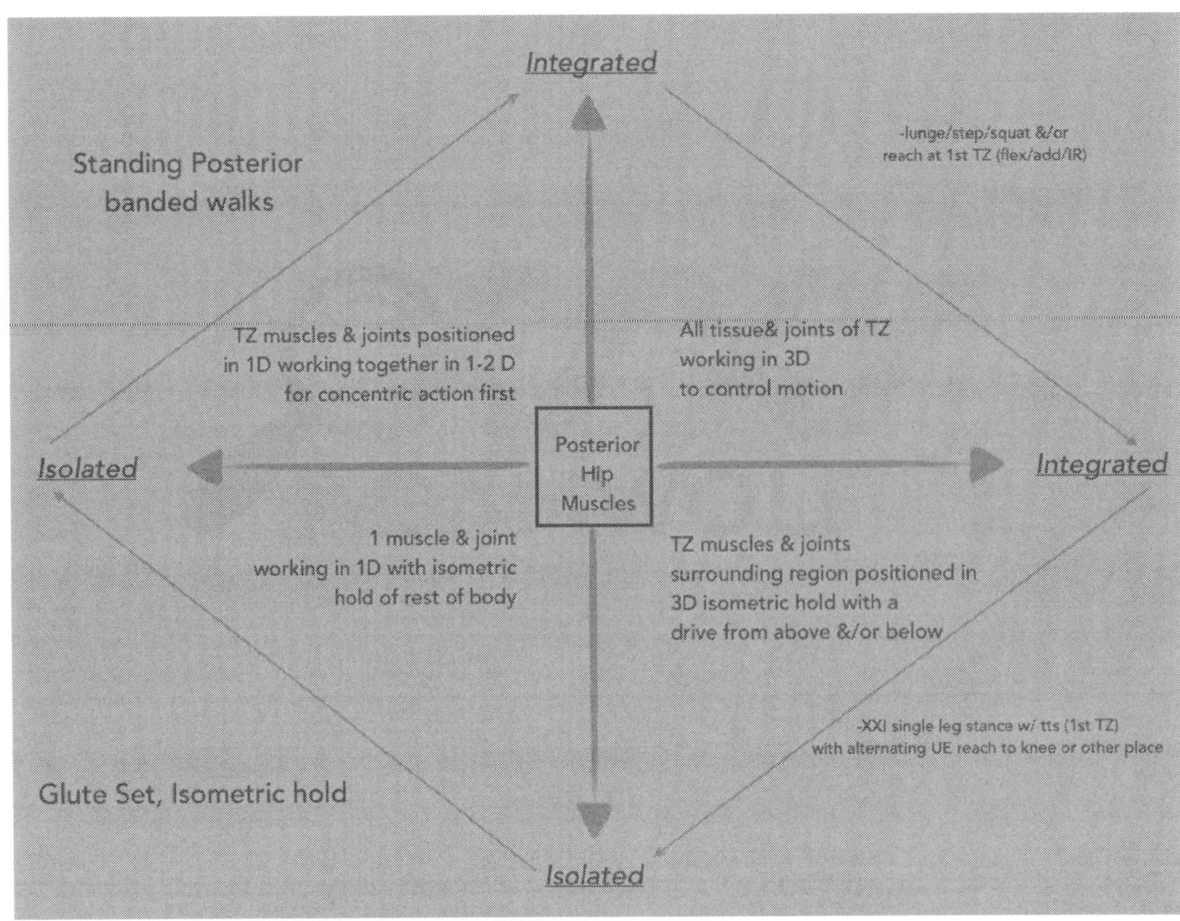

Isolated<>integrated spectrum for Posterior Hip musculature

Posterior Hip Musculature

The posterior hip muscles work in synergy with the lateral tissue to control and stabilize the pelvis during upright activities, however due to the fiber orientation, tends to control the transverse and sagittal planes more so than the lateral hip muscles, which control more frontal plane due to fiber orientation. Cadaveric studies confirm the gluteus maximus has the greatest capacity for controlling hip internal rotation, due to the orientation of the muscle fibers. Remember though, the differentiation between gluteus max, med, and min, is a manmade construct, comes from humans, and has to do more with fiber orientation. The body doesn't know a gluteus medius from a gluteus maximus, just slightly more posterior and transverse in orientation relative to the GlMed. Therefore, strategies for engaging the tissue are similar to the lateral hip, with variations consisting of positioning in and driving more sagittal and transverse plane instead of frontal.

In his book *Human Locomotion*, Tom Michaud states, "because it possesses significant lever arms for controlling transverse, sagittal, and frontal plane motion, the gluteus maximus and frontal plane motion, the gluteus maximus muscle very effectively dampens triplanar forces at the hip". Recall that when someone has deep posterior hip pain (often called "piriformis pain"), it is helpful to understand potential reasons why the glutes aren't controlling the transverse plane. With this in mind, driving transverse motion can be effective, noting that additional tweaks in the sagittal plane can create more or less gluteus maximus load depending on the threshold of the individual.

Michaud states, "Preece et al., demonstrate that this muscle places large external torques on the femur, ultimately leading to rapid deceleration of the tibia during early stance phase. ...the gluteus maximus plays a significant role in controlling transverse plane motions of the lower leg… during last stance phase of gait, the hip musculature plays a more important role in controlling rotation of the lower extremity than the foot and ankle." He continues with, "the largest portion of the gluteus maximus inserts into the posterior fibers of the iliotibial band, the gluteus maximus muscle provides significant stability to the hip and knee during contact and midstance". Clinically, this is relevant because ensuring the gluteus maximus has proper strength and function not only at contact phase, but throughout the gait cycle is important. *…(T)he gluteus maximus plays a significant role in controlling transverse plane motions of the lower leg and is primarily active during the gait cycle from just prior to heel strike through midstance.*

The following are suggestions for creating posterior hip load along the integrated<>isolated spectrum.

1. Isolated-Isolation can best be defined as one muscle and joint, working in one dimension, with or without an isometric hold of the rest of the body. This can best be thought of as most often what tradition teaches as 'muscle action' in isolation.
    - Relative to the Gluteus Maximus (Gmax), in isolation the Gmax is primarily considered a sagittal hip extensor, while also possessing numerous transverse plane fibers. While there are many strategies to engage the Gmax in isolated isolation, the most efficient is a glute-set or prone isolated hip extension.

A progression for isometrics for the gluteus maximus that mimic when it is active during the gait cycle include banded holds where the hip is flexed. A progression to this picture would be lifting the right foot towards the ceiling while keeping the knee where it is in space, creating a more internally rotated hip. It's important to coach to feel this in the gluteus muscles, and to alter the position if not.

2. Isolated-Integration can be defined as one or more muscles and joints working together in one plane of motion while working together in one or two planes and performing a concentric/shortening action first.
    - An isolated-integrated motion of the gluteus maximus includes banded posterior giant walks. In this instance, with an isometric contraction of the body, the glute max creates sagittal plane hip extension by swinging the limb posteriorly. In addition, the stance leg glute max is active from the moment the swing leg strikes the ground until just past midstance, as it stabilizes the pelvis in order to get the body up and over the stance leg foot in preparation to be swung posterior as the cycle repeats.

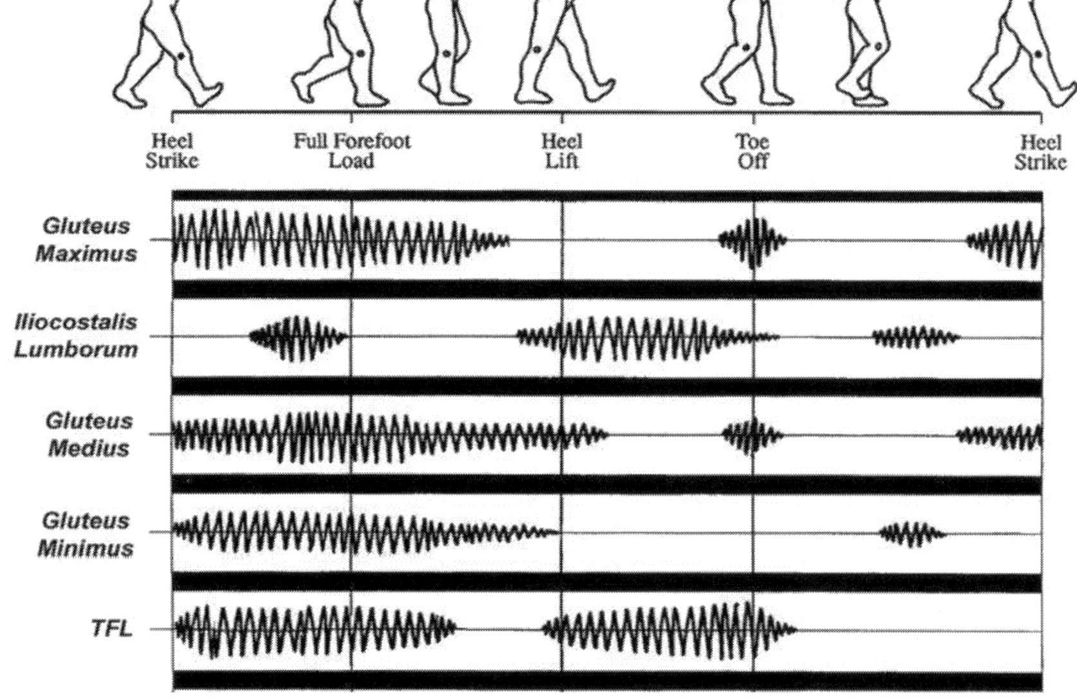

Banded posterior walks that include the posterior line and posterior X lines in the body.

- A second 'go-to', which is more advanced than above, but not quite dynamic enough to be considered Isolated-integrated is a 'prone ½ Controlled Articular Rotation (CAR).

This variation of a CAR helps to create glute complex activation through shortening motions.

1. Starting supine, resting head on hands, head facing right
2. Keeping shoulders and hips on ground through ENTIRE motion:
    a. Slide right foot and knee on ground, up to the right towards hip height, stopping when the right ASIS comes off the ground
    b. Lift right foot off the ground, towards ceiling (creating right hip internal rotation), making sure to stop when the spine moves or the right ASIS comes off the ground
    c. Isometrically engage entire body

3. Lift right knee off ground ONLY from right glute complex engagement
4. Squeeze the body, to isolate the motion to the right femur as much as possible
5. With right femur lifted, return to starting position,
    a. Release isometric engagement
    b. Repeat

Key Point

There are numerous potential compensations with this movement (see pictures), so coaching and ensuring the patient understands how to perform correctly is important. In addition, there are numerous progressions to this activity, including in quadruped or standing.

3. Isolated-Integration can best be defined as muscles and joints surrounding a region to be positioned in 3D isometrics holds, with a drive from above or below.
    - The most efficient way to engage the Gmax through isolated-integration is to position the lower extremity into a position that fully engages the triplane nature of the Gmax. While this can be performed in many ways, the easiest is:
        1. 1¼ stance, which is a single leg stance with a toe touch support
        2. Stance leg is toed in, for IR position of the lower extremity. Knee flexed at 30' isometric hold, hip flexed approximately 20', making sure to keep these positions.
        3. Alternating hand reach in sagittal plane to end range horizontal distance to thigh/knee/hip, emphasizing control of motion

Key Concept

This motion is positioning a body part and driving motion into it while engaging an isometric hold and contraction of the rest of the system. The alternating hand drivers should be as far forward and towards the ground as can be controlled, emphasizing the need to maintain the positions of the stance leg and the costo-pelvic and cervical relationships.

4. Integrated-integration. Can be defined as all tissue and joints of the TZ working together in 3D to control a specific motion.
    - Regarding the Gmax during gait, when the foot hits the ground with walking, running, jumping, lunging, up/down stairs, squatting, at the first Transformational Zone, the gluteus maximus loads into flexion/adduction/internal rotation along with the entire gluteus complex.

There are numerous ways authentically load the glute max and posterior chain, including anything that mimics heel strike through midstance. Isolated integration of the posterior hip would look similar to the lateral hip, however the driver of hands may be different in order to emphasize the sagittal plane. In this case, the reach is bilateral at knee height through bilateral overhead. Integrated isolation would include positioning below and driving the UE sagittal > transverse.

Scapulothoracic Relationships – Maintaining Shoulder Complex Capacities

The shoulder complex is made of four joints, the Acromio-clavicular (AC), Sternoclavicular (SCl), Glenohumeral (GH), and Scapulothoracic, and work in conjunction to allow the upper extremity to move in space. While not technically a joint, the scapulothoracic joint is the intersection of the thoracic spine and scapula, is considered a functional joint due to the slide and glide on the ribcage. Nineteen muscles attach the scapula to the humerus. Some are single joint and others multi-joint muscles, which work together to control the arm/hand in space. Single joint muscles, including the rotator cuff should be strong enough to stabilize the head of the humerus in the glenoid fossa while concurrently providing stability to the scapula for other muscles (including multi-joint) to pull against. Experience demonstrates often multi-joint muscles, which should eccentrically load to reduce force must also stabilize, causing overuse to the tissue and the cascade of events discussed in previous sections that result in sensitization. Specifically, often times the upper trapezius and pec minor do the work of the other scapular stabilizers, resulting in scapular upward translation of posterior tilt.

The Serratus Anterior and Low Trapezius Coupling

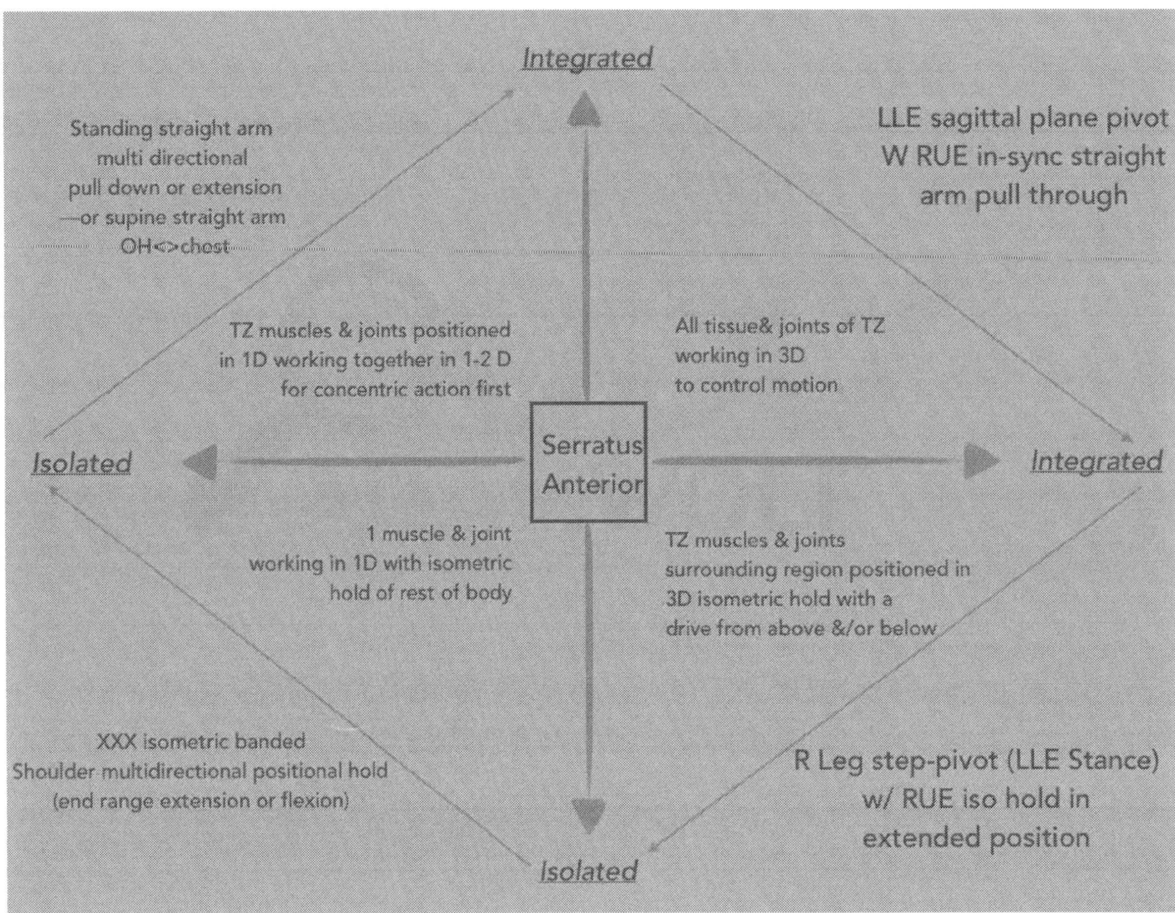

The serratus anterior is a muscle that is influential in the ability of the scapulohumeral complex to work efficiently and often demonstrates an opportunity for improved capacity, particularly with overhead activities. Along with the lower and mid trap, the serratus anterior should be able to work together to keep the scapula in the proper position to minimize scapular upward translation that often leads to glenohumeral pain. Clinically, the inability of the scapula to maintain a relatively neutral position against the spine and often results in shoulder pain. Often, the serratus anterior is a muscle that would benefit from strengthening and also training to stay engaged during shoulder movements, particularly overhead, in order to better control the scapula. Decreases in posterior tilt and increases in internal rotation of the scapula during humeral elevation have been demonstrated in subjects with shoulder impingement as compared to those without shoulder impingement (Lukasiewicz et al 1999). Remember, where the scapula goes, the humerus will follow, but where the humerus goes, the scapula doesn't have to follow.

One activity to ensure the correct muscles are working together without compensation is a light, bilateral farmer's carry. Typically, 20 pounds is enough, with the verbal cuing being "let your hands hang down and don't use your upper trap muscles". Not using the upper trap can be challenging because often those with shoulder or neck pain often use the upper trap through compensatory patterns. The potential result of the upper trap and pec minor to dominate these movements are varied and won't be specifically discussed here, however, strategies to get the upper trap and pec minor to relax with a co-contraction of the serratus anterior and low traps is imperative. Tactile cuing, including simply touching the upper trap or pec minor, can provide more input about if these muscles are dis-engaged. This sense of touch can also be utilized to ensure the low traps and serratus anterior muscles are engaged. Once the person has the ability to sense this, the movement is progressed, however periodically, especially when training someone in a new way, we come back to this activity to reinforce the sense of position about what is working. Coaching on engaging these regions as positional awareness exercises can also be helpful.

1. Isolated-Isolation can best be defined as one muscle and joint, working in one dimension, with or without an isometric hold of the rest of the body.
    a) The body needs to be 'long' with a 'tall' spine to correctly engage the serratus anterior in a manner that translates to being used with upright shoulder motions. This can be supine with feet on the ground or standing, as long as the pelvic/shoulder complex/head positioned is maintained. While there are many ways to emphasize this muscle, cables or bands are very effective.
    b) Standing tall, the tension of the band/cable should be from in front, where the hand is maintained at the side of the body with the elbow extended and wrist pronated. From this position, emphasize serratus and low trap involvement to pull without upper trap engagement.
        1. This movement can be progressed and layered on by placing tension into the pelvic complex musculature via a band around the femurs, emphasizing the glute complex while maintaining the proper relationships between pelvis/shoulders and head. Keep in mind the more intense input to various body parts, the more opportunity to create plastic changes is created.
        2. Can also be progressed via resistance at different angles, either a side or the band placed behind, still holding without movement

Coupling the serratus anterior with the lower trapezius via isometric holds helps to build somatosensory representation to help with proper shoulder movements. In the pictures above, ensuring proper costopelvic and cervical relationships before starting is imperative. In the left picture, emphasis should be placed on hands 'reaching for the ground with a long spine' with engagement of the serratus anterior and low/mid trap. The right picture is a variation emphasizing the same muscles engaging.

2. Isolated-Integration can be defined as one or more muscles and joints working together in one plane of motion while working together in one or two planes and performing a concentric/shortening action first.

a) This movement is essentially adding the movement to the position listed above, with the emphasis on continuing to maintain the relationship of the pelvis/shoulders and head. This can include a straight arm row, continuing to emphasize the contractions of the serratus anterior and low trap without engagement of the upper trap, and can progress to the same position with elbows flexed to 90.

b) Stand tall with resistance in band with the ability to maintain long position and shoulder/elbow extended next to body.

c) Perform a straight arm row, emphasizing maintaining long position without cervical protraction or upper trapezius recruitment.

I) Variations can be performed with unilaterally with the band to one side, and bilaterally with the band being place behind rather than in front.

II) Another activity could include a supine straight arm row, with the emphasis on overhead and pulling to chest height.

III) Emphasize maintaining the relationship between the pelvis, shoulder complex, and cervical spine. Compensation with this movement tends to be seen via thoracolumbar extension or upper cervical flexion.

Scapular exercises that assist to reeducate proper shoulder complex motions include various rowing progressions utilizing the serratus anterior and lower trapezius muscles with a neutral spine position. In the example above, the arms and body stay in one spot as the foot is stepped posteriorly, creating isometric stabilization with a bottom up drive into the system. Variations include unilateral work versus bilateral.

2. Isolated-Integration can best be defined as muscles and joints surrounding a region to be positioned in 3D isometrics holds, with a drive from above or below.

   a) Within the context of the serratus anterior, the starting position remains the same as above. The movement is progressed via a unilateral hold and adding a step, either anterior or posterior, or combining the anterior to posterior step to create a sagittal plane pivot with isometric scapular complex.

   b) The emphasis continues to be placed on maintaining serratus anterior and lower trap engagement while not engaging the upper trapezius, while maintaining an upright position and the arm staying in relatively one place in space. I) This is a challenging movement, requiring stabilization of a relatively fixed scapula on a moving body. Emphasize standing tall and not losing the pelvic, scapular complex & cervical relationships.

  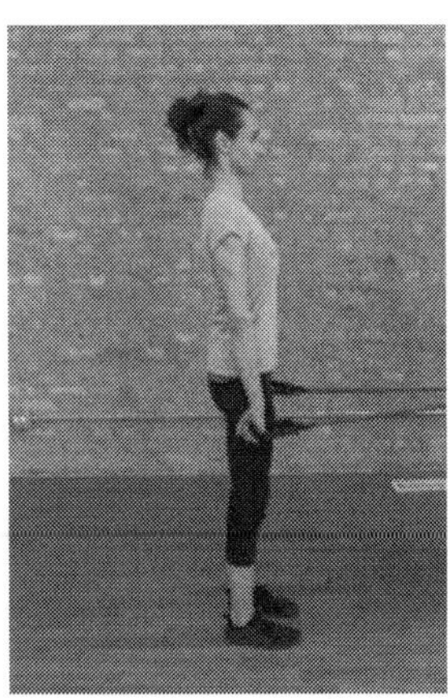 

Scapular exercises that assist to reeducate proper shoulder complex motions include various rowing progressions utilizing the serratus anterior and lower trapezius muscles with a neutral spine position. In the example above, as the foot steps posteriorly then anteriorly, the shoulder complex and upper body stays still, creating isometric engagement of the shoulder complex and 'core'. One coaching cue is ensuring stepping back heel to toe on a train track, not a tight rope, in order to keep a wide base of support.

4. Integrated-integration, can be defined as all tissue and joints of the TZ working together in 3D to control a specific motion.
    a) This movement could simply be a progression of the last movement, with the addition of an upper extremity row.
    b) For the right serratus anterior:
        I) Stand tall, band/cable in hand positioned anterior with shoulder slightly flexed approximately 20' with the left foot forward in a 'stand tall walking position'. Stand far enough back to have some tension in the band.
        II) While standing tall, take a step forward with the right foot and row the right upper extremity into extension, ending with the right shoulder extended and the right hip flexed.

            This movement incorporates the opposite hip/shoulder, creating an authentic load for the serratus anterior relative to the gait cycle and getting all other joints and tissue above and below to also loading authentically.

Scapular exercises that assist to reeducate proper shoulder complex motions include various rowing progressions utilizing the serratus anterior and lower trapezius muscles with a neutral spine position. In the example above, as the foot steps posteriorly, the shoulders extend, creating stabilization moments of the scapular complex as well as dynamic 'core' activation.

Thoracic & Scapulo-Thoracic Complex

Thoracic-centric exercises that create the proper side bending and rotation are important., and often 'yoga' exercises including down dog and a modified "child's" pose are helpful for enhancing thoracic extension. The thoracic spine tends to be limited on many people due to continually fighting gravity particularly while sitting, and those that can't achieve the full positions can still perform the movements in regressed positions, such as holding onto a chair during down dog.

Important exercises to consider, especially for those that work at a desk, includes proper ergonomic orientation, as well as movements that are geared towards enhancing the areas of the body that tend to become limited in mobility due to battling gravity, including the thoracic spine and hips.

Thoracic Extension

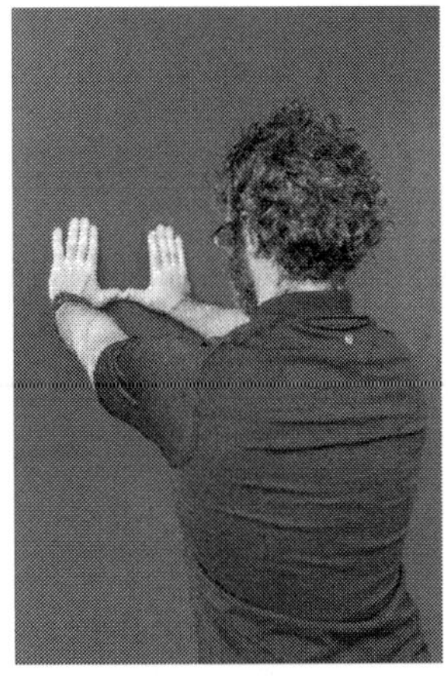

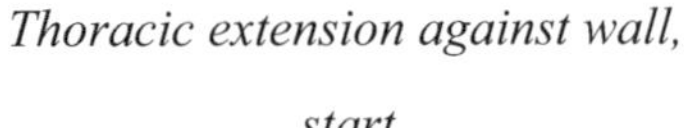

Thoracic extension against wall, start

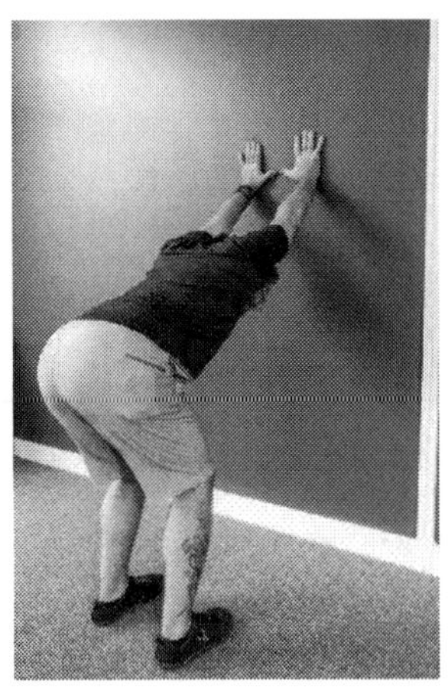

Thoracic extension with long spine, end.

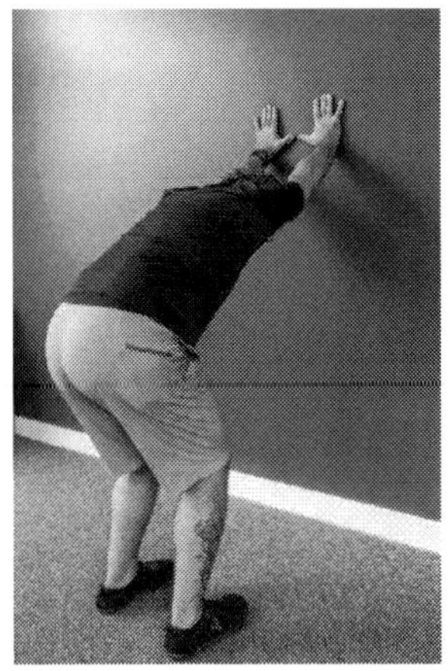

Thoracic extension compensation.

Compensations include increased mid-back 'rounding or kyphosis, and or flexing the neck. Notice the alignment of the head, shoulders and hips remain aligned and not rounded.

Chest Expansion

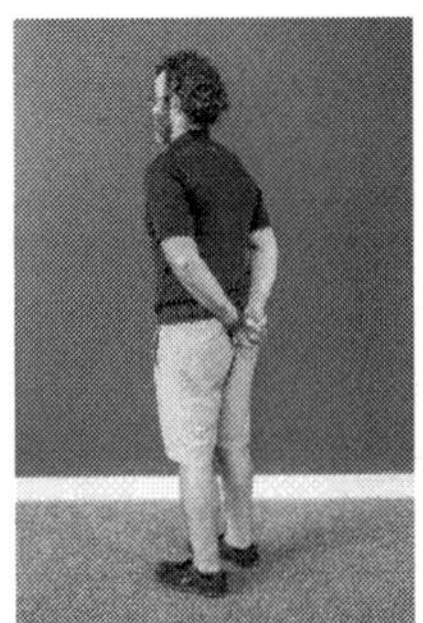

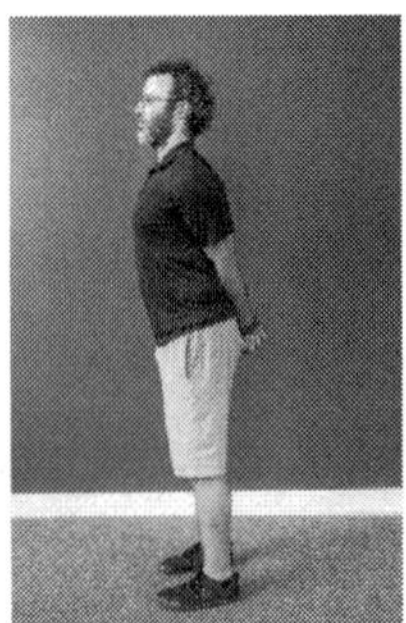

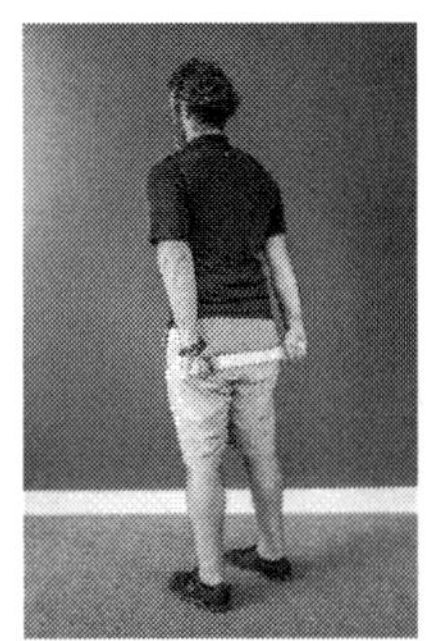

- Stand straight, feet parallel, shoulder width apart.
- Interlace fingers behind you
    - Regression is holding a strap or towel
- Straighten arms and "reach for heels" while putting the top of the head on the ceiling
- Energetically lengthen and pull clavicles laterally expand shoulders
- Progression: forward fold, pulling hands up and over the body.

Suspension Strap 'Fallouts'

Suspension strap 'fallout' for thoracic extension, start

Suspension strap 'fallout' for thoracic extension, end

Suspension strap 'fallout' with lumbar extension compensation

Child's pose with Type 2 Thoracic Spine (side bending/rotation to same side)

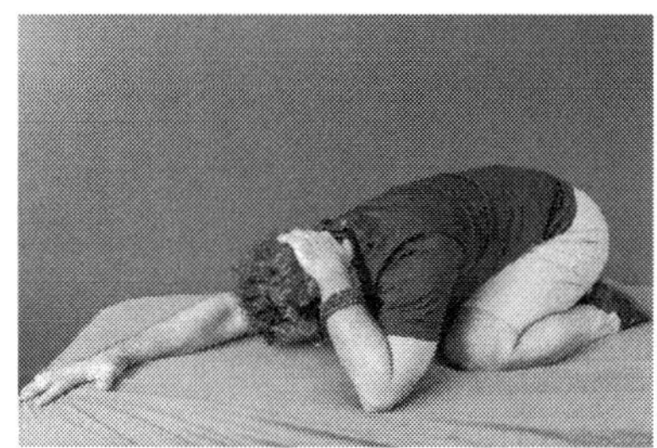

- Kneel on floor, touch toes together and sit on heels, & separate knees as wide as hips
- Exhale and lay your chest between your thighs. Widen the back of your pelvis and narrow the ASIS down onto the inner thighs.
- Reach hands overhead to shoulder are flexed (there should be no pinching in the closing angle of the shoulders)
- Spider crawl hands to the left, so the right hand is just to the left of midline. Take left hand and place behind the neck, with left elbow pointed down towards floor.
- With a long slow inhale (ideally through the nose), raise the left elbow up towards the ceiling, attempting to look at the ceiling under the left armpit
- With a long, slow exhale, return to the starting position
- The breath should last slightly longer than the movement

Down Dog

- From table top position (hands & knees), make sure knees are directly below hips and hands are slightly forward of the shoulders. Spread palms with middle finger pointed forward.
- Lift knees away from floor, pushing through hands and lifting the pelvis & ischial tuberosity up and towards the ceiling with knees slightly flexed and heels off the ground. The arms should be flexed and externally rotated, with a long neck.
- Breathe deeply, ideally through the nose, with long, slow exhales.
- Straighten knees, but don't' lock them and drop the heels to the ground.
- Envision keeping the pelvis and rib cage stacked over each other, relative to the position the body is in
- Attempt to create as much distance between the hands and the tailbone as possible, keeping proper alignment.
    - Down dog can be regressed by bending the knees and lifting the heels towards the ceiling. However optimal alignment of the spine and rib cage aligned over the pelvis is important.
- Scapula's should be down the spine, with a long neck in the front, back and sides.
- Down dog, or Adho Mukha Svanasana is a post of the Sun Salutation sequence in yoga.
- This movement is one I use, while interchanging between a plank and down dog, emphasizing breath and cuing to maintain a neutral spine.

Cervical Spine Capacities through Movement

The cervical spine is another region where 'movement leaks' can be observed during movement. Often, people demonstrate difficulty maintaining a retracted position through movement, and instead 'dump' into their cervical region, particularly with overhead activity. Movement in the cervical spine, particularly at the cervical-thoracic region is typically the result of a distal region not moving enough. Therefore, ensuring the ability to maintain a cervically retracted position when moving is necessary for optimal function, while also attempting to find the region that isn't moving enough. In addition, the cervical spine is directly related to otolithic dysfunction, and with chronic neck issues, the vestibulo-ocular system should be considered. Recall, the eyes are going to remain parallel to the ground, and if there is an eye issue, the cervical spine will often compensate to maintain gaze stability and optimal eye function often at the expense of cervical spine positioning.
The following are basic suggestions and capacities the cervical spine should be able to maintain through movement. When difficulty is observed, understanding there are numerous reasons why the cervical spine may be involved is helpful. This text won't get into the specifics of assessment, however it is absolutely necessary to ensure
successful integration. When there is difficulty, reeducating on maintaining this capacity often becomes the first thing to approach.

In the clinic, there are a number of tools I like to use to reeducate movement of the spine, including a Motion Guidance system. This system attaches to the head and is a useful tool for rehabilitation and reintegration. I find it particularly helpful in the cervical spine, particularly to provide visual feedback about how the cervical spine is moving, as well as to influence the vestibulo-ocular system.

Often, people with neck/shoulder pain aren't even aware of the coupling.

The following are other suggestions to ensure cervical spine positioning through movement.

- Standing Cervical Retraction
  - I often use Motion Guidance as a strategy to reeducate and bring awareness to the motion of cervical retraction, which can often be difficult to teach correctly. With the laser on the head, during retraction, the light from the laser should not move up or down and should stay in one spot through the motion. Movement of the light during the retraction motion is indicative of coupled flexion/extension of the upper cervical spine and should be further addressed because the motion shouldn't have to be coupled. On a larger scale,

coupled motion (or global motion) of the spine during local movement should be addressed, regardless of what motion. For example, I have observed with shoulder or hip flexion, there's often coupled motion of cervical spine or thoraco-lumbar junction as compensation for a local dysfunction. In these cases, finding the threshold of when the coupling begins should be assessed, along with strategies for improving independent movement of the region.

  - Motion Guidance was kind enough to provide a promo-code to those reading this book. Enter **MovementGuild** at checkout for 10% off their products.

- Supine retraction and deep neck strength via lift offs
  Deep neck flexor strength is often overlooked with cervical dysfunction.
  Ensuring a stable cervical spine often helps with long term cervical spine health.

  - In a supine position, retract the cervical spine (without flexion/extension coupling).
  - Maintaining this retracted position, lift the head off the ground and hold.

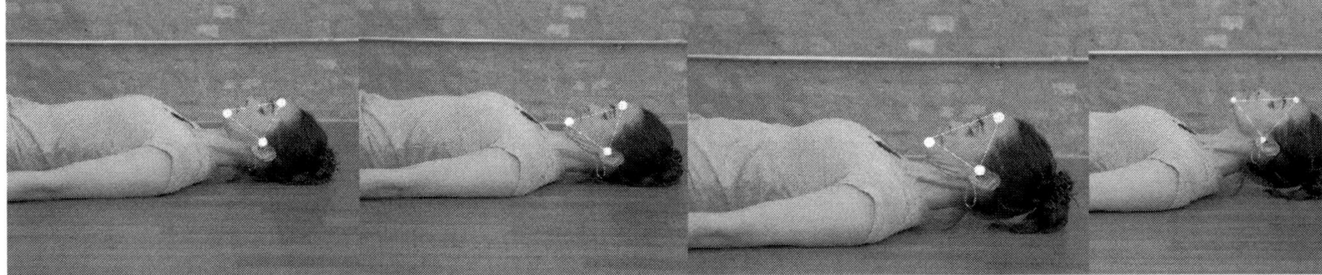

Deep neck flexor strength is often important for those with cervical dysfunction. Picture 1 demonstrates a 'long cervical spine', Picture 2 demonstrates a chin tuck, which picture 3 shows a chin tuck with 'deep neck flexor' engagement. Notice the orientation of the head to the body with correct positioning, versus picture 4 which demonstrates compensatory positioning, as the chin is higher towards the ceiling.

- Prone cervical retraction. Ensuring balance between the neck flexors and extensors ensures a better chance of proper length tension relationships in the cervical spine. Often the neck extensors are weak and short due to a forward head position.

Length and strength of the neck extensors helps to ensure proper length tension relationships. Picture 1 demonstrates a 'long spine' with neutral positioning, picture 2 illustrates upper cervical flexion with lower cervical extension, maintaining the 'long spine' position, while picture 3 demonstrates an often utilized compensatory pattern.

Brain-Based Applications This section is co-written by Mike & Adam

Visual, Proprioceptive, and Vestibular Integration

As an expansion to the above description of cervical integration through the use of the motion guidance system, this tool can be utilized to pair the sensory inputs of the vestibular system, visual system, and cervical proprioception. In order to move the head and neck appropriately through space the brain must be in full appreciation of where the head and neck is in space. The primary feedback and feedforward of these systems to calibrate appropriate movement is through the cerebellum as well as several nuclei in the brainstem. Any minor dysfunction in one or several of these systems will create symptoms such as dizziness, headache, head pressure, neck pain, neck tightness, and possibly blurred vision. While using the motion guidance laser as a stationary target to ensure minimal ancillary movement of the head during isometric holds, another strategy is using the laser guide proper smooth movement of the cervical spine.

The following is a progression of cervical, vestibular, and oculomotor/visual reintegration techniques that are best utilized when the cervical spine is the primary cause of dysfunction.

- Setup Progression – With the laser fixed to the forehead and setup at eye level:
    - Seated passive (Clinician standing behind the patient and guiding the head and the patient allows the passive movement)
        - This is the easiest on the system with the least amount of coordination
    - Standing passive
        - Standing involves higher level integration due to the maintenance of upright stability of the trunk and lower extremities.
    - Seated active
        - Once standing passive motion is smooth without extraneous muscle movement, move back to a seated position and progress to active movements. Before progressing to active standing, the movement must be smooth and rhythmic without symptoms.
    - Standing active
        - Depending on the severity of the case, this is often the point when breakdown in movement may occur. This position requires more integration to produce fluid movements.
    - Standing perturbed surface (foam pad) active
        - Removing solid surface innately makes this task more difficult, and also drives more of the vestibular system.
    - Dual tasking can be added to any of these movements to involve the frontal lobe, pairing movement with cognition.

- Movement Progression – Typically linear movement will be easier than multiplanar circular type movements. The progression is typically proper smooth linear movement followed by circular, figure-8, or butterfly type movements. Depending on the case these can be split up in a progression from visit to visit or performed in the same visit.
    - Horizontal linear movement
    - Vertical linear movement
    - Circular movement (clockwise and counterclockwise)
    - Multi-planar movement (butterfly pattern clockwise and counterclockwise)

The idea is to keep the laser on the designated line throughout all movements. Many will try to complete the task as quick as possible at the expense of accuracy. Therefore, focusing on accurate smooth movement without breakdown is important. If there is a breakdown in smooth movement or an increase in symptoms, step down in the progression to the last correctly performed movement. This application can be performed with the trunk, pelvis, and extremities as long as the proper movement patterns described earlier in this chapter are maintained.

***Clinical Note*:**

The above movement progression is often utilized when my findings include decreased rapid alternating movements on one side of the body or in numerous joints in an extremity.

Cognitive Coordination Training

As discussed throughout this book, the primary role of the brain is to tell the body where it is in space and allow proper movement through space. This is vital for all humans but is even more important for athletes. Proper placement of limbs can mean the difference in both performance aspects and injury avoidance. Learning to groove a movement is a large part of performance and takes regressive and progressive strategies. This is often described as "muscle memory" and while some may argue that there is some "memory" within muscles in relation to elasticity and contraction, most "muscle memory" is really neuroplasticity. With this in mind, it makes sense to train generic movement and sport specific movement with other brain activities simultaneously. All of the following exercises will train proper hand eye coordination which is really an integration of visual processing, upper extremity motor planning, and upper extremity movement execution. Adding in the cognitive aspect trains the athlete to be able to move and think at the same time. Many athletes are great at moving but as soon as they start to think, their movement breaks down and becomes less efficient and many times inaccurate. While most sports involve both upper and lower limb coordination, some rely on upper or lower extremity coordination more than others. The following section will outline upper and lower coordination exercises separately, but they very easily could, and for most athletes, should be combined as a progression.

Upper Extremity and Hand-Eye Coordination

Knowing where the upper extremity is in space and moving it appropriately to varied approaching stimuli is hallmark in many sporting activities. For this activity it is important to start slow to allow the athlete to build initial neuroplasticity, or learn the activity, then progress quickly. Depending on the skill level of the athlete, this will progress at varying speeds. Equipment can be as simple as a tennis ball or whiffle ball with various letters, numbers, and shapes drawn on them in various colors. If you want to spend a few dollars, another great piece of equipment is a Hecostix, a three pronged foam device with each prong being a different color. I use these in my clinical with many patients and have had great success with them. Below are a couple examples using each tool.

Hecostix –

- The faster that the Hecostix is spun, the harder it will be to catch appropriately.
- Rules: Catch the color that is called out as the hecostix is in the air with the hand that is specified.
- Examples: Left hand blue, right hand black, or both hands yellow
- I will also use these with locomotor drills including a ladder.
- Progressions include: varying call cadences and waiting till the tool is closer before calling. Also, combining hand/color combination (i.e. left red, right blue)
- Use WOLFPT10 for 10% off your purchase from Hecostix

Whiffle Balls –

- Use 12 baseball sized whiffle balls with four various shapes drawn in red, green, and blue.
- Draw circles on three, squares on three, triangles on three, and stars on three.
- Draw all circles on one ball in red, all circles on the second ball in green, and all circles on the third ball in blue. Repeat for the rest of the shapes.
    1. Rules: Catch red shapes with the right hand, green shapes, with the left hand, and blue shapes with both hands.
    2. Progressions:
    3. Call out the colors or call out the shapes while the ball is in the air.
    4. Eyes closed until the thrower says "go" as the ball is in the air.
- Stand on a balance board or unsteady surface like an upside down BOSU ball.
- Use strobe glasses which disrupt vision momentarily in one or both eyes.
- Any combination or all of the above.

Lower Extremity Ladder Agility Drills

As discussed with the integration of upper extremity and cognitive coordination, the same is true with the lower extremity. Lower extremity coordination becomes more important when looking at injury prevention. Use of the lower extremity is not always dependent on upper extremity movement, but in almost all cases, use of the upper extremities relies on stability and proper placement of the lower extremities. For example, when playing soccer, proper arm coordination will aid in more controlled dribbling and kicking the ball, but it is not vital. In contrast, when throwing a pitch in baseball, the coordination of leg drive and foot placement is imperative for force generation and timing. For this reason, training proper awareness, agility, and coordination of the lower extremity is vital, as is coordinating the upper and lower extremities together (as a progression). It is also of upmost importance that these and any movement is performed efficiently and subconsciously as to not draw energy away from other movement of the body. In addition to setting up a proper foundation for upper extremity and trunk movement, proper awareness of the lower extremity is crucial for limiting injuries, especially of the lower extremity.

One drill that is useful for proper lower extremity awareness is the floor ladder agility drill. The ladder is a simple device that can be purchased for little or made from masking tape. The rungs are typically 12-18" apart making a square with the outer ropes, with the length of the ladder about 15' long. Just like the upper extremity drills, the ladder exercises can be greatly varied with almost countless options for rules. A simple search on YouTube will provide many variations of foot drills. Simply moving the athlete through variations of foot drills will begin to integrate better lower extremity awareness and movement. Once the patient/client can effectively navigate the ladder without errors, a dual task activity should be added. This can be as simple as saying every other letter out loud while performing the activity or as complicated as completing math problems that are called out during the movement. The following is an example of a progression through the floor ladder.

Ladder Drill –

Rules:

1) Start with the left foot and make sure that each foot touches inside of each box only once while moving forward through the ladder. Move as fast and effectively as possible.

2) Start on the left side of the ladder, move laterally to the right placing the right foot in the box, followed by the left foot, then move the right foot outside of the box on the right side of the ladder followed by the left foot. Follow this pattern back through the ladder to the left and repeat in a zig-zag patten down the ladder. The athlete should be in an athletic stance position throughout the drill and should be moving as fast but as controlled as possible.

Progressions:

1) Incorporate dual tasking while moving through the ladder. Say every other month out loud while moving. Count down by 7's from 52 while moving through the ladder. Name the state capitals. Call out specific names of memorized plays in the athlete's specific sport and describe the play. Creativity and variation is the key.

2) Add upper extremity tasks with the movement through the ladder. Take the upper extremity tasks from above and layer them on top of the movement through the ladder.

3) Perform upper extremity and cognitive dual tasks at the same time.

Conclusion

The point of this section is a jumping off point to conceptualize where on a movement spectrum someone should start, and by no means represents a complete list. In addition, the idea about how to begin to 'layer' brain-based approaches into a musculoskeletal paradigm should be apparent. Sometimes, the best approach is to layer one intervention (such as an eye exercise) in conjunction with another intervention (joint position hold or movement) and do them together, while other times it makes sense to do one, followed by the other. Other times, it makes sense to perform one repeated for multiple sets in a row. Only through an understanding of thresholds and what is trying to be done can this question be answered. In addition, specific brain based applications, other than very superficially have been avoided.

Additional Readings:

- Goode A, Hegedus EJ, Sizer P, Brismee JM, Linberg A, Cook CE. Three-dimensional movements of the sacroiliac joint: a systematic review of the literature and assessment of clinical utility. *J Man Manip Ther*. 2008;16(1):25-38. Doi:10.1179/106698108790818639
- Sacroiliac joint motion in patients with degenerative lumbar spine disorders. Nagamoto Y, Iwasaki M, Sakaura H, et al. J Neurosurg Spine. 2015;23:209–216
- The influence of gluteus maximus on transverse plane tibial rotation. Stephen J. Preece, Philip Graham-Smith, Chris J. Nester, Dave Howard, Hermie Hermens, Lee Herrington, Peter Bowkerm Gait Posture. 2008 May; 27(4): 616–621. Published online 2007 Sep 27. Doi: 10.1016/j.gaitpost.2007.08.007
- Lukasiewicz AC, McClure P, Michener L, Pratt N, Sennett B. Comparison of 3-dimensional scapular position and orientation between subjects with and without shoulder impingement. *J Orthop Sports Phys Ther*. 1999;29(10):574–586. PubMed ID: 10560066 doi:10.2519/jospt.1999.29.10.574
- Osar, Evan; *Corrective Exercise Solutions to Common Hip and Shoulder Dysfunction*
- Destafano DO, Lisa A; *Greenman's Principles of Manual Medicine, 5th Edition*

CASE STUDY #1

This case study is simplified in its descriptions in order to keep a narrative that fits the influence of the nervous system in governing the musculoskeletal system. What is described below is complicated information that has been simplified to illustrate the importance of learning the central systems and how they interact. A specific input should result in a specific output, which directs treatment.

Jim is a 45 year old undercover detective and competitive Brazilian Jiu Jitsu participant who practices yoga. He came to see me after already seeing other practitioners for right low back pain and met me through a class my wife was then teaching. He described more pain in the mornings that developed insidiously, and also increases with BJJ and other strenuous activities. Recently, he hadn't been participating in BJJ due to pain and fear of hurting it more, in addition to working more.

Due to his work, he was late for the first session, and our Initial Evaluation was therefore more abbreviated than normal. In these cases, the key becomes to anchor to a few pieces of objective information and then get going, recognizing the evaluative process in ongoing activities. It is easy, however, to get a couple pieces to anchor to in both the 'orthopedic' and 'neurological' realms, understanding these become potential indicators by which to measure progress.

Like most sessions, our first started with a videoed gait analysis, observing specific capacities of the gait cycle. Overall, Jim was relatively flexible and strong, and gait analysis still proved to be helpful in identifying significant differences one side to the other. The biggest discrepancy observed was in the frontal plane at midstance and best viewed from behind. At that point, his left leg demonstrated far less midstance control compared to the right as seen by videotaped gait analysis. Although he described being 'tight in the LB' in the AM and pain in the hamstring, his passive range (supine on table), was rather symmetrical, with the largest difference being in midstance control as seen weight bearing. In his case, and in many instances like his where motion isn't controlled, or there is pain with movement, understanding the combinations of tissue that lengthen together to control motion is helpful in directing treatment.

Gait Assessment Findings Include

- Overall unremarkable, with limited stride length bilaterally and decreased arm swing on left vs. right.
- At midstance > 5 degrees of left hip adduction (236pprox.. 10) compared to the right midstance, which was 5 degrees.

Movement Assessment

- Right leg posterior lunge aka Active Hamstring Stretch
  - The patient complained of left hamstring tightness compared to opposite side.
  - Full ROM with bodyweight squat
    - Able to sustain good spine position during end range squat.
  - Overall, good mobility of thoracic spine and hips observable.
  - 6" step down
    - demonstrated more compensation stepping down with left foot compared to right (see picture for discrepancies).

Picture 1 on the left depicts a posterior lunge with anterior reach, or 'active hamstring' exercise. Picture 2 demonstrates a step down, which should be compared to the other side to identify frontal plane control of the pelvis.

On Table Assessment

- (-) SCOUR, (-) FABER
- 90/90 Hamstring WFL
  - Patient verbalized tighter sensation in left hamstring at end range, despite similar ROM
- Hip IR with 90' of hip flexion
  - R: 20', L: 35'

Motor Control and Neuro Assessment

- (-) Romberg, (-) Tandem Romberg (leaned left)
- Rapid Alternating Movement: unremarkable
- 'Basic' Vision:
    - pursuit: saccadic intrusion with right pursuit
- 2 point Discrimination
    - 3" lateral to spinous process at level of pelvic crest, vertical measurement
        - Left: 8"
        - Right: 4"
- Musculoskeletal motor testing:
    - NO (weak in clear): left glute medius, maximus, TFL, proximal hamstring, right QL, right low trap, right serratus anterior, right & left lumbar erectors

Tissue Mobility

Limited superficial tissue mobility in low back/thoracolumbar region, specifically following the right superior cuneal nerve distribution.

Clinical Impression, Based on Findings

These findings combined with clinical experience leads me to think perhaps due to his inability to control midstance in his left glute complex, the right 'QL"/low back region overwork to help stabilize the pelvis. Increased shearing forces in the hip, knee, and low back, and can easily create a situation where increased tissue trauma results in a chemical process due to overworking tissues that causes a drop in tissue pH, aggravating and sensitizing the superficial nerves. He also loads the low back tissue while 'rolling' in Jiu Jitsu. It is also of value to note that this is the story I tell myself, based on treating many patients. In my head, it fits into a model that appreciates neurological processes, pain science, and biomechanics, integrating it into a workable format.

First Treatment

Clinical experience has shown that, at midstance, there often tends to be consistency in the muscles that tend to overwork, with an understanding that discrepancies exist and it is very individualized. In the case of a midstance insufficiency, when the glute med demonstrates a delay in the timing (a latency), often the opposite QL region has an increased connection. Other times it might be the same side (or opposite side) adductor group that creates the inhibition, and only through assessing can this be 'best guessed'.

Utilizing an ABA protocol described in the motor control section determined that right low back muscles were overworking, specifically the right QL, feeding into the dysfunctional inability of the left glute complex to control midstance. Recall at midstance on the left leg, the left gluteus complex, along with the right QL, work to control midstance, and often times one can overwork and create difficulties in the others also optimally working. In this case, I believe the QL was overworking at midstance, forced to concentrically produce forces to stabilize the pelvis in the frontal plane to compensate for the insufficient stance leg gluteus medius.

Manual therapy was performed, specifically along the superior cuneal nerve distribution in order to improve superficial tissue mobility. Upon palpation, the patient verbalized a more restricted and intense sensation along the right superior cuneal nerve distribution. We also attempted to mechanically liberate the peripheral nerves innervating his hamstring, specifically the posterior femoral cutaneous nerve. A 'level one isometric glute set' was then assigned, emphasizing lateral glute complex engagement. This creates cortical space in order to more effectively control midstance and was assigned as homework. He verbalized how difficult the isometric sequence was, and education was provided explaining the holds being as intense as possible in order to fire as much 'input' up into the brain as possible. At the end of the first session, he had a 50% reduction in pain and felt less restricted, and was also excited about potentially not having pain.

Second Session

The second session was unremarkable and began with the question, "How can I help you today?" which in itself is an interesting question. Jim verbalized feeling better overall, with improved confidence with BJJ participation. He mentioned consistently performing his glute sets, and while he still felt right low back tenderness, it wasn't as tender, and was more localized in nature. Emphasis was placed on explaining and educating about the positive signs he described, as the symptoms were less and more localized.

On a larger scale, assessment and reassessment provide the foundation for direction and intervention. The trick becomes to obtain multiple objective measures to anchor to, including some the patient/client can feel. For me, this typically includes a few integrated movements starting with stability, and systematically removing it to see when and how the overall shape of the movement changes. Changing shape during motion is indicative of stepping over a threshold. Observing movement can be challenging because it happens so fast and is a reason to record movement (Spark Motion is my preference, use WOLF to get a discount from Spark Motion). Upon reaching a threshold, understanding what combinations of tissue and joints work to control the motion is useful. With this information, I noted that I need to check the combination of tissue in other ways, including on the table.

Session Three

Session three took place seven days after the second. He described less pain overall, yet his hamstring trouble continued. Jim started with isometric glute exercises as I finished up with a patient. An FNOR model dictates layering input to emphasize specific parts of the brain as tolerated and is why assessment and understanding of the neuromusculoskeletal system directs treatment. We continued to layer input to the gluteus and added scapular setting to emphasize serratus anterior and low trap engagement.

At this point he had been doing his homework rather diligently and reported the low back pain was significantly less compared to the first session. He described slight 'tightness' described when waking up in the morning, that resolved with light mobility. His hamstring was the main complaint at this point, and with this understanding I introduced concepts of Functional Range Conditioning (FRC). FRC is a system organized in thought by Dr. Andreo Spina and involves a systematic approach to utilizing independent (rather than interdependent) joint motion. His movements included hip controlled articular rotations (CARS), and progressive/regressive angular isometric loads (PAIL/RAIL), for the hips in a 90/90 position for the hips and hamstrings.

Author's Note

I chose to incorporate FRC at this point because of his motivation and its effectiveness to improve mobility, particularly with this police officer who was very active and high level. It is typical in Session 3 or 4 that patients are introduced to 'stuff' that isn't daily activities and rather would be done a few days per week as 'extra'. With those who say there isn't time to perform the exercise, we use the concepts of "stealing" time while doing something else, such as sitting in a meeting, standing in line, or talking on the phone. Most people in pain require behavior change, and tasks that drive reminders and reinforcement of the desired change are a large part of my approach. The activities can include breathing as well as simple hip stretches or engagements Patients are coached that "every time you send an email" or "when standing in line, do this" particular activity.

Session Four

Session four turned out to be a breakthrough, occurring a week after session 3. Jim continued to get better and participate more actively without issues in BJJ and described minimal low back pain in the a.m. He continued to report soreness in the proximal aspect of the tissue, especially with increased exertion, despite the mobility work. He also mentioned that the last session of BJJ, there were a couple moments when he was on his back defending himself and became disoriented and unsure where he was in space.

It was then it occurred to me that I hadn't completed the more neurological aspect of his assessment, including a generalized understanding of vestibular, cerebellar, and ocular function because he was late on the first session.

Clinical Note:

It was at this point in time I decided a 'bedside neuro exam' should be included with everyone, early in the first session, despite if 'clinical' neurological symptoms were present.

While my clinical exam skills continue to improve with experience, and information looked at varies from patient to patient, at this point at the minimum it typically includes analysis of cerebellar activity via various exams including Romberg and Tandem Romberg, rapid alternating movements (RAM) compared bilaterally in the upper and lower extremities, and also basic assessment of visual reflexes. Visual reflexes typically assessed include vestibulo-ocular reflexes, VOR cancellation, pursuits, saccades, and fixations. I also try and gain insight about motor output and general frontal lobe activity via muscle testing and dynamometer measurements, and sensory through different sensation measurements including two point discrimination and point localization, focusing more on the parietal lobe. In an effort to obtain as much objective info as possible, I also typically utilize a Btracks to obtain mCTSIB, limits of stability, and other information that can be used to 'test against', and see what potential changes occur with various inputs. That being said, even the basic information can have profound impact, and I encourage everyone to learn more about the neurological processes of the cerebellar and vestibulo-ocular systems in addition to strategies to assess and treat these dysfunctions.

Author's Note

While writing this case study I am able to reflect upon the difficulty in integrating newly learned information into my then current treatment paradigm that had worked for me. Yet there were enough that didn't, and because one cannot 'unlearn', once I was exposed to a brain-based thought process I knew I had to know more. My experiences are that things recently learned begin to be seen with an inability to understand where 'it' is coming from or what to do about it. After a while, with continued study, integrating new information becomes more natural and less awkward. Until that point, it is nice to fall back on old habits and techniques. It also illustrates the importance of continuing to learn and add to a clinical knowledge base. I try to recognize clinical 'holes' and plug them with knowledge in order to make me as well rounded an outpatient clinician as possible. At the time of this publishing, I am working towards a certificate of competency in vestibular rehabilitation.

Jim's comment about not knowing where he was in space guided further neurological function investigation, which was telling and further guided treatment. Findings included difficulty with rapid alternating movements on his left shoulder, wrist, finger, knee, and ankle reflexes. In addition, he leaned left on Romberg and lost his balance by falling to the left with Tandem Romberg within six seconds of starting. He also had difficulty with pursuits to the right, in the horizontal plane, and also moving right from Up left<>down right. He exhibited limited pursuit convergence in the left eye, and when placed into the vestibular canals demonstrated an improvement in outcome measurements while placed in the left posterior canal and more difficulty in the right anterior canal, which was verified against other exams and also verbalized by patient sensation.

What I have learned from various 'rehab' communities including those in the worlds of FNOR, Functional Neurology, Applied Functional Science, and also simply being a PT in general, is that testing and retesting to see what changes with a specific input stimulus has huge value, and is hard to master. Relative to movement, it is what
happens when the foot, hand, or other body drives a motion as a way to observe the reaction. With neurological processes it is the same thing, just different in that the inputs to test specific mechanisms need to be more specific and include eye, head, and other movements to see what outcome measurement changes with that particular stimulus. All of this is in an effort to direct a course of treatment.

Brain-based stimulI are immediate, therefore can direct treatment with a process of following success. For example, when placed into the left posterior canal, when pursuit convergence was retested, left eye convergence improved and when placed into the right anterior, didn't improve. In addition, rapid alternating in both the upper extremity (alternating pronation/supination) and lower extremity (heel tap against opposite tibia), improved when the head was placed into the left posterior canal and didn't in the right anterior. In other words, when testing cerebellar and ocular function against the vestibular system, both changed. This leads me to suspect the vestibular (and therefore ocular) system had an opportunity to improve the way the brain was perceiving afferent information, and a discrepancy existed between the

proprioceptive, vestibular, and ocular system. This can often be improved via driving afferent to a specific system. In this case, the test improved and was made worse with specific input, and therefore driving layered input to specific body parts and specific systems became the strategy.
What is described above is a similar thought process to testing muscles against each other to see what changes the second time they are tested, as is the simple intervention that was determined by the outcome of the previous stimulus. Treatment included attempting to balance and drive input to specific canals, in addition to movements to drive convergence of the left eye. We also layered complex movements into the glute holds he was already performing in an effort to influence the left cerebellum.

He was sent home with fifteen minutes of intense movements designed to drive input to specific parts of the brain, particularly the left side. If this patient had come earlier in my career, the treatment would have continued hammering away at the hamstring and trying to fire the glute. My paradigm of thought would have been solely from a musculoskeletal perspective, and reflecting back upon patients who didn't get better, there is likely a good chance they also demonstrated an opportunity to improve the way the brain was reconciling sensory information. His fifteen minutes also included vestibulo-ocular specific "active rests" and layers during his hold positions, in addition to education about 'stealing time' during the day by performing brief episodes of vestibulo-ocular exercises combined with complex UE/LE movements driving cerebellar activity. The idea was to layer the isometric holds of various regions with eye exercises to maximally drive safe input into the brain to create neuroplastic changes that feed forward into a positive feedback loop. After this session, Jim voiced less tension in his hamstring, and what was exciting was, it was the first session we didn't specifically 'go after' his hamstring.

Following session four, Jim reported feeling better and overall, less tension in his hamstring. He continued to have slight irritation but less as he creates the appropriate mobility and ability to control his end range motions, coupled with a balanced vestibulo-ocular system. The next two sessions were spaced a week apart, and continued along much the same path, driving as much input as possible in order to improve the way his brain was interpreting afferent input.

Jim was seen for a total of eight sessions, with the last one being approximately three weeks after the seventh. At his last session, he described feeling a lot better with far less low back pain and hamstring pain and reported continuing to perform the vision exercises. He also incorporated the other exercises into his warmups at training, including the FRC based 'joint' isolation exercises.

A big win was the recognition of what he can do to get himself out of pain. He is actually a classic example of those with musculoskeletal pain who isn't driven from musculoskeletal issues. In his case, his system perceived gravity in a specific way that resulted in his weight being shifted back and to the left, irritating his hamstring. Once aware of the dysfunction and how to correct it, his vestibular system became more balanced and his brain perceived effects of gravity more evenly and efficiently.

Author's Note

Over the years, I have become guarded against letting others place it upon me to make them better. There have been strategies I have developed to guard myself from this and also identify those who demonstrate this tendency. At the start of most sessions, I ask 'How can I help you today', or 'What do you need from me today?' It is an interesting question to ask because typically the answer is either "I'd like you to work on me a bit, then let's exercise and progress," or it is "you tell me, you're the professional". In my experience, it is more of the second group who tend to take less responsibility for doing their exercises and more often the ones reporting inconsistency with their homework. I've also noticed those not assuming responsibility for their progress tend to apologize for not doing assigned homework. Early on, this bothered me, and on some level would attach to their outcome, which I believe literally contributed to making me sick (I developed an inflammatory bowel disease). I have since developed a level of equanimity and honestly do not care if they get better or not, recognizing this sounds harsh. However, I have since rationalized that if my full effort was given for the 45 minute session, and they aren't compliant, or not invested fully in their outcome, it's not my responsibility to get them better. In other words, my responsibility is to show the proverbial horse where the water is. I am hesitant to be called a healer because I am not and do not heal anyone. I simply know many cool tricks, study a lot, and have enough experience working with people to identify patterns.

CASE STUDY #2

Having a multidisciplinary healthcare team to refer when progress is limited (or non- existent) is a necessary part of practice because nobody is an island unto themselves. This was difficult for me to understand as a younger clinician, however, the more I practice the more the necessity of knowing when to refer to another professional who complements my practice becomes apparent. To do this effectively requires an understanding of personal clinical strengths and weaknesses and where a clinical practice requires more knowledge to successfully intervene. Lifelong learning shouldn't be limited to information solely within your field of practice and should include interviewing and interpersonal skills. This highlights the benefits of learning from those not immediately in your profession.

Mark is a late twenties professional dancer referred to physical therapy for headaches and dizziness, that was affecting his ability to perform his work and daily life effectively. He was referred from a massage therapist to specifically see if I could help him get over the hump. Despite the soft tissue work and relief he experienced temporarily after the massage sessions, dizziness always returned. Mark described having at least a low level dizziness consistently for the past two years, which increased with dancing. Dizziness proves especially challenging because he is a professional dancer and needs to quickly move and spin through space on the regular. He says the dizziness started on the bus, when he was looking down at his phone and reading, and since then, it hadn't gotten better, despite the numerous medical professionals he had been to see. As mentioned, Mark describes some relief with massage, particularly on days when his neck gets really bad, which happens often when he was dizzy.

His physical therapy evaluation revealed the following:

Musculoskeletal:

-ROM grossly WFL, with limited thoracic kyphotic curve, although mild.
Strength: Grossly 5/5 except: right mid & low trapezius, right serratus anterior ⅘, gross right neck flexors and extensors ⅘.

Motor Control & Neurological Testing:

Romberg & Sharpened Romberg:
-positive: leaned left. Tests changed with head/canal positioning
Cerebellum (Rapid Alternating Movements): unremarkable

Oculomotor:

Saccadic intrusions with left to right pursuits.
Difficulty with gaze stability in all directions. No further tests secondary to slightly dizzy.

Mark's evaluation demonstrated vestibular and overall sensory integration dysfunction, expressed as dizziness. It became evident to me my limits of intervention would be reached quickly. This was for a couple reasons, including my depth of knowledge with applying neurology, and limited tools to identify specifics of his dysfunction would inherently make it more challenging. My strategy, therefore, which is consistent with all patients regardless of diagnosis, is if he not making improvements or moving in the right direction after three or four sessions, to refer to another provider. My strategy, as it is with everyone, is to identify where to drive plasticity in the brain. In Mark's case, it was to try and find improved representation for both his scapular stabilizers as well as the vestibulo-ocular apparatuses.

My paradigm regarding neck and shoulder pain was shifted through understanding that anyone with shoulder and neck pain has, at some level, vestibular dysfunction due to the path nerves take from/to the joint to the higher brain through the medial vestibular nucleus. This was hammered home by Dr. David Traster, who illustrated that the eyes and neck are reflexively one unit. Specifically, the shoulder, via the rubrospinal tract, passes through the external accessory cuneate nucleus, which has a branch, along with the vestibular nucleus, into the otoliths.

Clinical Concept

One great strategy for gaze stability and to drive input for the visual system is with the Motion Guidance system. Use TheMovementGuild for 10% off.

After the evaluation, and based on our findings, we attempted to reposition the inner ear relationship between his left posterior (which increased symptoms), to the right anterior canal. Prior to intervention, he was educated about our findings and the path of intervention, including a chance of being dizzy upon completion. What was clear upon evaluation was the discrepancy between proprioceptive, vestibular, and ocular systems. Based on our findings, we provided some exercises designed to generally drive input to improve the general vestibulo-ocular reflexes, in addition to performing manual therapy to his cervico-thoracic region. After manual work, targeted input was focused towards maintaining proper cervical spine and shoulder complex positioning with emphasis on engaging via isometric holds of the serratus anterior and low trap combination. These isometric holds were geared towards providing intense, novel, and safe input to bring awareness to and improve the ability of those muscles to engage efficiently and without compensation.

After the first session, Mark experienced relief in his neck and was compliant with his home program. He also described the headache as being more into his forehead rather than behind his eye. After his second treatment session, he described being about the same as he was prior to the first, but his headache sticking around a bit more with continued dizziness. He also described increased dizziness when looking up. We then made the decision to refer him to a chiropractic neurologist well versed in the thought processes associated with applying neurology as taught at the Carrick Institute.

I was able to attend the first session with the doctor and also the patient, which lasted close to three hours and was performed at the Neurological Wellness Institute. To be perfectly honest, the entire experience for me, as a physical therapist that only touches on this expansive world, left me quite humbled, and also motivated to continue to learn about functional neurology

CLINICAL INTEGRATION DYSFUNCTION: THOUGHT PROCESSES & CASE STUDY

Introduction:

This section is primarily written by Mike, with an emphasis on applying the same thought process to a more clinical integration dysfunction. In this section, Adam will provide his insight with *Italicized highlights*, and the non-highlight sections are written by Mike.

The majority of this text has focused on the subclinical orthopedic dysfunction. Recognizing these subclinical findings and treating the patient by improving movement function following the ideas presented throughout the book will undoubtedly lead to better outcomes. The next part will take a deeper dive into clinical integration dysfunction that may be more complicated than the typical patient coming into a standard rehab clinic but will give a glimpse into assessing and treating complicated patients, such as complex regional pain syndromes, post-concussion, and transverse myelitis. What is common is the concepts applied clinically are, for the most part an extension of what is used in with more 'complicated' patients that aren't musculoskeletal in nature.

Often when starting down the path of integrating neurology principles into practice, many practitioners look for algorithms or cookie-cutter approaches to evaluate and treat their patients. Unfortunately, there is no easy way to have an algorithm for this type of therapy and thought process because the brain is very dynamic, and movement is individualized to each patient. Of course, there are typical patterns for disease processes but as with anything there are nuances that vary among patients. The patients we typically see have often exhausted standard practice therapies and medicines with little success. In the concussion and TBI world, what may be a perfect treatment for one patient may make another patient feel terrible, and when dealing with neurological symptoms, feeling bad happens quickly, depending on the fragility of each individual patient. The neurological fragility of someone dealing with musculoskeletal injuries secondary to poor movement patterns will be very different relative to someone who is one week post-concussion. Due to differences in fragility, layering multiple neurological stimuli on top of movements is often helpful for the musculoskeletal dysfunctional patient, yet a neurologically fragile patient may be able to handle one simple stimulus before needing a long break between sets.

Therefore, the spectrum with a more fragile patient is often broad and the clinician must be acutely aware of this with each patient. If a patient is severely compromised, start slow and easy, and if they are strong and looking for better performance, work them hard. Below outlines a thought process compiled from teachings from various clinicians and experts in functional neurology, physical rehab, chiropractic, and psychology. Every patient is different, and the primary complaint and the primary condition of the patient drives the thought process, but in general this hierarchy has provided favorable outcomes. The following chart attempts to illustrate the levels in order of importance. The top tier is most important and each of the categories in the tiers have about equal importance to each other.

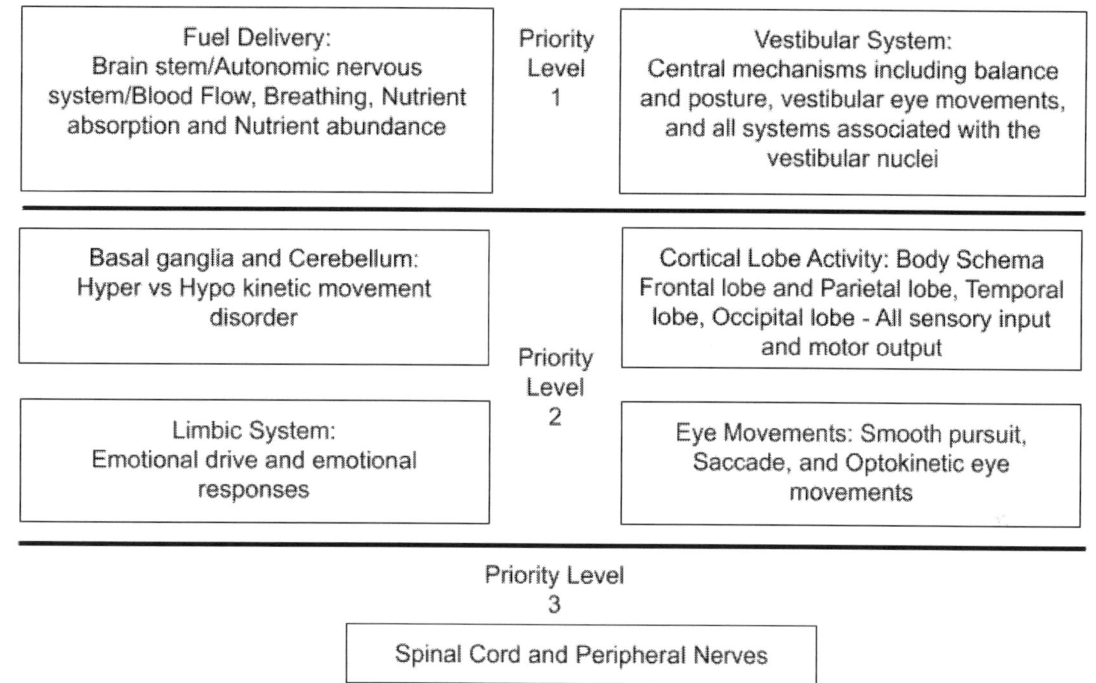

Priority Level 1:

Fuel Delivery

The first two systems or areas of importance are the fuel delivery systems and the vestibular system. The first one should make sense to everyone, as fuel delivery is vital to sustaining life while the second may need some explaining. Fuel delivery won't be focused on in the context of this book, however it is an important component. First and foremost, for every patient, fuel delivery to tissues must be addressed because it doesn't matter what the treatment is, without proper blood flow, oxygen delivery, and nutrient delivery, the tissue will not be able to handle the activity. In daily practice I see many patients who deal with dysautonomia, more specifically POTS (postural orthostatic tachycardia syndrome). These patients are the most severe when it comes to the example of fuel delivery. They do not have the ability to keep proper blood flow to their brain upon standing from a supine or seated position. Their symptoms will typically include lightheadedness, dizziness, nausea, headache, confusion, and sometimes giddiness. Although these are some of the most severe cases of improper fuel delivery, the same thing can happen for patients without severe dysautonomia. The most important aspect of fuel delivery is blood flow, which is governed by the autonomic nervous system (ANS). With blood flow, oxygen delivery is most vital to survival of tissues but glucose (or ketones) and other nutrients are crucial to tissue health.

This concept makes sense for those with autonomic pathologies, including 'gut' issues, such as myself. As Mike points out, lack of proper fuel delivery to the stomach and intestines is part of the sympathetic dominant pattern and for those predisposed often results in inflammatory bowel issues.

During initial assessment it is important to look very closely at the autonomic nervous system. ANS function can be assessed with multiple tools, including a fundoscopic exam which is performed on every patient and gives many clues into the overall health of the system. There are many reasons for looking at the fundus of the eye, but primarily looking at the A:V (artery:vein) ratio as it is the only area of the body where you can see the tone of the artery without obstruction of skin. Normal A:V ratio should be 2:3. Checking blood pressure bilaterally to assess the right vs left sided sympathetic tone will also give clues into the health of the higher order control of the ANS. Descending reticular formation neurons modulate blood pressure ipsilaterally. In other words, the right frontal cortex controls blood pressure on the right side of the body via the hypothalamus and pontomedullary reticular formation, while the left frontal lobe works on the left side of the body. When assessing the blood pressure and heart rate, it is important to check seated, supine, and standing. This gives an idea of how the patient handles orthostatic changes. While not necessarily important or accounted for in the general musculoskeletal population, when checked is not uncommon to uncover a cardiac issue that may have gone unnoticed. In the case of concussion or post-concussive patients, especially young female patients, orthostatic intolerance and autonomic issues are very common and must be treated first to provide adequate blood flow to the other damaged tissues of the brain.

Assessing blood flow is a given for patients with POTS but it can be a game changer for musculoskeletal pain patients as well. For example, a patient with a chief complaint of right sided low back pain with a history of migraines and hypertension. In functional MRI studies, sensory and motor activity of a specific area create increased activity and therefore increased blood flow in the associated area of the brain homunculus. As discussed in part 4 of this book, when a patient has chronic pain, the cortical representation of that area decreases. This is known as cortical smudging. With cortical smudging, the specific maps (homunculus) of the body become blurred. If the map is blurred in the brain, blood flow to the specific area of the brain and subsequent blood flow to the associated part of the body will be decreased. In this case, the right sided low back which already has a proportionately small homunculus representation, may have an even further reduction in cortical representation. On top of other dysautonomia findings such as migraine (constricted cerebral blood flow) and hypertension (turbulent and pressurized blood flow), the result is often more challenges to rehab the low back because the brain area associated with the low back will not be receiving optimum fuel. In these situations, treatment strategies to consider should include decreasing sympathetic tone with breathing exercises, gargling, humming, and even meditation if the patient can properly meditate.

The term meditation, to me, has much pressure. I've 'sat' regularly on and off through my life but feel I've only 'meditated' once. Upon realizing I was meditating I lost it and haven't 'found' it since. The term I prefer, which I heard from Richard Rohr is contemplative sitting. It feels like there's less pressure around that term. Regardless, the act of being present and observing yourself and the thoughts that pop in is helpful.

All of these exercises will aid decreasing pain, hypertension, and migraine through activation of the parasympathetic centers of the brain which will ensure that the patient is in a state where they are better able to heal. In addition, proper breathing techniques increase tissue oxygenation as well as increasing parasympathetic vagus nerve tone, as discussed in Part 9. I would also include performing graphesthesia training over the area of pain to improve the cortical representation.

Clinical Note:

The best way to perform graphesthesia training is to draw a letter on the skin over the area of pain, have the patient guess the letter, if incorrect tell them the letter, and redraw it until they can perceive the letter. If they improve, make the letters smaller. Warming up with these activities prior to getting into standard therapy protocols will greatly enhance the likelihood of success by treating the brain at the same time as treating the low back. Some people may argue that they are not able to treat the brain because of their scope of practice or knowledge base, but what has to be remembered is that whenever you provide any stimulus to the body, you are providing stimulus to the brain.

The blood flow has to be appropriate to the tissues, but it also has to be nutrient and oxygen dense. Many people have poor diets, do not supplement properly, and have terrible breathing mechanics, often leading to increased inflammation, joint and muscle pain, fatigue, and decreased ability to recover from injury. If the practitioner skips the thought of fuel delivery, he/she may be fighting against a nagging injury with a patient who just doesn't seem to resolve, not because the techniques and therapies are improper, but because the fuel to the brain and the fuel to the tissue being rehabilitated is inadequate.

This highlights the importance of having people on your 'team' who can address these needs when out of the scope of an individual's practice.

The Vestibular System

The vestibular system should be thought of at the same time as the autonomic system because it is so vital to our entire being. Most clinicians think about the vestibular system and associated disorders from a peripheral standpoint. Meaning, vertigo or dizziness associated with BPPV (Benign paroxysmal positional vertigo) or vestibular neuronitis. Balance is only a small portion of the vestibular system, and the vestibular system is in nearly all living beings that have self-driven movement. Even very simple organisms, such as zebra fish, have rudimentary vestibular mechanisms to keep them upright in water.

The vestibular nuclei are located in the very middle of the brainstem. Not only in a rostral-caudal central location but also nearly at the midline of the brainstem. The vestibular system is part of the most primitive portion of our brain, meaning it is old in our evolutionary process. All of our brain systems rely on an intact vestibular system. In order to maintain upright balance our vestibular system has to send signals from the vestibular apparatus to the vestibular nuclei which sends the fastest neuronal signals via the vestibulospinal tract to our feet, legs, core, and all other stabilizing muscles. And that is just to allow us to stand upright and still.

The vestibular system must have signals to the autonomic system to cause tightening of vessels in the neck and an increased heart rate in order to maintain blood flow and blood pressure against gravity when we sit or stand from a lying position. Without this immediate response, gravity would pull all of the blood out of your brain and you would pass out. Everyone has experienced this to some extent when laying down for a long time then quickly jumping up. That feeling of lightheadedness and even disturbed vision is due to a sluggish response between the vestibular and autonomic systems. If someone was to ask you to solve a math problem at the same time as being in this lightheaded and distorted visual state, it would be very difficult. Now you may understand the difficulty that a patient with POTS has on an everyday basis.

Another important part of the vestibular system includes the connections with the eyes and cerebellum, as well as ascending connections with the cortex, specifically the parieto-insular-vestibular cortex (PIVC) located at the junction of the parietal, temporal, and occipital lobes. As discussed throughout this text, the brain's job is to tell you where you are in space, where space is around you, while allowing you to navigate through that space. A major portion of this is derived from the information that is fed to the PIVC from the vestibular system. The testing for the vestibular system can get extensive with expensive equipment such as a VNG (Videonystagmography) unit, posturography platforms, caloric machines, and other electrodiagnostics. If you have access to the aforementioned tools it may be easier to assess the vestibular system, but it is also important to assess the health of the vestibular system during the exam, in real time.

Clinically, the dividing line of when to refer out is often the point when the patient isn't progressing as readily as desired and would benefit from the specificity the special tests such as VNG, caloric machines and electrodiagnostics can provide.

Author's Note:

While fuel systems & nutrition delivery is an important component and in the thought process of Mike's thought process, it purposefully isn't discussed in this text. However recognizing it's importance and having someone on your clinical team who can assess this information is recommended.

Priority Level 2: Basal Ganglia and Cerebellum, Cortical Activity, The Limbic System and Eye Movements

This area has the most thought process in the sense that it has the highest quantity of clinical thought work. I think of each of these next four areas equally. 1) The basal ganglia and cerebellum, 2) Cortical lobe activity, 3) The limbic system, and 4) Cortical and sub-cortical eye movements.

Basal Ganglia

The basal ganglia is a very complicated area in the brain that will be briefly touched upon. The basal ganglia is essentially the movement governor in the brain, allowing movement via the direct pathway and inhibiting movement that isn't desired via the indirect pathway. An easier way of clinically assessing the basal ganglia is delineating hyper vs hypo kinetic movement disorder, recognizing all disorders are movement disorders.

When I see an anxious patient, I think of them as having a hyperkinetic movement of thought whereas depressed patients are typically hypokinetic in thought. Irritable bowel syndrome can be hyperkinetic whereas constipation is hypokinetic, and this thought process can be applied to nearly all clinical conditions. While assessing a patient one question addressed is if the patient hypokinetic or hyperkinetic. The hypokinetic patient will appear down, depressed, slow moving, slow talking, slow thinking, confused, apathetic, and unmotivated with decreased muscle tone, whereas hyperkinetic appears anxious, high strung, highly motivated, agitated, fast moving, fast talking, unable to sit still, unable to maintain focus, fast thinking, and oftentimes in pain with increased muscle tone.

Clinical Note:

A complicated disorder of the basal ganglia is Parkinson's Disease which is a mixed hyper and hypokinetic movement disorder. Hypokinetic in that there is bradykinesia and hyperkinetic in that there is associated tremor.

The basal ganglia is a purely reflexive area of the brain that controls habit formation and timing of movement. Treatments vary for the basal ganglia and can be complicated depending on which area of the basal ganglia being treated. Typically treatment involving a metronome can be very beneficial for both types of errors in the basal ganglia.

Clinical Note:

For the hypokinetic patient, i.e. in early stage Parkinson's, setting a metronome to a cadence faster than their typical gait pattern and walking to that beat can greatly increase gait speed. Likewise, in anxious and hyperkinetic people, offering a slow metronome beat while they clap to that beat or tap feet to the slow beat can greatly enhance an ability to slow down the hyperkinetic nature of their movement disorder.

Cerebellum

As discussed in previous parts, the cerebellum receives sensory input from the body and helps fine tune all movement and allows complicated movement to be smooth and controlled. Often when the cerebellum is not functioning well, precise coordinated movement suffers. Breakdown in cerebellar function can also result in tremors. These tremors are typically referred to as kinetic or movement tremors as they are worse during movement, as compared to a parkinsonian tremor which is often times worse at rest. I assess the cerebellum through a variety of tests but most commonly through rapid alternating movements.

The cerebellum is an extremely important area of the brain for the manual therapist of any kind to consider. First, any decrease in optimal function of the cerebellum is going to result in abnormal movement patterns. This can be seen as described in the above test, but it can also be seen in balance, eye movements, sit to stand speed, coordinated extremity movement, trunk movement, and even thought process. Athletes with cerebellar dysfunction will experience repetitive injuries to the same joint or repetitive injuries to the same side of the body. The cerebellum receives sensory input and controls movement to the ipsilateral side of the body. Easier put, the right cerebellum is connected to the right side of the body.

Clinical Consideration:

Someone with a chronically sprained ankle may have "weak ligaments" in that ankle, and it is extremely important to assess if the cerebellum on that side is not functioning appropriately. The cerebellum may be the cause of the continuous sprains. Treatment of the cerebellum would consist of any complicated movement training. This could include nonlinear complex movement, oftentimes in a figure-8 motion performed passively or actively. Other treatments to consider would be complicated motor tasks such as specific footwork patterns, gait training, finger and hand movements, and could also include the layering of vibration, gyroscope devices, and body-blades.

Limbic System:

The limbic system and basal ganglia are linked through the reflexive nature of both systems, and the limbic system is the brain's primary emotional center. When broken down to most simple terms, the limbic system drives all activity subconsciously from waking in the morning until going to bed, and arguably even while we are sleeping. Many patients have dreams that mirror emotional states that occurred during the day, as anxiety and fear will be expressed in dreams and also motor output during sleep. For example, with chronic physical or emotional pain will grind teeth at night with resultant TMJ pain and dysfunction.

Emotional drive is what causes us to seek out food, water, procreation, meaning in life, happiness, and all other desires, and should be considered with every patient. It is also what is working during times of anger, frustration, sadness, pain, and despair. All these things happen subconsciously and drive our outward actions to seek pleasure and avoid pain. A positive emotional connection will give the patient a much better chance at successful outcomes, regardless of the injury, than the patient who has a negative emotional connection. A positive limbic connection can be developed simply when the patient feels that the practitioner has their best interest in mind. Red flags in the limbic system are the "sixth sense" that everyone talks about.

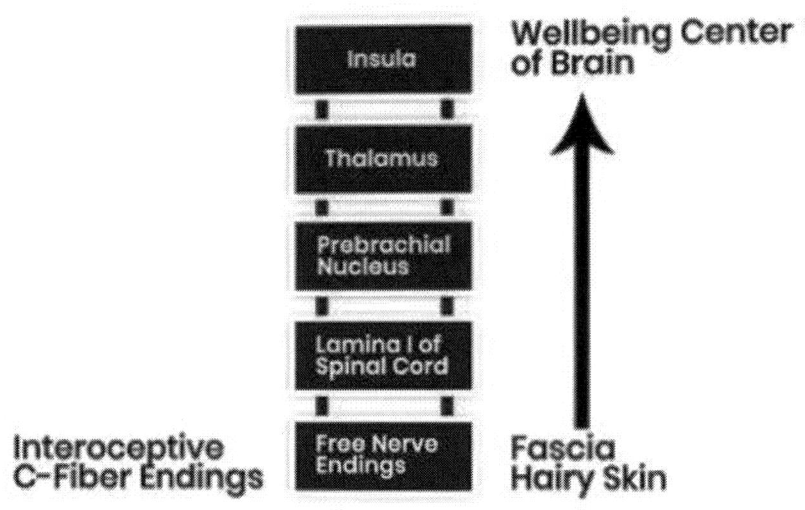

This also is part of interoception, and understanding that the sixth sense is housed in the limbic system and consists of the anterior cingulate cortex and insula is helpful.

In practice, I don't specifically assess the limbic system. However anxiety, depression, history of bi-polar disorder, abuse, and chronic pain will all result in a dysfunctional limbic system. Autonomic dysfunction, as described earlier in this chapter, has been shown to have connections with the limbic system and should be considered. While out of the scope of many to specifically treat the limbic system and should be performed licensed psychiatrists, psychologists, and social workers, it should be taken into account. Reducing a patient's pain and making them "feel good" and cared for will inherently improve limbic system function. While there is sufficient evidence that vestibular therapies can improve psychological disorders, they should never be performed as the sole treatment for the limbic system.

Cerebral Cortex Function

Cerebral cortex function includes environment perception, self-perception, cognitive function, and cortically based eye movements. I think of all these areas together even though they are separated in the chart. While all the higher level cortex functions are linked with the cerebral cortex as the origin of all these functions, the eye movements have significant connections in the brainstem as well. Cortex based eye movements including smooth pursuit, saccade, and optokinetic movements can point to areas of dysfunction in the cortex or can have errors if the connections through the brainstem and peripheral oculomotor nerves are affected.

This highlights the importance of understanding the anatomy and pathways into and out of the brain. While the first step may be understanding and identifying that there is a dysfunctional eye movement, such as a saccadic intrusion with a pursuit, further understanding of the 'why' behind the 'what' requires a deeper layer of understanding and knowledge.

As I am interacting with the patient throughout the history and exam, I am assessing the integrity of his/her cortex. Do they make eye contact? Do they understand what I am saying? Are they easily agitated or confused? Do they make sense in their account of their own history? How is their posture? Do they get distracted by their own thought process? Do they perseverate on specific topics or symptoms? If I notice abnormalities in any of these areas I will often move to their opposite field of view and quietly re-assess the abnormalities that they exhibited earlier. Standing in the patient's right field will bias their left cortex and vice versa. If I find they are more confused or agitated when I am standing in their right visual field, then become more relaxed in their posture, exhibit more spontaneous smiling, and are generally more at ease when I move to their left field of vision, I have already gathered a great deal of information about how the patient perceives their environment from a cortex standpoint.

Author's Note:

It is recommended to go back and review the specifics of the lobes of the Cerebral Cortex in Part 4: Capacities and Movement Thresholds. In that section, a review of strategies to assess and identify function of each part of the cerebral cortex occurs, along with ideas about progression and layering. While Mike uses this information with higher level "clinical dysfunction", the information is the same across the board and can also be applied towards a 'subclinical' population, which is the reason it is found in that section.

Priority Level 3:

Peripheral Nerves

The last area of thought process during my assessment is the spinal cord and peripheral nerves. It's not that these areas are not important, they are extremely important, but the amount of integration is much less in these areas. Of course, if the patient presents with a primary spinal cord lesion or peripheral nerve lesion, these areas move up the hierarchy quickly, but I still go back to fuel delivery even when dealing with primary cord or nerve lesions. Are the nerves and spinal cord receiving adequate blood flow? Is there a B-12 deficiency? Is there mesolimbic wind-up present causing sympathetic overload and autonomic/brainstem errors? What is the condition of the cerebral cortex associated with the cord or peripheral nerve? While assessing all of these other areas, of course if there is a primary cord issue or peripheral nerve entrapment/inflammation, it must be directly assessed and treated.

As mentioned earlier, fuel delivery to the peripheral nerves is vital, and diabetic patients are at great risk for peripheral neuropathy, as is anyone with micronutrient deficiencies, especially B-vitamins. Outside of these two scenarios, autoimmune disorders, alcoholism, and genetic disorders can cause peripheral neuropathies. All of these typically result in global or regional signs and symptoms such as burning, numbness, and/or tingling. In the case of nerve trauma, mononeuropathy, compression, or severing of a nerve will cause loss of function distal to the injury site. Compression can happen from long term repetitive disruption to the nerve such as meralgia paresthetica, which is caused by compression of the lateral femoral cutaneous nerve, commonly in those who wear weighted belts for work. This is common in police officers and carpenters. Compression can also happen acutely to peripheral nerves such as in lumbar radiculopathy where an intervertebral disc ruptures and compresses the nerve root against surrounding bony prominences of the spine. Severe acute nerve injuries can happen due to traumatic accidents as well as surgical intervention.

Knowing superficial nerve paths and common compression sites is like having a cheat sheet for the patient. If inflamed peripheral nerves are the pain generators, finding and relieving the compression and inflammation will be like a miracle for the patient. I typically will test the common entrapment sites by applying slight pressure over the nerve and asking the patient if it increases or decreases their pain. If it increases or decreases the pain, this is where I will work. If there is no change in the quality of the head pain, I do not work on that nerve. I have found that it is important to address both the compression and the inflammation at the same time.

When assessing peripheral nerve injuries and irritations it is very important to understand various types of pain. Knowing what type of pain is generated from various structures can not only keep you from banging your head against the wall with tough patients, it may even save their kidney, which is exactly what happened to one of the more profound peripheral nerve pain patients that I have treated.

Clinical Case Study: Chronic Transverse Myelitis

For most people reading this book, an acute spinal cord injury assessment will not be taking place. Usually this happens in the hospital immediately following a cord injury. After being stabilized, rehab takes over. Knowing the level of the cord lesion can be easy with advanced imaging, but functional deficit may be more complicated and may appear different than where the lesion is seen on imaging. For example, a chronic stage transverse myelitis case came into my office a couple years ago. The patient was suffering from what he thought was a heart attack due to the massive amount of pressure in his chest. He was admitted to the hospital and MI was ruled out but he was kept for monitoring. At roughly 2 am that night, he woke up suddenly with what was described as feeling "like a red hot knife was piercing my upper back in the middle of my spine." Immediately after this, he lost feeling and movement of anything below his neck. It was likely that the infection had been starting to affect his descending spinal cord tracts and compromising his postural and respiratory muscles. The infection progressed through the cord as he slept causing what was his final condition of transverse myelitis. On imaging, the infection transected the majority of his spinal cord at T2 but functionally this patient had changes in motor and sensory changes that varied from side to side and were sporadic between C5 down to T2, with near complete loss below T2.

Assessment Findings:

I used a specific standardized spinal cord injury assessment tool to determine all the areas of deficit which included complete motor loss below T4 with varied motor loss from C6-T4 bilaterally. His sensory loss was more sporadic. He had no sensation of temperature, pressure, light touch, vibration, or pinprick in either of his legs. His trunk sensation was sporadic from his hip crease up to his nipple line with some pinprick, some pressure, and minimal light touch. All of these did not follow an exact dermatomal pattern. From his nipple line and superior he had near full sensation to his shoulders. In his arms he could feel more on the left than the right although it did not fit a clear transection pattern. He had sensation at C7 on the left but not C6 or C5 dermatomes. On the right he could feel all sensation from C6 through C8 but nothing below that.

Key Concept:

This is where having a good spinal cord assessment is key. It is not always textbook motor and sensory loss. The best assessment tool for spinal cord injuries is the ASIA (American Spinal Injury Association) International Standards for Neurological Classification of Spinal Cord Injury. This tool breaks down all sensory and motor deficits with a grading system and level of the lesion assessment based on dermatome.

When he presented to our office he had been transferred out of his long term rehab facility and been told that he had reached maximum medical improvement (MMI). He wanted to get back to normal, but I knew it was very unlikely that he would be able to walk again. At this point he was wheelchair bound with minimal use of his hands other than using them to control the motorized chair navigation stick. My goals were to improve any hand and arm function as well as core stability which was significantly affected by the cord lesion. He had been told that he would not improve beyond his current state. I told him I could not promise anything, in fact, I couldn't promise any improvement due to the nature of his injury. I did tell him that I have seen many people regain the ability to walk who had been told they never would, therefore I also told him that I never rule anything out until I exhaust all of my options.

Treatment:

With limited access directly to the spinal cord, much of the treatment consisted of working from top down, cerebral cortex activation component including saccade and pursuit eye movement training over the areas of paralysis and optokinetic stimulation with a bias of downward activity performed in an attempt to reflexively activate extensor postural muscles. I also was over-the-top encouraging throughout all of his treatment, almost to the point that it was comical. I would congratulate him on very small accomplishments which usually returned a hard eye roll along with some variety of grumbling under his breath and usually a display of not being able to use his hands or legs yet. A bottom-up approach was also taken with a significant amount of repetitive peripheral somatosensory stimulation (RPSS) with the use of a somatosensory evoked potential (SSEP) machine. Much of the therapies were layered and performed simultaneously in an attempt to create any and all neurogenesis and neuroplasticity through the spinal cord.

The hour drive each way to get to the office became too hard to maintain for him and his wife which is why his treatment inevitably ended. Towards the end of his treatment cycle he had regained the ability to sit up on his own, he regained all sensation of both arms, decreased spasticity in both legs, decreased the upper motor neuron signs in his upper and lower extremities, and regained some hand function bilaterally with more use of his right hand. Often, he would express his gratitude for not giving up on him, he was happy to come to the office, and his overall mood improved. He still cursed God and his situation, but the talk of suicide had vanished. Unfortunately, motor activity in his legs did not return. This is an extreme example of a spinal cord injury, but most cord injuries are extreme. It is also a good example of thinking outside of the box, and how using all areas of the nervous system can create positive neuroplasticity, even when all hope seems lost.

Case Study: Complex Regional Pain Syndrome

This particular patient presented to the office I was working in at the time with one of my mentors and good friend, Dr. Nathan Keiser, as a "last ditch effort before having a kidney removed." The patient was suffering from severe pain in her right flank that was described as intense burning and stabbing pain that covered an area about the size of her spread out hand just below her ribs on the right and sometimes wrapped around to the anterior side of her abdomen. This pain had been chronic and worsening over the last year. She had MRI imaging performed and it was revealed that she had floating kidney syndrome. Although rare, it is a condition where the connective tissue of the kidney is not adequate or non-existent and allows the kidney to move around in the abdomen more than it should. She was convinced by a surgeon that this must be where the pain was coming from despite the fact that her pain was specific to a pinpoint area, described as burning and sharp. Typically organ pain will be nondescript, deep, and aching pain. The surgeon told her that it would be easy to laparoscopically attach the kidney to her 12th rib and securing it should stop the pain. The surgery was supposed to involve three small holes. When she woke up she had a four inch incision just under her ribs on the right on a 45 degree angle just below her 12th rib due to the surgeon changing his mind halfway through the surgery. The pain was twice as intense as it was originally and throughout her recovery over the next few weeks the pain continued to worsen. At one point she bent forward and heard a loud snap, feeling what she described as being flicked hard at the bottom of her ribs. Upon another MRI it was found that the wire connecting her kidney to the 12th rib failed. Her pain continued to worsen to the point that just the weight of her shirt on her side would cause immense pain that was unrelenting. Again the blame was placed on the floating kidney. She was set to have her right kidney removed from a major university hospital before her best friend, another patient of ours, told her that she needed to come in as one last shot at stopping the pain. It became evident quickly that the patient was suffering from superficial nerve pain that was exacerbated by the incision and subsequent scarring that was very close to the lateral cutaneous branch of the tenth thoracic nerve.

It was theorized that she was suffering from an entrapment syndrome of the superficial sensory nerve that caused the sharp, burning pain in the first place. The large incision near the already aggravated nerve caused scar tissue binding and further inflammation and irritation. Due to the long term nature of the pain, repeated injury, mesolimbic wind up and an overall sympathetic dominance, the patient developed CRPS (Complex Regional Pain Syndrome) a severe pain syndrome. This typically arises after an injury where the brain can't turn off the pain signal due to an overwhelming state of sympathetic nerve output.

Treatment:

The treatment for this patient consisted of both a bottom-up approach of addressing the site of the pain and a top-down approach of calming the sympathetic nervous system and activating areas of the brain that inhibit pain. Specifically the left side of her body was stimulated through various activities including RPSS and non-linear complex movements of the proximal joints. She also performed specific eye movement exercises consisting of saccades (fast eye movement) from her lower right to her upper left on a 45-degree angle followed by a pursuit (slow tracking eye movement) from upper right to lower left visual fields on the same angle. The RPSS, non-linear movements, and eye exercises were all targeting the right cerebral cortex through the various sensory pathways.

Clinical Correlation:

One question to ponder is why treat the left side if the pain was on the right? Another is why eye movements when the patient had an obvious peripheral nerve lesion? Through ipsilateral descending pathways primarily starting in the right frontal lobe and involving the periaqueductal grey and the pontomedullary reticular formation on the right, pain is inhibited. The main goal was to decrease her pain, but due to the severity of pain with any sensation to her skin, pain inhibition had to come from the top-down. Once her sympathetic nervous system began to calm after a couple treatments, light touch about six inches from the incision scar could be tolerated.

At this point a combination of light touch pain desensitization with auditory stimulation was performed to increase further toleration of touch. With this technique I typically use bone conducting headphones with a sound frequency of between 17-25 Hz while using a tissue to stroke over the painful area as well as a non-painful area, typically on the contralateral same area of the body. This specific technique was taught to me by Dr. Fili Talamantez, as he discovered it with many of his pain patients. This frequency is below the sound threshold so the patient will not hear it but the brain will pick it up. To find the specific tone needed, test from 25Hz and work down until finding a frequency that diminishes pain. In her case the right side of her upper and lateral abdomen (the painful side) and her left upper lateral abdomen (the non-painful side). I performed this tedious task at one second strokes for hours over the week that I saw her, stopping when she was unable to tolerate the pain.

On a larger scale, I've been utilizing the bone conducting headphones on myself to stimulate parasympathetic responses. Utilizing a frequency generator on a sweep from 80Hz-500Hz to stimulate both the utricles and saccules, I keep them on while performing breathing exercises. Special Thanks to Eric Cobb from Z-Health for that strategy.

As the treatments continued, I was able to slowly move closer to the scar and the affected nerve. Oncc she could handle touch directly over the nerve and the scar, ProloGel was utilized with both manual neurofascial release of the nerve as well as instrument assisted scar release over the incision site. After treatments of 3x/day for a week the patient was mostly pain-free and able to handle light and deep pressure into the area that a t-shirt would previously bring her to her knees. She ended up cancelled her nephrectomy surgery. I have performed this type process on many peripheral nerve entrapment and CRPS patients since this with great success. I cannot state enough gratitude to those who taught me these techniques.

Conclusion

As mentioned earlier, the goal is to look at complicated concepts and cases from a clinical setting, then utilize those concepts to improve subclinical musculoskeletal cases in everyday practice. I cannot stress enough how understanding neurological pathways, structure, and function will make your life easier as a clinician and will improve your patient's outcomes.

Conclusion

This is the end, beautiful friend, the end.

-Jim Morrison

This text was started shortly after completion of my first book, without a specific end place in mind, or knowledge of the direction it would take. However, there were still topics I wanted to cover, and I began by filling out a chapter on pain that I chose not to include in the first book. As a then first time author, I was nervous to expose myself too much, and so left out what I perceived to be more of the 'heated' topics of the time. The second chapter I put together was Part 9 on Integration<>Isolation, which was something I was throwing around in my head at the time as a way to logically progress through the spectrum of movement.

Around this time I was challenged by my friend and a mentor, Lenny Parracino, (Soft Tissue Therapist for the Los Angeles Clippers and Gray Institute educator) to put together my fundamentals of intervention, partially because we were co-teaching a class and it would make for a good discussion. Fundamentals of intervention became the working title of this book, and from there an outline was created that essentially follows the order of this book, and I continued to consistently write (a large portion between 4:30-6:30am).

Fortunately, I type fast, and when learning I have developed a system where I typically take notes on my computer during a course, often times transcribing exactly what the lecturer says. I then go back and reconcile those notes and with the accompanied lecture's presentation deck and create a new source to build from. I typically read and learn from many resources around one topic, pulling out relevant information to fill out my knowledge base. Ultimately, the result is what you see here.

The process wasn't always smooth sailing, however, and it was put down for over a year for a couple reasons, including me being depressed and not in a great head space, as written about in Part 6. My excuse at the time was needing to learn more about the higher level integration information to write about it in a way that felt authentic and real to me in a way the rest of the book did. While true to a certain extent, in retrospect, it coincided with a bit of depression and me being 'off my' ideal game. Eventually, an upward spiral began as I was simultaneously treated by Dr. Drzewiecki for a few sessions. As Mike and I were already friends, we continued to work together on this project with Mike taking the role of 'neuro editor'. He and I worked for close to a year, and when the quarantine of 2020 began, kicked into high gear to complete it. As a frame of reference, this section is the last to be written, and we are at week eight of social distancing.

Part 1 of this book discussed a simple idea that even though pain or dysfunction may not be biomechanically driven, biomechanics can be a useful entry point into the nervous system. Therefore, biomechanics is an important part of the process because understanding movement and what should happen sets up situations to see if it is happening. Part 2 dove deeper into the concepts of real vs. relative motion and why it's a fantastic framework in which to work. Bones move, joints feel and perceive, muscles react, and the nervous system governs and controls the movement. Human movement needs to be a synchronous dissociation of body segments, and if bones move in the same direction at the same speed the joint won't feel any movement.

Part 3 went further into the ideas of treating capacities instead of anatomy and went into the specifics of the gait cycle. A discussion about why understanding the motions of gait and what angles joints should be in at specific phases allows a thought process that anchors to attempting to improve the gait capacities rather than just focusing on the part that hurts. Part 4 continued a discussion surrounding working with capacities instead of anatomy, diving further into the specifics of the brain and nervous system. We discussed that like 3D movement, understanding neuro anatomy and what each part is responsible for, and supposed to do, sets up a situation to see if it's happening or not. What gets challenging however, is understanding the pathways that connect with numerous brain regions and produce an observed output. Said differently, when assessing the brain there is no way to isolate out one section or system because it's so interrelated. Therefore, a summative assessment is required to identify where the opportunity for improvement lies. This can only occur with a thorough understanding of anatomy.

The conversation in Part 4 continued with a discussion of the different musculoskeletal capacities that can be associated with human movement, including the costo-pelvic region, the shoulder complex and cervical spine region. Part 5 was a discussion around working with pain, and the idea that pain is an output and input can be influenced. We discussed the various multisystem inputs that can be provided in order to change output, including stretch, muscle engagement, pressure, tension, vibration, heat, cold, thoughts and emotions, along with what they likely do to the nervous system and why each intervention might be utilized.

Part 6 was a discussion about my personal central integration dysfunction, and some of my path into wanting to understand the brain more in depth. This chapter was co-written by Mike, who utilized my objective test as examples to describe his thought process and intervention strategies. Part 7 was a discussion about mobility and in a larger context motor control. It included a definition and also strategies to incorporate mobility into a movement paradigm. The discussion about using mobility in manual therapy and integrated stretching led to a discussion about differentiating between various sensations and an order in which to intervene. Part 8 continued a discussion about motor control, talking about how to utilize principles of motor control for an assessment strategy of motor output via muscle testing. In this chapter, basic principles of muscle testing were outlined and defined, along with a beginning process to using a muscle testing thought process to identify what areas to work, along with if those areas should be up or down regulated. In Part 9, a discussion about the integrated to isolated spectrum in general led to examples for each body region, and specific suggestions from isolation through integration including the foot, costo-pelvis, shoulder complex, and cervical spine. In addition, suggestions about utilizing 'brain-based' applications to enhance the way the brain takes up information from the three major systems was discussed.

The book finishes with two musculoskeletally driven 'sub clinical' integration case studies of patients I've seen in practice. It is followed by Mike's thought process while working with a clinical integration population such as what he sees in clinical practice.

As my professional practice has grown, some of what I struggled with is the feedback that 'I can't reproduce myself', meaning nobody else would have gotten them better. My response has always been that's not true, it is the thought process not the person. In that spirit, some of my desire to put my thoughts into words was to provide a thought process that has personally been very successful. It was developed in the clinical trenches, working for myself for over 11 years at the point of this writing. What that means is that it has been proven, because if patients didn't get better, they'd likely go to one of the numerous big box PT companies found in Chicago, or one of a few other independent practitioners scattered around like myself. Without marketing, which I haven't done up until recently (and that's for my practice, The Movement Guild, not myself) it becomes necessary to provide a different thought process that gets people better rapidly. That's been marketing enough.

Reflecting upon this book and writing these words, I feel I gave my best effort to put into words that which makes me the clinician I am, one who is curious and continually learns and integrates new material. This text has helped me to synthesize and reconcile my own thought process as a movement professional. I hope it illustrates that different thought processes that seem quite different and opposite can actually be reconciled.

I still am nervous to put this book out yet I am also excited about the final product because it does represent a solid summary of my foundations and what makes me the clinician I've become. Thank you for reading this, and I hope you have found it helpful.

Works Cited

1. Barral, J. P., and Pierre Mercier. *Visceral Manipulation*
2. Beck Randy, F*unctional Neurology for Practitioners of Manual Therapy*
3. Björnsdotter M, Morrison I, Olausson H; (2010) Feeling good: on the role of C fiber mediated touch in interoception. Exp Brain Res **207**:149–155.
4. Bove GM, Harris MY, Zhao H, Barbe MF. Manual therapy as an effective treatment for fibrosis in a rat model of upper extremity overuse injury. *J Neurol Sci.* 2016;361:168-180. Doi:10.1016/j.jns.2015.12.029
5. Butler, D, Mosely, L: *Explain Pain Supercharged*
6. Butler, D, Mosely L; NeuroOrthopedic Institute; www.noigroup.com
7. Brodsky, Michael C. et al; Skew Deviation Revisited, Survey of Ophthalmology, Volume 51, Issue 2, 105 – 128
8. Brooks, Vernon; The Neural Basis for Motor Control
9. Bremner JD, Vythilingam N, Vermeetn E, Adil J, Khan S, Nazeer A, Afzal N, McGlashan T, Elzinga B, Anderson GM, Heniger G, Southwick SM, Charney DS.. Cortisol response to a cognitive stress challenge in posttraumatic stress disorder (PTSD) related to childhood abuse. *Psychoneuroendocrinology* 2003;28(6):733–750.
10. Bubic, A., von Cramon, D. Y., and Schubotz, R. I. (2010). *Prediction, cognition and the brain. Frontiers in human neuroscience*, (*4*, 25.Doi:10.3389/fnhum.2010.00025
11. *Chaitow, Leon; Maintaining Body, Balance, Flexibility &* Stability: A Practical Guide to the Prevention and Treatment of Musculoskeletal Pain and Dysfunction
12. Chinkulprasert C, , Vachalathiti R, , Powers CM. and Patellofemoral joint forces and stress during forward step-up, lateral step-up, and forward step-down exercises. J Orthop Sports Phys Ther. 2011; 41: 241– 248. http://dx.doi.org/10.2519/jospt.2011.3408
13. Coan, J. A., Schaefer, H. S., & Davidson, R. J. (2006). Lending a Hand: Social Regulation of the Neural Response to Threat. *Psychological Science*, *17*(12), 1032–1039. https://doi.org/10.1111/j.1467-9280.2006.01832.x
14. Cook, G. *Movement Functional Movement Systems: Screening, Assessment, Corrective Strategies*
15. Craig, B; *How Do You Feel? An Interoceptive Moment with Your Neurobiological Self*
16. Dalcourt, Michol, Institute of Motion https://instituteofmotion.com/
17. Destafano DO, Lisa A; *Greenman's Principles of Manual Medicine, 5th Edition*

18. Egeblad M, Rasch MG, Weaver VM. Dynamic interplay between the collagen scaffold and tumor evolution. *Curr Opin Cell Biol*. 2010;22(5):697-706. Doi:10.1016/j.ceb.2010.08.015
19. Feldenkrais, Moshe; Body & Mature Behaviour: A Study of Anxiety, Sex, Gravitation and Learning
20. *Frantz, C, Stewart, K, Weaver, V; The extracellular matrix at a glance*; J Cell Sci 2010 123: 4195-4200; doi: 10.1242/jcs.023820
21. Frost, Robert; *Applied Kinesiology: A Training Manual and Reference Book of Basic Principles and Practices*
22. George, David, Fife, Stuart. www.fnor.net
23. Goldberg, S; *Clinical Neuroanatomy Made Ridiculously Simple*
24. Goode A, Hegedus EJ, Sizer P, Brismee JM, Linberg A, Cook CE. Three-dimensional movements of the sacroiliac joint: a systematic review of the literature and assessment of clinical utility. *J Man Manip Ther*. 2008;16(1):25-38. Doi:10.1179/106698108790818639
25. Gray, G. *Functional Video Digest Series. Vol 3.4 Functional Manual Reaction- The Foot and Ankle, Vol. 3.8 Proprioceptors.*
26. Gray, G. Tiberio, D, video blogs on www.GrayInstitute.com
27. Gunnar MR. Quality of early care and buffering of neuroendocrine stress reactions: Potential effects on the developing human brain. *Preventive Medicine: An International Journal Devoted to Practice and Theory*. 1998;27(2):208-211.
28. Gunnar MR, Donzella B. Social regulation of the cortisol levels in early human development. *Psychoneuroendocrinology* 2002;27(1-2):199-220.
29. Gunnar MR, Larson M, Hertsgaard L, Harris M, Brodersen L. The stressfulness of separation among 9-month-old infants: effects of social context variables and infant temperament. *Child Development* 1992;63(2):290-303.
30. Gunnar MR, Lamb M, Barthel M. Transition to childcare: associations with infant-mother attachment, infant negative emotion and cortisol elevations. *Child Development* 2004;75(3):639-650.
31. Heim C, Newport JD, Mletzko T, Miller AH, Nemeroff CB. The link between childhood trauma and depression: Insights from HPA axis studies in humans. *Psychoneuroendocrinology* 2008;33(6):693-710.
32. Henderson, Luke et al Chronic Pain: Lost Inhibition, Journal of Neuroscience 24 April 2013, 33 (17) 7574-7582; DOI: 0.1523/JNEUROSCI.0174-13.2013

33. Hertenstein, M. J., Keltner, D., App, B., Bulleit, B. A., & Jaskolka, A. R. (2006). Touch communicates distinct emotions. *Emotion, 6*(3), 528–533. https://doi.org/10.1037/1528-3542.6.3.528

34. Hertsgaard L, Gunnar MR, Erickson M, Nachmias M. Adrenocortical responses to the strange situation in infants with disorganized/disoriented attachment relationships. *Child Development* 1995;66(4):1100-1106.

35. Hoheisel U, Mense S, Simons DG et al. (1993) Appearance of new receptive fields in rat dorsal horn neurons following noxious stimulation of skeletal muscle: a model for referral of muscle pain? Neurosci Lett 153:9–12

36. Holzer P, Holzer-Petsche U: Pharmacology of Inflammatory Pain: Local Alteration in Receptors and Mediators. Dig Dis 2009;27(suppl 1):24-30. Doi: 10.1159/000268118

37. Jacobs, Diane; Dermoneuromodulation

38. Kandal, E., Schwarts, J. Jessel, T.; *Principles of Neural Science*

39. Korb, Alex; *The Upward Spiral: Using Neuroscience to Reverse the Course of Depression, One Small Change at a Time*

40. Lee, Seo & Kim, Jin-Hyuk. (2007). Involvement of substance P and calcitonin gene-related peptide in development and maintenance of neuropathic pain from spinal nerve injury model of rat. Neuroscience research. 58. 245-9. 10.1016/j.neures.2007.03.004.

41. Lehman, G: Recovery Strategies Pain Workbook; http://www.greglehman.ca/

42. *Liebenson, Craig; Rehabilitation of the Spine*

43. Lewit K, Simons DG. Myofascial pain: relief by post-isometric relaxation. Archives of Physical Medicine and Rehabilitation. 1984 Aug;65(8):452-456

44. L.S. Löken, M. Evert, J. Wessberg Pleasantness of touch in human glabrous and hairy skin: order effects on affective ratings, Brain Res., 1417 (2011), pp. 9-15

45. Loken, L. S., Wessberg J., Morrison, I., McGlone, F. & Olausson, H; (2009). Coding of pleasant touch by unmyelinated afferents in humans. *Nature Neuroscience,* **12**, 547–548

46. Lukasiewicz AC, McClure P, Michener L, Pratt N, Sennett B. Comparison of 3-dimensional scapular position and orientation between subjects with and without shoulder impingement. *J Orthop Sports Phys Ther*. 1999;29(10):574–586. PubMed ID: 10560066 doi:10.2519/jospt.1999.29.10.574

47. Mansour AR, Farmer MA, Baliki MN, Apkarian AV. Chronic pain: the role of learning and brain plasticity. *Restor Neurol Neurosci*. 2014;32(1):129-139. Doi:10.3233/RNN-139003

48. Michaud, Thomas; *Human Locomotion*

49. Nagamoto Y, Iwasaki M, Sakaura H, et al, Sacroiliac joint motion in patients with degenerative lumbar spine disorders.. J Neurosurg Spine. 2015;23:209–216
50. Oliver, Jocylen, https://neuromuscular-reprogramming.com/
51. Osar,Evan; *Corrective Exercise Solutions to Common Hip and Shoulder Dysfunction*
52. Pienta K.J,. Coffey DS; Cellular harmonic information transfer through a tissue tensegrity-matrix system, Medical Hypotheses Volume 34, Issue 1,1991,Pages 88-95
53. Pisotta I., Molinari M.; Cerebellar contribution to feedforward control of locomotion; 2014 *Frontiers in Human Neuroscience*, 8 (JUNE) , art. No. 475
54. Preece, Stephen J, Graham-Smith, Philip; The influence of gluteus maximus on transverse plane tibial rotation. Stephen J. Preece, Philip Graham-Smith, Chris J. Nester, Dave Howard, Hermie Hermens, Lee Herrington, Peter Bowkerm Gait Posture. 2008 May; 27(4): 616–621. Published online 2007 Sep 27. Doi: 10.1016/j.gaitpost.2007.08.007
55. *Ray, Albert, Treatment of Chronic Pain by Integrative Approaches*
56. Rolf, Ida P., and Rosemary Feitis. *Rolfing and Physical Reality*
57. Root, Orien, Weed, *Normal and Abnormal Function of the Foot*
58. *Scarr, Graham; Biotensegrity: The Structural Basis of Life*
59. Schleip, Robert; Fascial plasticity – a new neurobiological explanation: Part 1, Journal of Bodywork and Movement Therapies, Volume 7, Issue 1,2003,Pages 11-19,ISSN 1360-8592, https://doi.org/10.1016/S1360-8592(02)00067-0.
60. *Schliep, Robert Website: www.somatics.de*
61. Schwartz, Joseph https://dna-assessment.com/
62. Scott J. E. (2003). Elasticity in extracellular matrix 'shape modules' of tendon, cartilage, etc. A sliding proteoglycan-filament model. *J. Physiol.* 553, 335-343
63. Shadmehr, Reza, Maurice A. Smith, and John W. Krakauer. Forthcoming. Error correction, sensory prediction, and adaptation in motor control. Annual Review of Neuroscience 33.
64. *Siegel, Dan; Whole Brain Child*
65. Spina, Andreo; https://kinstretch.com/pails-rails-good/
66. Spina, Andreo; https://functionalanatomyseminars.com/
67. Takakusaki, K. (2013), Neurophysiology of gait: From the spinal cord to the frontal lobe. Mov Disord., 28: 1483-1491. Doi:10.1002/mds.25669
68. Thie, John F., Thie Matthew; Touch for Health: A Practical Guide to Natural Health with Acupressure Touch
69. Tottenham NH, Hare TA, Quinn BT, McCarry TW, Nurse M, Galvan A, Davidson MC, Thomas KM, McEwen B, Gunnar M, Aronson J, Casey BJ. Amygdala volume and sensitivity

to emotional information following orphanage rearing. Journal of Child Psychology & Psychiatry. In press.

70. Wand, Benedict M. et al Tactile thresholds are preserved yet complex sensory function is impaired over the lumbar spine of chronic non-specific low back pain patients: a preliminary investigation,., Physiotherapy, Volume 96, Issue 4, 317 – 323

71. Wessels, Tina & Tulder, Maurits & Sigl, Tanja & Ewert, Thomas & Limm, Heribert & Stucki, Prof. Dr. med. Gerold. (2006). What predicts outcome in non-operative treatments of chronic low back pain? A systematic review. European spine journal : official publication of the European Spine Society, the European Spinal Deformity Society, and the European Section of the Cervical Spine Research Society. 15. 1633-44. 10.1007/s00586-006-0073-4.
72. *Wright P, Drysdale I; A comparison of post-isometric relaxation (PIR) and reciprocal inhibition (RI) muscle energy techniques applied to piriformis, International Journal of Osteopathic Medicine, Volume 11, Issue 4, 2008,Pages 158-159*
73. Wolf, Adam; *REAL Movement: Perspective on Integrated Motion & Motor Control*
74. Yehuda R, Halligan SL, Grossman R. Childhood trauma and risk for PTSD: relationship to intergenerational effects of trauma, parental PTSD, and cortisol excretion. *Developmental Psychopathology*. 2001;13(3):733-753.

About the Neuro Editor

Dr. Michael Drzewiecki has a strong passion for helping those who have been "everywhere else" and have seemingly lost hope in their condition. By using groundbreaking clinical neuroscience research and applying them to his patients, Mike helps his patients regain their quality of life.

Having treated many complex neurological cases from around the world, Mike teaches nationally and internationally as an instructor and consultant for other physicians. He earned his Doctor of Chiropractic from Life University in Marietta, Georgia, and has earned the highest level of training in Functional Neurology by earning his Diplomate Degree in Chiropractic Neurology / Functional Neurology. He is also one of the only four Fellows in the state of Illinois from the American Board of Brain Injury and Rehabilitation, and is a certified Chiropractic Sports Physician. Mike has treated numerous professional, semi-professional, college, and high-school athletes and has a great passion for working with these athletes.

Born in Houston, Texas, and raised in Grand Blanc, Michigan, Mike is an avid hockey player and coach and holds a strong appreciation for biomechanics and injury prevention. He graduated from the University of Michigan with a degree in Business Administration and holds a Master's degree in Sport Health Science from Life University.

About the Author

Adam's professional credentials include Licensure in Physical Therapy (IL) and Massage Therapy (IL) and Fellow of Applied Functional Science (Gray Institute)(09). Some of his certifications include Enhance Running Technician, Functional Range Conditioning (FRC), Dry Needling Certified, Neurokinetic Therapy level 3(NKT), Functional-Neuro-Orthopedic Rehab (FNOR) provider, and has his certificate of competency in vestibular rehabilitation.

As a Physical Therapist of over 15 years in Chicago, he is the owner of REAL Physical Therapy and founder of The Movement Guild, a multi-disciplinary facility focusing on integrating movement disciplines including physical therapy, massage therapy, personalized training, yoga and recovery services. The Movement Guild's mission is to bridge the gap between rehabilitation, performance, and recovery by providing a seamless and an individualized experience.

His first book, *REAL Movement: Perspective on Integrated Motion & Motor Control* was published in 2016. Adam is a Master Instructor on the Rocktape Education Team for the past six years, and teaches nationally, internationally, and online, both for Rocktape and his own material.

For more information about Adam & his offerings, please visit www.movementguild.com .

Made in the USA
Monee, IL
17 September 2020

42762189R00151